Theological Fragments

Theological Fragments

Explorations in Unsystematic Theology

DUNCAN B. FORRESTER

t&t clark

T&T Clark International
A Continuum imprint

The Tower Building, 11 York Road, London SE1 7NX
15 East 26th Street, New York, NY 10010

British Library Cataloguing-in-Publication Data
A catalogue record for this book is available from the British Library.

ISBN: HB: 0-567-03077-6
          PB: 0-567-03023-7

Library of Congress Cataloging-in-Publication Data
A Catalog record for this book is available from the Library of Congress.

Typeset by Free Range Book Design & Production
Printed and bound in Great Britain by MPG Books Ltd, Cornwall

Contents

Preface   ix

Chapter 1. Theology in fragments   1

Part I: Understanding people

Chapter 2. The mystery of the human person in community   25

Chapter 3. Good and gay?   35

Part II: Public theology

Chapter 4. Divinity in use and practice   49

Chapter 5. The pastoral significance of Mary: a Protestant
           perspective   56

Chapter 6. Biblical interpretation and cultural relativism   65

Chapter 7. The Church and the concentration camp: some
           reflections on moral community   78

Part III: Understanding worship

Chapter 8. Lex orandi, lex credendi   95

Chapter 9. The liberation of worship   103

Chapter 10. The end of sacraments?: sacramental action
            and discipleship   112

Chapter 11. Worship, ethics and unity   122

Part IV: Issues

Chapter 12. Politics and reconciliation   137

Chapter 13. The media and theology: some reflections   147

Chapter 14. Welfare and human nature: public theology in
            welfare policy debates   158

Notes   175

Bibliography   187

Index   195

In Memoriam

J. Ian H. McDonald 1933–2004

A wise Scholar, an Inspring Teacher, and a Loyal Friend

Preface

This book of essays hopes to show that there is an important place today for a modest and unsystematic theology, consisting of 'theological fragments' rather than some grand theory. Theology, I believe, is something that one *does* rather than simply reads about. I think the Scottish idiom whereby one speaks of *doing* a subject, even if that subject be metaphysics or theoretical physics, as contrasted with the English tendency to talk of *reading* a subject even when it is engineering or field ornithology, has much to be said for it! The most relevant theology, I believe, involves disciplined reflection on practices and happenings, on specific ethical dilemmas, life choices and experiences, all in the light of the great tradition of faith and the witness of Scripture.

This is why I have chosen over a number of years to speak of 'theological fragments'. These are not like the bits of a jigsaw, with the theologian's task being to fit them all properly together so that in course of time the puzzle may be solved and all the pieces find their proper place in the great picture of things. Theological fragments, as I try to show in the introductory essay, have their own integrity and mystery, and can provide illumination, encouragement, challenge or warning.

Theological fragments, as I understand them, arise from, and relate to, specific situations, problems, contexts, issues and communities. But often insights from one specific situation are found to be of more general relevance. A theology of fragments hopes to contribute to throwing some light on what is going on, and challenging to constructive and faithful practice today.

The essays in this book come from different stages in my life, and engage with a variety of my continuing concerns as a teacher in India, at Madras Christian College, at the University of Sussex, and for 23 years at New College in the University of Edinburgh. I try to wrestle in these essays with questions like these: What do the practices of Christian worship have to teach us about ethics? How can a word of reconciliation be heard in Northern Ireland? Does the relationship between Dachau concentration camp and a little country church just outside the perimeter wire warn us to avoid the ecclesiastical triumphalism at present so fashionable? Are the modern mass media a threat or an opportunity for Christian communication? How can we responsibly read the Bible in a multicultural context? These are the kind of issues discussed in this book of theological fragments, which I am sure some readers will find irritating or provocative, while others, I hope, will find stimulus and encouragement within these pages.

There are too many of those who helped me on my way and encouraged, criticized and supported me in dealing with these, and other theological fragments, to make proper acknowledgement possible here. I have been privileged to have had a succession of wonderful students, friends and dialogue partners from many lands, while I taught in India, England and Scotland. I owe them a huge debt for their support, and for the vigorous way in which from time to time they put me right.

But above all, the love and the support and the wisdom and the good sense of Margaret, my dear wife, have shaped and reshaped the way I think about God and the world, and deal with theological fragments. I am more grateful to her than I can say.

Duncan B. Forrester

1

Theology in fragments

Theology, I wish to suggest, is not some great theory of everything to which believers are expected to give their consent. Nor is it, as so many people regard it today, a pretentious theory of nothing at all, or of matters so irrelevant to the life of the world that they can be safely disregarded while we get on with living and organizing our societies. It is not discussion of topics as urgent and complex as how many angels can dance on the point of a needle, or how to interpret the number 666 in the book of Revelation. Clear and comprehensive understanding is not even the goal or objective of theology, although Christian theology sustains a grounded hope that at the last there will be fullness of wisdom and understanding. Meanwhile we live with and by fragments of truth and insight, making a variety of patterns, and offering important, disturbing and challenging glimpses of illumination, guidance, encouragement and hope. Theology and theological ethics are more like improvisation than acting according to a set and predetermined script, to borrow the notion of improvisation from the fine recent book of my friend, Samuel Wells.[1]

Socrates and Jesus

The title of this book is adapted, with due acknowledgement, from Søren Kierkegaard, that strange and fascinating Danish nineteenth-century thinker. Central to Kierkegaard's massive literary production was his little book, *Philosophical Fragments* (1844), in which he compared the stories of two disturbing and questioning figures, Jesus and Socrates. Both were notable for asking questions, telling stories, probing received opinions, challenging existing orthodoxies, and communicating 'indirectly', that is, disturbing, shocking people into a

1

new self-awareness, and engagement with the truth. Both dealt with fragments rather than complex and co-ordinated wholes. Both demonstrated the need to live in truth and witness to the truth. And both sealed their witness by and in their dying. Neither produced a 'system'.

Socrates regarded himself, with good reason, as 'a sort of gadfly, given to the state by God... And all day long and in all places [I] am always fastening upon you, arousing and persuading and reproaching you'.[2] His sting made people waken from their dogmatic slumbers and face reality. Likewise, Jesus disturbed and challenged received certainties and was in constant dialogue with the authorities and with his disciples. He was accused of 'perverting the people',[3] just as Socrates was accused of misleading the youth and encouraging them to question the official theology of the city.

Both Socrates and Jesus communicated through fragments. Neither produced anything that could be called a system, or a systematic theology or philosophy. Both attended to the concrete, to particulars, and above all to people, with all their complex needs, hopes and confusions. And Kierkegaard, many centuries later, devoted a great deal of attention to attacking the systems and system-builders of the day – pre-eminently Hegel and his disciples. There was, claimed Kierkegaard, an unreality about such grandiose philosophical and theological systems that claimed universality. Truth, he taught, is something to be done, to be lived and loved and celebrated, not simply to be contemplated or thought about. As John's Gospel puts it: 'Those who do what is true come to the light, so that it may be clearly seen that their deeds have been done in God.'[4] Systems, on the other hand, characteristically claim some kind of finality and completeness. They are hard to 'indwell'. 'In relation to their systems', Kierkegaard wrote, 'most systematisers are like a man who builds an enormous castle and lives in a shack close by. They do not live in their own enormous systematic buildings. But spiritually that is a decisive objection. Spiritually speaking a man's thoughts must be the building in which he lives – otherwise everything is topsy-turvy.'[5]

Both Socrates and Jesus taught, with appropriate differences, that the truth was something to be lived and loved, not simply reflected upon or studied. Kierkegaard launches a fearsome attack on 'the professor of theology'. It is impossible, he suggests, for a professor of theology to be saved – words I have tried to keep before me throughout my time as a professor of theology![6] The professor characteristically, but not universally, according to Kierkegaard, seeks to understand by detachment, by stepping back, by attempting to bracket off himself and his own frame of reference, his own feelings and emotions, from the situation so that he may grapple with the 'objective truth' directly. And this, suggests Kierkegaard, is entirely the wrong approach to Christian truth. In a subject like mathematics, the example, the personality and emotions of the teacher may be irrelevant. But authentic Christian theology, according to Kierkegaard, is for disciples, and cannot tolerate detachment:

> Ethico-religiously, and Christianly in particular, there is no doctrine that can be regarded as essential while the personal life of the teacher is accidental; here the essential thing is imitation. What nonsense then that one, instead of following Christ and the Apostles, and suffering what they suffered – that one instead of this should become a professor. Of what? Why, that Christ was crucified and the Apostles scourged.[7]

It is not only in theology that there is an emphasis on involvement rather than detachment as the path to truth. In some of the social sciences a rather similar emphasis is to be found. In a remarkable essay, 'On Intellectual Craftsmanship', C. Wright Mills argues that scholarship 'is a choice of how to live as well as a choice of career'. One becomes through life experiences a good workman; one is personally involved, rather than detached, in one's intellectual endeavours. The imagination is to be kindled, if good work is to result; the whole person is involved in the intellectual enterprise.[8] In many of the social and human sciences it is well recognized that empathy and involvement rather than detachment and objectivity are the paths to understanding, and that the task is not so much to fit reality into a system as to discover fragments, and allow fragmentary patterns in personal and social life to reveal themselves. The participant observation of the social anthropologist, for example, really depends on the development of a strong affective bond between the observed and the observer. Loving, or at least a strong emotional relationship, is the condition and the context for knowing.

Systems and particulars

Stephen Hawking, the eminent scientist, is reported to have declared that modern science is on the verge of producing a 'theory of everything'. When that happens, he declares, God will have become redundant. His is, of course, an extreme reaction. But in all spheres of life theories and systems, despite the extravagant claims they often make, are, with appropriate cautions, important for understanding and as guides to action. We have to have them; but they are dangerous, and easily become oppressive or misleading. The ghastly systems of Nazism and Communism showed appallingly how political systems can generate destructive violence on a scale unthought of in earlier centuries. And these earlier centuries, like today, are littered with systems of belief and practice which became oppressive and diabolic, one of which was the Inquisition, carried through by piously religious friars. It was not surprising that Voltaire issued a call: *écrasez l'infâme*.[9]

And yet we need systems and theories to focus our thinking and our acting if we are to understand our world and respond to the challenges of the day with understanding and effectiveness. But universalizing systems and theories which are intended to help us to understand, and provide guidance for action easily become titanic, not so much revealing reality as forcing reality into a particular predetermined mould, and denying their own limitedness. Mahatma Gandhi issued a profound challenge to Enlightenment universalizing when he challenged Kant's theory of the 'universalizing of one's maxim', that is, asking what would happen if everyone acted as I propose to do. Gandhi said that if one wanted to know whether a proposed act was moral, one should ask how this act would affect the poorest, weakest, most vulnerable person one can imagine. The right action is that which would help that particular person the most. Most of the time we have no more than glimpses of the truth, fragments of insight, concrete and specific challenges to action. But these are often rich and valuable resources for action and for understanding. And fragments can often be helpfully subversive of what are generally believed to be received certainties.[10]

The kind of theologizing that I find most congenial and productive is that which starts from the concrete, the particular, the person, or the issue, and seeks insight from Scripture and the tradition, and also attends to God speaking to us through the 'secular' sciences, and their theories. This is far more than theological 'scavaging'![11]

Every sphere of life seems to require at least some theory or theories, systems of ideas and aspirations, if it is to operate effectively, and learn from experience. But the theory that practitioners need to support their practices and make sense of their commitments, can also conceal what is really going on, acting as a kind of smokescreen to stop people seeing what is happening. I well remember, for example, a group of people with a range of experience of the criminal justice system meeting to discuss imprisonment and other forms of punishment. We went through the major theories of punishment – retribution, rehabilitation, and so forth. Then a few people with intimate involvement with the life of Scottish prisons commented sharply that none of the theories, or even all the theories together, explained much of what was happening in Scottish prisons. In particular, under the fashionable banner of 'rehabilitation', multitudes of prisoners were still 'slopping out'; there was a great deal of brutality and intimidation, and little that could really be labelled 'rehabilitation' was going one. The fashionable – and in many ways admirable – theory of rehabilitation distracted the gaze of the public and the politicians from what was really happening. And then, after a long and fascinating discussion, there was general agreement in the group that Christian understandings of forgiveness, reconciliation and the healing of relationships were a kind of 'public truth' that both helped us to understand the criminal justice system, but also – and more importantly – how it should be made more humane and constructive.

Commitment to great moral or political idealistic theory can sometimes conflict directly with a proper ethical attitude to the concrete Other, to the neighbour God has given us to love, as with Dostoevsky's doctor, who said:

> I love humanity,…but I wonder at myself. The more I love humanity in general, the less I love man [sic] in particular. In my dreams…I have often come to making enthusiastic schemes for the service of humanity, and perhaps I might actually have faced crucifixion if it had been suddenly necessary; and yet I am incapable of living in the same room with anyone for two days together, as I know by experience… In twenty-four hours I begin to hate the best of men… But it has always happened that the more I detest men individually the more ardent becomes my love for humanity.[12]

And in the film of Pasternak's great novel, *Dr Zhivago*, the young student idealistic revolutionary who appears with blood streaming down his face after the Cossacks have charged to break up a demonstration for justice and liberty, appears later in the film as the ruthless commissar who moves around the steppes in an armoured train, destroying villages and massacring villagers suspected of sympathizing with the Whites. Idealism and captivity to a universalizing theory have eroded any kind of altruistic commitment. The best of theories and ideologies which claim to start from the universal or the general rather than the concrete can easily degenerate into the inhumane.

Unsystematic Christianity

Christians in the pew often assume that faith is primarily a matter of intellectual understanding, consent to a creed or confession. That, it is thought, is the qualification for church membership. Christianity is a system which must be taken whole or not at all: as Hobbes wryly suggested long ago, 'For it is with the mysteries of our religion, as with wholesome pills for the sick, which swallowed whole have the virtue to cure; but chewed, are for the most part cast up again without effect'.[13] Infant baptism might well be seen as the refutation of this position, since infants are admitted to membership of the Church before they are consciously aware of what is happening, before they can be said to have faith, or the ability to repeat or understand the ancient baptismal creed, commonly called the Apostles' Creed. Interestingly enough, the emphasis in most baptism rites is not so much on theology (by its very name a form of theory) as on story. In my own Church the child at baptism is addressed by name with these words:

> For you Jesus Christ came into the world:
> for you he lived and showed God's love;
> for you he suffered the darkness of Calvary
> and cried at the last, 'It is accomplished';
> for you he triumphed over death
> and rose in newness of life;
> for you he ascended to reign at God's right hand.
> All this he did for you, N....,
> though you do not know it yet.
> And so the word of Scripture is fulfilled:
> 'We love because God loved us first.'[14]

It is a very different thing to be incorporated into an ongoing story, a narrative, rather than accepting consciously the truthfulness and adequacy of a theory or a system. A central part of the difference is this: from childhood until old age we can enter into stories, live out stories, graft our own personal story onto broader stories, making them our own. Stories are particular; theories are, or usually claim to be, universal.

Loving and knowing

For Kierkegaard the truth is to be lived and loved. This priority of loving in knowing is one of the most distinctive and compelling features of the tradition with which we are concerned. In love and in loving the truth reveals itself. In the First Letter of John it is declared that we should love one another because love is from God, and then, amazingly, the passage continues: '*Everyone* who loves is born of

God and *knows God*. Whoever does not love does not know God, for
God is love.'[15] And then, a few verses later, come these words: 'God
is love, and those who abide in love abide in God, and God abides in
them.'[16]

The apostle Paul in his great 'hymn of love' in 1 Corinthians 13 says
a great deal about the nature of our knowledge of God, much of
which seems to be lost sight of when we engage with the great
theological systems of today or of the past. Theologians and believers
often are seen as rather arrogant, people who claim to have a comprehensive grasp of God's truth which puts them in a privileged position.
But Paul himself, at least in the passage with which we are at present
concerned, seems to be very modest.

Now, in the present age, Paul suggests, our knowledge is
fragmentary, enigmatic, often confusing, like dim images in a distorting
mirror. The Greek word often translated 'dimly', or 'darkly', is perhaps
better rendered as 'in a riddle', or 'as an enigma' – and *enigma* is indeed
the Greek word used here. Our grasp of the truth in the present age is
necessarily uncertain, incomplete and hazy. We now know only in part;
beyond our present knowledge there is a dazzling and attractive
mystery which we are called to live and love. Love is the one thing that
lasts forever – prophecy, tongues, even knowledge itself will come to
an end. But love lasts for ever, and in love all things find their
fulfilment. Yet here and now we live and move in the hope of the
fullness of knowledge that has been promised at the end.

The knowledge in question today and at the end is *personal*
knowledge. It is not detached, objective, unyielding, but it is the kind
of knowledge which reveals itself in the context of love, and which
always remains an entrancing mystery. At the end, and only at the end,
we can hope for undistorted knowledge, when we will know God and
others as clearly as we are ourselves known to God. True and complete
knowledge is beyond mystery, the face-to-face encounter with God,
which God promised to Moses, for which we also may hope:[17]

> And [God] said, 'Hear my words:
> When there are prophets among you
> I the Lord make myself known to them in visions;
> I speak to them in dreams.
> Not so with my servant Moses; he is entrusted with all my house.
> With him I speak face to face – clearly, not in riddles;
> and he beholds the form of the Lord.

A fragmentary theology assumes that in this life we never see save
'in a mirror dimly', and only at the end 'face to face'.[18] This might

make us more generally cautious about regarding theology as some grand coherent modernist theory rather than a series of illuminating fragments which sustain and nurture the life of the community of faith, and which claim also to be in some sense 'public truth'. After all, the gospels and even the epistles do not present a 'system'. Rather, they are full of parables, stories, epigrams, injunctions, songs – fragments, in short. The system-building came far later, and it is still not easy to co-ordinate the material into a coherent consistent system. Perhaps theologians should sympathize with the postmodernists' suspicion of systems and system-building! Is it perhaps enough, with the man born blind, to know one thing, one fragment, with assurance: 'once I was blind; now I see' (John 9.25)? But that fragment is all-important.

Are there today theological fragments which might be recognized as public truth and serve to give some coherence and integrity, even in 'the desolation of reality that overtakes human beings in a post-religious age that has grown too wise to swallow the shallow illusions of the Enlightenment'? (John Gray) And might these fragments perhaps be the aptest way of confessing the faith in the public realm today?

My colleague and friend, Michael Northcott, has commented that I do not see truth-telling in fragments as a way of confessing the faith today. My aim, he suggests, is 'to bend the ear of the Powers in such a way as they may hear an element of Christian truth quarried, but necessarily detached from the realms of Christian faith and practice'. My whole notion of theological fragments, he argues, 'carries with it the clear implication that theologians have no business to tell the story of the Gospel in the public square in a secular or postmodern society'. Why should Christians be expected, Northcott asks, to refrain from proclaiming their beliefs as a whole in public?[19]… Despite the fact that Northcott cites Yoder on his side, and apparently believes that the kind of fragments with which I am concerned are mere lubricants for the existing social and political order, I think he misunderstands my point. I too believe that the central role of public theology is to confess the faith. But one does not confess the faith in its wholeness all the time, and in every context. Hobbes was wrong in suggesting that Christianity was like a pill that had to be swallowed whole or not at all. The theological fragments of which I have had experience are often sharp and disturbing, but often also constructive, helpful and healing. And again and again they invite those who have been challenged, encouraged or disturbed to trace the fragment back to its source, the quarry from which it was hewed. But perhaps the real difference between Michael Northcott, Yoder and myself is that I do not believe that the gospel is *always* confrontational. Along with its task of announcing the good news there certainly goes a responsibility for denouncing lies and lovelessness. But it also has a function of encouraging and forgiving those who have responsibility for the wellbeing of others.

A new Dark Ages?

Kierkegaard in a real sense anticipated a world that is as postmodern as it is post-Christian. The condition of postmodernity is a pluralist society in which not only are many theories and world-views allowed and tolerated but there is a profound suspicion of grand theories and theologies, of systems which make exclusive claim to truth. These are essentially seen as coercive and inadequate to reality. Society, *pace* Rawls and others, does not need a consensus to survive, according to the postmodernists. Indeed, consensus can only be achieved by force or manipulation. It inherently involves a limitation of freedom, which in a fairly straightforward sense becomes the great central value of postmodernity. There is, in Lyotard's words, a profound 'incredulity towards metanarratives'.[20] The postmodern mind knows itself to be homeless; but it also recognizes that no home exists. The mindset is melancholy and anxious, but it is also willing to come to terms with the fragmentation of reality and refuses to impose an artificial and fragile order upon it.

Postmodernists typically see the East European communist dicta-torships that collapsed nearly a decade ago as both an exemplification of the Enlightenment project and its nemesis. Václav Havel would probably decline to call himself a postmodernist, but his analysis of Czechoslovakia under the communists has a postmodernist flavour. Havel saw the death throes of the old communist regimes as indicative of a far more extensive and profound crisis that could perhaps be called the collapse of modernity, the Enlightenment project having run its course. The sad communist systems were 'a kind of warning to the West, revealing its own latent tendencies'.[21] The East holds up a mirror to the West; both are modernist societies in deep crisis. The system – and Havel clearly means both the old Marxist systems, where decay, decadence and demoralization were easy to discern, and the societies of the West, where decline is more concealed – depends on *ideology*, whose function 'is to provide people...with the illusion that the system is in harmony with the human order and the order of the universe'. Ideology legitimates power and oppressive dictatorship, for it pervasively suggests that 'the centre of power is identical with the centre of truth'.[22] Ideology – overtly in the old Marxist regimes, more covertly in other modernist societies – is thus the main pillar of the system which effectively creates and internalizes a false reality: 'It is built upon lies. It works only as long as people are willing to live within the lie.'[23]

Havel's diagnosis may be, at least superficially, postmodernist; but his response is not. He does not despair of knowing and living in truth, of witnessing to truth, either in unitary ideological despotisms or in conditions of pluralism and thoroughgoing relativism. He comprehensively rejects the modernist project of rebuilding the world according to some great rational scheme, especially a scheme that promises the overcoming of the human condition and a future contrived perfection. But Havel affirms the primary importance of people and of 'togetherness', particularly that form which is 'being for' others.[24] And in this he reminds us of the unavoidable centrality of the Church in Christian theology.

Others, such as Alasdair MacIntyre, see the postmodern condition as a *predicament*. Modern society, for MacIntyre, is morally fragmented since there are no generally accepted criteria for the resolution of moral disputes and conflicts.[25] No widely recognized moral framework exists; the situation is volatile, for behaviour lacks a rationale, or a place in a larger scheme which makes some claim to truth. The moral fragments that survive today were embedded and embodied in various traditions and practices which are, for the most part, dismissed as discredited and irrelevant survivals among deviant minorities. We cannot understand moral standards properly, MacIntyre believes, without situating these fragments in the context of the traditions of moral enquiry from which they originally came, and from which they have become detached. Only if we take seriously the ancient comprehensive traditions of moral enquiry, he believes, may we be able to make progress towards resolving key issues of today.

Both MacIntyre and the postmodernists recognize that fragmentation is characteristic of the contemporary world. The postmodernists celebrate this fact; MacIntyre laments it as a grave predicament. I would argue that from the angle of the Christian mission we should recognize that fragmentation presents opportunities and challenges which are at the same time fresh and also have striking similarities to the situation in the ancient world when the Christian faith was born. We can learn from the early Church how to witness to the truth in a fragmented age. Whether fragmentation is a predicament or an emancipation, the gospel can be proclaimed in a fragmented age. That is the immediate task. Whether MacIntyre is right in suggesting that we should work towards a new Christian consensus on Aristotelian and Thomist foundations is a question we may leave aside for the while. My own inclination is that the establishment or restoration of some general consensus based on Christian foundations is inconceivable for the foreseeable future, and probably in the light of historical experience undesirable. Today we have to witness to the truth in a world in fragments.

Disputes which appear to be irresolvable about justice and goodness represent not only academic difficulties but major problems of practice, for people 'on the ground', as it were; hence they become pressing issues for Christian mission and public theology. Politics and policy-making easily degenerate into, in MacIntyre's telling phrase, 'civil war carried on by other means',[26] an arena in which interest groups compete for control, using ideas as weapons rather than constraints, and as justifications for volatile policy changes which in fact are little influenced by overarching moral considerations. Or the ideological pendulum swings from one extreme to another without the reasons for the change being clear or generally acceptable.

Practitioners often feel that they are making do with fragments of moral insight, and fragments which are frequently in unacknowledged conflict with other fragments, or are not recognized in the way the system or institution is run. And practitioners sometimes recognize that the fragments which are most important for them as insights into reality, as in some sense *true*, and which are central to the sense of vocation which sustains them in their practice, are derived from a tradition which was and is nurtured and sustained in a community of shared faith to which they may or may not belong, and which is now a minority view in society.

Liberal democracy

MacIntyre's rather apocalyptic scenario of the new Dark Ages, in which the public square is an arena for a game without rules or referee, and his nostalgia for a rather romanticized and wistful understanding of the Christendom of the high Middle Ages, implies also a radical critique of the kind of pluralism which is characteristic of modern liberal democracies. These societies cannot, it is true, call upon any coherent and generally accepted body of religious and moral understanding which may authoritatively resolve the ethical dilemmas which face any community on a daily basis. Often enough there are quite fundamental disagreements; say, on the status of the early foetus or the unborn child, or on human reproductive or therapeutic cloning, or on the morality of homosexuality.

Such moral diversity must be, and can be, handled in plural societies wisely and even productively. Larry Rasmussen is, I think, over-pessimistic in suggesting that Western society lives from moral and community fragments which are 'being destroyed faster than they are being replenished'.[27] Jeffrey Stout has argued for the significance and constructive role of what he calls 'moral bricolage' rather than 'moral Esperanto'. Moral Esperanto is the construction of an artificial – and secular – moral language which it is hoped will be acceptable to everyone, and claim its place as the universal language of morality. Bricolage is altogether less orderly. Here the resources at the beginning are 'bits and pieces' – or fragments – of traditional material and inherited insights. The process starts from problems that need solving and examines relevant resources. For Stout it is of the greatest import-ance that religious resources are not excluded from this discussion, and here he differs from many other Western philosophers who have concerned themselves with these matters. In the process of bricolage it is necessary that the various parties, representing different views and offering different resources, should modestly attend to the viewpoints of others as well as presenting their own, and see whether some kind of at least short-term working solution may be arrived at.[28] There will always be the need for an element of a common morality, even if this is less prominent than it was in much of the past. But new situations raise new ethical problems, and a decent and free society has to develop ways of resolving problems, or continuing a responsible debate until some acceptable conclusion may be reached.[29]

In such a situation there are clear duties laid upon Christian believers to contribute fragments of what they know to be true, and hope that they may both play a significant role in resolving, even if only temporarily, the kind of ethical dilemmas which surround us today, and encourage people of integrity to engage not only with the offered fragments, but also with the quarry from which they have come.[30]

Communities of shared faith

As we have seen, Havel emphasized in his confusing situation as a dissident in communist Czechoslovakia the importance of 'togeth-erness', and responsibility to and for one another. Alasdair MacIntyre, in his famous conclusion to *After Virtue,* proclaims that the barbarians have taken over, and in the new Dark Ages people of shared faith should gather together in communities to preserve and examine the tradition in preparation for the coming of happier times. The broader community cannot be sustained merely by fragments of a lost coherent culture. Fragments are incapable of holding together a decent society. With fragmentation the whole basis of civility is destroyed; a society that no longer has a shared grand narrative cannot survive coherently for long. But in these new forms of dissident community 'the moral life could be sustained so that both morality and civility might survive the coming ages of barbarism and darkness'. He continues:

> What matters at this stage is the construction of local forms of community within which civility and the intellectual and moral life can be sustained through the new dark ages which are already upon us. And if the tradition of the virtues was able to survive the horrors of the last dark ages, we are not entirely without grounds for hope. This time however the barbarians are not waiting beyond the frontiers; they have been governing us for quite some time. And it is our lack of consciousness of this that constitutes part of our predicament. We are waiting not for a Godot, but for another – doubtless very different – St Benedict.[31]

It is, I think, the case that MacIntyre affirms rather than demonstrating that a decent community must have a shared grand narrative, a canon, or a common tradition which it explores and which is in some sense normative. Diversity is not seen as enrichment and challenge. This passage, or the mindset that it typifies, has been seized upon by a variety of modern theologians with great enthusiasm. The Church of today is seen, like the monasteries of the original Dark Ages, as an alternative society, exemplifying and exploring an alternative way of being

It is surely significant that Barth, in a context in which theology was firmly embedded in the university, saw a necessity to speak not simply of *Christian* dogmatics, but *Church* dogmatics and *Church* ethics in order that theology might recover its integrity, fulfil its vocation, and grapple with the issues of the day. In facing a modern situation in which he feels there is a danger of Christian ethics losing its distinctiveness and dissolving into academic ethics in general, the American theologian Stanley Hauerwas has developed Barth's point by arguing that the church not only has, but *is* a social ethic. The primary ethical task of the Church, he argues, is to *be* the Church as a community of faith, of worship and of service.[32] In expounding the thought of the Mennonite John Howard Yoder, Hauerwas suggests that 'practical reason is not a disembodied process based on abstract principles but a process of a community in which every member has a role to play'.[33]

Such a community of character, even in its sinfulness, is both a community of moral discourse and an exemplification of the moral orientation sustained by the biblical tradition. For Hauerwas, the only theology and the only ethics that matter are rooted in the life of the Church and serve the development of Christian character and faithful practice, participating in the Church's function of witnessing to the truth.

This does not mean that Hauerwas sees theology as a kind of in-house discourse, the language game of the Christian community which has no claim to truth in a more general sense. He engages in his writings with issues on the public and the academic agenda, with medical ethics, war and peace, the position of the handicapped, and many others. He comes at these questions from an unashamedly theological, ecclesial and Christian angle, and in so doing often brings a strange freshness to tired controversies, directing the attention to commonly forgotten dimensions and neglected resources. But Stout is right when he affirms that 'The church is one place where truths are spoken. It is also, however, a place where many falsehoods are spoken.'[34]

Hauerwas has been accused by James Gustafson and others of 'sectarian withdrawal' from engagement with the moral tensions and ambiguities of what some people call 'the real world'. The charge does not, I think, stick, although I am more sympathetic to the suggestion that Hauerwas tends towards a rather romanticized and even triumphalistic understanding of the Church. His position might be strengthened if he spoke more clearly of how a sinful Church in a fallen world can nevertheless be a sacramental sign of God's love and truth. Hauerwas is determined not to allow Christian ethics to dissolve into a general ethics of Americanism, and he has increasingly concentrated on the churchliness of Christian ethics. Hauerwas both affirms the crucial significance of the Church, and remembers that God's purposes and God's practice encompass the whole creation. .

The danger in the Hauerwasian emphasis on the Church, which builds particularly on the work of MacIntyre and John Howard Yoder, is that it can be seen as pointing to the Church as an exemplar of the theological verities, where truth and love are to be found in abundance. The problem with this rather triumphalistic understanding of the Church is twofold. On the one hand, it courts disillusion, as people find that a local congregation is very far from being exemplary of the Christian gospel. On the other hand, it tends, particularly as developed by advocates of 'radical orthodoxy', to suggest that all truth is to be found in the Church, and nothing but lies and confusion in 'the world'. As I discuss in the essay, 'The Church and the concentration camp', later in this book, this position is defective, precisely because it expresses too narrow an understanding of the Church and too limited an understanding of God's ability to address and challenge us through the events of the day or the wisdom of the secular world.

The Church is called to be a manifestation of God's love and truth, but does not always live up to her call. The Second Vatican Council rather daringly declared: 'By her relationship with Christ, the Church is a kind of sacrament or sign of intimate union with God, and of the unity of all humankind. She is also an instrument for the achievement of such union and unity.'[35] The wording is quite cautious, but it is unambiguous in suggesting that the Church is, or is *called* to be, an exemplification of a kind of community which God intends to encompass all humankind, and of which the Church is also to be an instrument, helping to bring such inclusive community into existence as well as providing a preliminary manifestation of it. The term 'instrument' suggests that the Church has been given a servant role, helping with the overcoming of ancient hostilities and the establishment of the kind of reconciled community in which human beings may flourish together in love and justice.

The Uppsala Assembly of the World Council of Churches in 1968 adopted similar language, declaring that 'The Church is bold in speaking of itself as the sign of the coming unity of mankind.'[36] It was increasingly emphasized that the 'sign' was 'a calling and a task', not something that was already complete and perfect, fully expressed in the visible Church. The Church could only become an instrument for the healing of the nations 'as a community which is itself being healed'. Despite its divisions, which so often in fact reflect and exacerbate the divisions of the world, the Church may be 'the foretaste of a redeemed creation, a sign of the coming unity of [hu]mankind, a pointer to the time when God shall be all in all'.[37]

These are vast and daunting claims made for the Church – but more realistic than those sometimes made by the Hauerwasians and the radical orthodox theologians. The Church is a community of forgiven sinners which is *called* to be an anticipation of God's Reign, an earnest or down-payment, enabling people to glimpse and experience the authentic flavour of God's Reign. It is called to be an exemplary community, existing for the sake of the world. And more, it is to be an instrument, not so much for bringing or building God's Reign as for spreading throughout human society the values, social structures and attitudes which are characteristic of the Reign of God, which is still to come as gift and as grace in its fullness. But the Church, in using such language, is committing itself to being a community which seeks to follow and exemplify the kind of inclusive fellowship which was characteristic of the disciples and others who gathered around Jesus. Only thus may the Church be a sacrament, sign and instrument of the unity of all humankind.

Fragments today

In its concern with the concrete, with action and existence, and with freedom, and in its suspicion of grandiose and impersonal schemes and systems, postmodernity presents opportunities and challenges to the mission of the Church. Indeed the recognition of fragmentation opens a whole range of evangelistic opportunities.

I have suggested the deployment of 'theological fragments' not because I buy into the postmodernist scenario (although I find it quite illuminating, particularly in its view of grand theories as oppressive), but because in a situation where most people are both ignorant and suspicious of Christian doctrine and practice there is really no other way forward than modestly presenting or offering 'fragments' which may be seen as relevant, true, illuminating and helpful for just practice.

A theologian should not, I think, be ashamed of offering, initially, in public debate, in the conditions of postmodernity and radical pluralism, no more than 'fragments' of insight. Postmodernists (and sociologists of knowledge) are, after all, right in affirming that systematic, carefully developed theories can sometimes conceal practices which are inhumane and brutalizing; ideologies can serve as the emperor's new clothes, so that the theologian's task, as a little child, is to cry out, 'But the emperor's got no clothes on!' – a fragment of truth reveals that to which most people have allowed themselves to be blinded. Truth-telling in a consistent but fragmentary way becomes even more important when the scheme to conceal the emperor's nakedness is something that is hurting people and destroying community.[38]

Moral and theological fragments come from specific quarries, or traditions, if you prefer that terminology. We know that theological fragments by which Christians live and which shape their practice have their home in a community of shared faith, the Church, which, if it is true to its calling and its mission, does not wistfully look back to an unrecoverable past, but looks forward with expectation to God's future, and meanwhile offers its fragments as a contribution to the common store and seeks to embody its insights in its life. Only at the end will the fragments, the 'puzzling reflections in a mirror', give way to a face-to-face encounter with the Truth.

When a fragment is recognized as in some sense true, one should expect an interest in its provenance, in its embeddedness in a broader truth. Is a compelling task and opportunity today the bringing together of 'theological fragments' which have been illuminating, instructive or provocative in grappling with issues of practice 'on the ground', reflecting on them, and on their embeddedness in the structure of Christian faith, and enquiring whether this gives clues as to a constructive contribution in the public realm today? This may perhaps be the way towards the renewal and recovery of Christian social vision in the conditions of today.

By 'fragments' I mean a wide range of things – the importance of forgiveness in any decent criminal justice system, confessional statements such as the 1934 Theological Declaration of Barmen which established the German Confessing Church in opposition to Nazism; Reinhold Niebuhr's challenging reflections on the politics of his day; the recent suggestion of Frank Field, the former Minister for Welfare Reform in Britain, that a 'Christian' view of human nature is necessary for a viable welfare system; and many others. Fragments may be irritants (the grit in the oyster that gathers a pearl?), stories/parables, the Socratic questioning of received assumptions, even the 'road metal' for straight paths.

Fragments, of course, come from somewhere; they have been quarried. My purpose in talking this way about real happenings and possibilities is partly evangelical: some people who recognize a Christian fragment as true may trace it back to the quarry from which it comes. But I am also increasingly aware that fragments detached from the quarry are particularly liable to be abused or misunderstood and distorted. Thus the theological task is, I believe, twofold: injecting or offering theological fragments in public debate and, simultaneously, labouring in the quarry or mine – work that may be largely invisible and regarded by most as irrelevant, but which is in fact essential. This, I believe, is precisely how Barth behaved in the 1930s: hard, unrelenting work on the *Dogmatics* 'as if nothing had happened' (his phrase), and simultaneously bombarding the Nazis and the German Christians with a fusillade of fragments which for many people provided a strong discernment of what was actually happening, and how a Christian should respond. What I am profoundly opposed to is a facile presentation of idealistic commonplaces as if they were theological fragments!

Bread in fragments

Another parallel analogy which in some ways is a corrective to the fragments and quarry image, and is far more deeply rooted in Christian thought and liturgical practice, is that of the loaf and the crumbs or grains. The separate grains are ground and kneaded and baked into bread, the one loaf which is the sign of the Body of Christ, both the body broken on the cross and the body of believers who gather and are dispersed in the world to bring forth fruit. For the work of salvation, for the work of God in the world, the body/loaf must be broken into crumbs, only to be gathered together into one at the end of time. At the heart of Christian faith and action is the breaking of the bread for the nourishment of God's people. The fragments are food, nourishment, for a pilgrim people. And not just for the faithful: Jesus said that the bread that he will give is 'for the life of the world', not just for the nourishment of the faithful.[39]

This all boils down to a conviction that ways of doing public theology which seemed to work in earlier times when Christian assumptions were widely shared, when many people were well acquainted with the 'quarry' and approved of it, are irretrievable. And I am also increasingly uneasy about any suggestion that a secular theory can do service as a surrogate for public theology. I am also uneasy about early liberation theology's over-eagerness to baptize Marxism, and the Vatican's (and Christian democracy's) presentation of an alternative *system* of social doctrine, true everywhere and for everyone. Reality is too messy and too confused for either.

The question how a fragmentary approach avoids theory obscuring what is actually going on intrigues me. I certainly do not want to say that all theory obscures what is going on. To the contrary, I am sure that theory is indispensable. But theory must constantly be scrutinized with suspicion, and be subjected to Socratic questioning. What I think is quite essential – and terribly seldom done – is to attend to the 'victims'; and the reflective practitioners and how they view the situation. I have been much shaken by having poor people denounce leading liberal or left-wing experts on poverty, saying, 'You don't know what you are talking about.' And I have heard similar complaints in other contexts. Often it is precisely at this point that a theological fragment might be offered which just might make some sense of a muddled and ugly situation, help reopen communication, and encourage people resolutely to do justice. I've seen it happen. But not often.

Back to the quarry[40]

Theological fragments can play many roles in public theology – as irritants, as illumination, as road metal, as lenses, as fossils, reminders of the past, and ultimately, perhaps, as building blocks once again. I want to suggest that serious theological work is rather like working in a quarry, and quite specifically the kind of quarry which we find in India, where men and women, and often young children, in the heat of the day hack away at the rock-face with simple implements, exposing themselves to danger, and committing to the task all their reserves of energy, intelligence, determination and strength.

I am not thinking of the modern fully mechanized quarry, where everything is done at a safe distance, at the flick of a switch, or the pressing of a button, where danger and sweat are minimized, and people do not themselves engage directly with the rock-face. That might be an image of the modern academic assumption that we are most likely to encounter truth in detachment, that objectivity is all, that commitment is a distraction, or leads to distortion of the truth.

No, I am thinking of the kind of quarry that we find in India and elsewhere, where:

- the work is hard, demanding, exhausting
- the work does not bring high status or tangible rewards, indeed the very opposite – you work because of an inner compulsion or constraint
- most of the work is invisible, rarely noticed or applauded – people in their cars pass by the quarry with hardly a glance as they go about their business.
- the work is sometimes dangerous, full of unexpected hazards
- co-operation is essential – no one can work the quarry alone; one must work as a team with others
- the quarriers seldom see the end-product – the stones they quarry are normally used and fashioned far away
- often the task involves sorting and arranging fragments, not so much like pieces of a jigsaw so that a unified picture may emerge from interlocking pieces, but rather that the fragments may effectively be put to use in various ways for the welfare and salvation of women and men

The cliff-face in our theological quarry is the Bible and the rich resources and insights into truth to be found in the Christian tradition, and the other world faiths and ideologies that have interacted with the Christian tradition.

If we are faithful in our quarry work in the heat and sweat of the day, we produce rough blocks of stone, which others may fashion and shape and use for building strong and lasting edifices – homes, and hospitals, schools and churches, places of welcome and of service, places of stability, constancy and love, built of living stones. Some blocks are given to sculptors, who fashion works of beauty for all to delight in. Often these carvings seem almost to be *released* from the stone by the sculptor's art.

And from our quarry we also produce the small rubble stones called *road metal*, used for making firm, straight paths on which God's people may move forward.

Occasionally we find a gemstone in our quarry, which delights by its beauty, sparkling in the sun; generating a vision that many can share – glimpses into another world.

From time to time an intricate and wonderful fossil emerges, a vivid reminder of times past, and of evolving purposes, and the importance of origins.

Sometimes we come across a crystal, acting like a lens, helping us to see more clearly into the depth of things, to glimpse another world.

And then, as in every quarry, there is much grit and dust, apparently useless, untidy, pervasive, irritating the eyes and coating the nose and throat. Some of it goes to make cement and concrete. But if perchance a piece of that grit might ultimately find its way into an oyster, it gathers around the irritant layer upon layer until the grit becomes the nucleus of a pearl. The grit stands for the awkward, probing, irritating questions that a lively theology should address to church, society and culture.

Some fragments are like pieces of glass or gems that catch the light and display its wonderful colours, or generate a vision that many can share – glimpses into another world. It is perhaps better that visions and hopes of utopias should be generated in this way than by one of the huge ideologies that seem now to have collapsed. People and societies need to be liberated from being confined in the prison of 'the real world', unable to dream the dreams which will shape the practice of tomorrow and become ultimately the practice of the Reign of God. The point is made very powerfully by F. A. Hayek in a 1949 essay:

> The main lesson which the true liberal must learn from the success of the socialists is that it was their courage to be Utopian which gained them the support of the intellectuals and therefore an influence on public opinion which is daily making possible what only recently seemed utterly remote. Those who have concerned themselves

exclusively with what seemed practicable in the existing state of opinion have constantly found that even this has rapidly become politically impossible as a result of changes in public opinion which they have done nothing to guide. Unless we can make the philosophic foundations of a free society once more a living intellectual issue, and its implementation a task which challenges the ingenuity and imagination of our liveliest minds, the prospects of freedom are indeed dark.[41]

So back to the quarry, to obtain the fragments that give us road metal, that provoke the oyster to make pearls, that concentrate the light into visions, that generate utopias, that build up jigsaws of meaning, and that nourish the activity of truthfulness, love and justice which is the practice of the Reign of God!

I

Understanding people

2

The mystery of the human person in community[1]

I want in this chapter to think about the *mystery* of the human *person* in community, rather than about something called 'human nature'. The concept of human nature, some unchanging, ahistorical essence that all human beings possess, is a philosophical rather than theological or biblical notion. It tends to understand human beings, the human person, in isolation, apart from the relationships which in fact make us who we are, and in the absence of which we cannot be truly human. So I am glad that the title includes the term *mystery*, as a salutary reminder that we cannot comprehend human beings, understand them fully, any more than we can comprehend the mystery of the triune God. A mystery, even the great central mystery of God, is to be known by being lived and loved; it cannot be captured in words. St Augustine pointed to the way of personal knowledge in relationship when he prayed:

> Let me know you, who know me, let me know you even as I am known. Do you, the power of my soul, enter into it and fit it for yourself, that you may have it and possess it without spot or wrinkle. This is my hope, this is my prayer, and in this hope do I rejoice... For behold you love the truth, and 'he that doth the truth comes to the light'. I wish to do it in confession, in my heart before you, in my writing before many witnesses.[2]

Equality and Imago Dei[3]

The creation account in Genesis 1 declares that human beings, *all* human beings, are made in the image and likeness of God:

> Then God said, 'Let us make humankind in our image, according to our likeness; and let them have dominion over the fish of the sea, and over the birds of the air'... So God created humankind in his image, in the image of God he created them, male and female he created them. God blessed them, and God said to them, 'Be fruitful and multiply, and fill the earth and subdue it.'[4]

The Imago Dei has, of course, been much discussed down the ages, and continues to be debated today.[5] For our present purposes just a few points need to be made. First, the universality of the image, the fact that it has been conferred on all human beings, needs to be stressed. In this passage from Genesis, writes Jonathan Sacks, 'What was new was not that a human being can be in the image of God, but that *every* human being is. From its inception, Judaism was a living protest against hierarchical societies that ascribe to some, but not all, dignity, power and freedom. Instead it insisted that if any individual is sacred, then every individual is, because each of us is in the image of God.'[6] The Imago Dei stands resolutely against any social system which demeans or despises human beings, such as apartheid, Fascism, or slavery.

We should be cautious about regarding the image as some quality that may be possessed by human beings, like reason. Certainly it is not an achievement that we work on. The image is given by God, but often hidden or obscured, like the watermark on a bank-note. And that analogy reminds us that the image of God, given to every human being, is the basis for asserting and recognizing the equal worth and value of every human being, the wise as much as the person with severe learning difficulties, the physically handicapped as much as the outstanding athlete. People, because they are created in the image of God, should be treated with reverence – but often are not. This is a point made splendidly by Joe Corrie, the Scots miner-poet:

> The image o' God
>
> Crawlin' aboot like a snail in the mud
> Covered wi' clammy blae,
> Me, made after the image o' God –
> Jings! But it's laughable tae.
>
> Howkin' awa' 'neath a mountain o' stane,
> Gaspin' for want o' air,
> The sweat makin' streams doon my bare back-bane
> And my knees a' hauckit and sair.
>
> Strainin' and cursin' the hale shift through,
> Half-starved, half-blin', half mad;
> And the gaffer he says, 'Less dirt in that coal
> Or ye go up the pit, my lad!'
>
> So I gie my life to the Nimmo squad
> For eicht and fower a day;
> Me! made after the image o' God –
> Jings! But it's laughable, tae.[7]

The Imago Dei speaks both of the importance of equal relationships and of the need to give equal respect, treatment and indeed *reverence* to all, for all bear the image, even if now only in partial and broken form. Equality is ascribed by God in the work of creation; it is not a human achievement or an empirical characteristic of human beings. The contrast here with some other traditions could not be starker. The Hindu creation myth, for example, suggests that hierarchy is a given part of the created order. Some are born pure and others polluted, perhaps as reward or punishment for behaviour in a previous existence. In this mortal life the hierarchical order is beyond question. The lowly and impure must simply thole their condition while those of higher status and greater purity may enjoy their reward without troubling their consciences. But for Christians equality before God and with one another is the original and proper human condition, and is an aspect of the promised culmination of all things. Meanwhile it must find real, if partial, expression among faithful people and in godly societies, indeed wherever the dignity and worth of human beings should be affirmed and celebrated. The image of God is thus a way of affirming and interpreting human dignity. I cannot put the basic conviction better than in G. K. Chesterton's vivid image: people are equal in the same way pennies are equal. Some are bright, others are dull; some are worn smooth, others are sharp and fresh. But all are equal in value for each penny bears the image of the sovereign; each person bears the image of the King of Kings.[8]

And this point has a direct bearing on a range of contested issues in our increasingly secular societies, which have great difficulty in justifying equal treatment of people who for one reason or another cannot make a productive contribution of the usual sort to the wellbeing of the community. The American philosopher, Robert Veatch, has aptly suggested that modern secular thought does not have the resources to deal with fundamental questions such as the moral claims and status of those with severe and uncorrectable physical or mental incapacities. In such situations, Veatch suggests, decent and moral practice calls out for help and support from Christian theology.[9] So, in particular, we must proclaim the good news that such people are made as much in the image of God as we, the able-bodied and intelligent, and they should be treated as such. People should be treated with reverence because they bear, often invisibly, the mysterious image of God, an insight that underlies Jean Vanier's wonderful work with people with severe learning difficulties, and the development of care for the dying in the Christian hospice movement, in a culture in which death and dying people are a major source of embarrassment.

Interestingly enough, the equal worth affirmed by the Imago Dei does not erase the precious differences between people, which should be celebrated and honoured, as Jonathan Sacks, the Chief Rabbi, suggests in his remarkable book, *The Dignity of Difference*. 'Can we recognize God's image in one who is not in my image?' asks Sacks. In the new global age in which our world has become a society of strangers, can we find in the human other, the person or people who are different, a trace of the Divine Other? This, Sacks suggests, is 'not a threat to faith but a call to a faith larger and more demanding than we had sometimes supposed it to be'.[10] Those who recognize that God has conferred God's image on all human beings should be able to celebrate the precious differences which enrich society and make it interesting and varied. Difference, rather than degree, is to be affirmed, expressed and delighted in.

Trinity and Imago Dei

It has often been noted in the Genesis 1 passage that the plural is used both of God and of those who bear the image. For Jews, like Jonathan Sacks, this presents a problem, for they believe that prior to the creation, particularly of human beings, God was alone.[11] But Christians who believe in the Triune God believe that God has never been alone, that even before the incarnation the Godhead was three persons bound together in perichoresis, the great eternal dance of love. God is love, and always has been love, and always will be love. And the affirmation that God is love carries with it the conviction that there is a loving relationship which is integral to the life of God.

In Genesis 1 this is indicated by the plural pronouns used of the God who says: *We* will create human beings in *our* image and likeness. And then man and woman are created *together* in the image of God, as if to emphasize that the image is not an attribute of human beings in isolation, but only in relationship with one another and with God. The narrative in Genesis 2 is different. It does not use the plural of God, and Eve is created after Adam, but there is the same emphasis on the human need for relationships: it is not good for Adam to be alone. He needs Eve, and neither is complete without the other. People are created in and for relationship with God, with one another and with the natural environment. People are made to love and to be loved. The relationship of women and men is paradigmatic. It is central in both Genesis 1 ('male and female he created them') and in Genesis 2, where God declares, 'It is not good that the man should be alone; I will make him a helper as his partner'.[12] The image is not to be regarded as an inherent or acquired status or quality; it is a nature or status and vocation graciously given by God. When it is marred and dishonoured it may be restored by participation in Christ. The Imago Dei is thus not some abstract quality that each human being possesses, but it relates to the human capacity for relationship.

Human beings are essentially relational, made for loving.[13] It is in human relationships of love, solidarity and equality that the image of God is most clearly manifest. We are made in order to reflect and participate in the life of the triune God. The image is not so much a quality as a calling and a capacity for a certain kind and quality of relationship. Just as the Blessed Trinity is bound together in the inclusive dance of love and delight, so women and men should allow themselves to be drawn into the life of the Trinity so that we in our turn are enabled to draw the unloved and the unlovable into the ambit of our love. As in Rublev's famous icon of the three visitors that Abraham entertains by the oak of Mamre, so in loving the lover and the beloved give undivided attention to one another.

Ecce homo: behold the human being

Luther's great hymn includes this verse:

> With force of arms we nothing can,
> Full soon we were down-ridden;
> But for us fights *the proper Man*,
> Whom God Himself hath bidden.
> Ask ye who is this same?
> Christ Jesus is His Name,
> The Lord Sabaoth's Son;
> He, and no other one,
> Shall conquer in the battle.[14]

Jesus Christ, the second person of the Trinity, is 'the proper human', so that Pilate was inspired when he presented Jesus to the mob that was howling for his blood, proclaiming *Ecce Homo*, 'Behold the Man'. Paul teaches that Christ is the true and perfect image of God.[15] And in as far as Christ is the perfect image of God, a Christian understanding of the human person may aptly be developed, as by Karl Barth, in the closest integration with christology. Barth concentrates on 'the concrete existence of Jesus Christ'. We cannot speak of God apart from Jesus, or of Jesus apart from God. Nor can we speak of human beings apart from Jesus Christ, or of Jesus Christ apart from all human beings, for in Jesus 'God was there for all persons'.

Barth's theology centres explicitly on the 'royal man', Jesus Christ, and therefore is also implicitly reflection on all humanity:

> According to Barth, humankind can never receive its due as long as it seeks it within itself.... We can conceive what God intends for humankind only by reflecting on the one human being that God himself has uniquely intended and directed, and in whom his own divine being is taken up: Jesus Christ. He is the royal man. And his royalty does not exclude, but includes, us. *All humankind is reflected in him.*[16]

Jesus Christ alone displays true humanity, according to Barth. Something like Pascal's affirmation is at issue here:

> The knowledge of God without that of man's misery causes pride. The knowledge of man's misery without that of God causes despair. The knowledge of Jesus Christ constitutes the middle course, because in Him we find both God and our misery.[17]

And such a strong christological emphasis is, of course, perfectly compatible with a trinitarian approach; indeed it demands and assumes such an emphasis.

God in Christ does not simply assume human nature in general. His identification especially with the weak, the poor, the oppressed and the forgotten is a special theme of the hymn in Philippians 2, a kind of summary of New Testament teaching on the incarnation, which is often echoed in contemporary theological anthropology:

> Let the same mind be in you that was in Christ Jesus,
> who, though he was in the form of God,
> did not regard equality with God
> as something to be exploited,
> but emptied himself,
> taking the form of a slave,
> being born in human likeness.
> And being found in human form,
> he humbled himself
> and became obedient to the point of death –
> even death on a cross.
> Therefore God also highly exalted him
> and gave him the name that is above every name,
> so that at the name of Jesus
> every knee should bend,
> in heaven and on earth and under the earth,
> that every tongue should confess that Jesus Christ is Lord,
> to the glory of God the Father.[18]

So theological anthropology has distinctive and challenging things to say in the general discussion of human nature today. It cannot say these things, or confess the faith in the public forum, unless it avoids the temptation simply to reflect the 'received certainties' of the moment, and speaks boldly on the basis of its faith in God. That does not necessarily mean using technical theological language, but it does mean attending to the problems and possibilities of contributing Christian insights into humanity in language which can in fact communicate in the particular context of an age, a culture, a language and the specific issues of the day. And in such discussion theologians should expect to listen as well as speak, to learn as well as teach.

When we affirm that God was in Christ we are not only acknowledging that the second Person of the Trinity became incarnate and walked our dusty roads while remaining in the closest fellowship with the Father and the Spirit; we are also affirming that Jesus' extraordinary loving openness to the weak, the marginalized, the forgotten and the excluded both demonstrated the scope and nature of the love of God, and provided a model of Christian fellowship, of the Church. John Zizioulas's *Being as Communion* explored this theme in the Fathers and the Orthodox tradition.[19] For Zizioulas, human nature can only be understood in communion, and communion is essentially ecclesial: The Church, for Zizioulas and others, is not simply an institution. She is a 'mode of existence', *a way of being...* Ecclesial being is bound to the very being of God... This way of being...is a way of *relationship* with the world, with other people, and with God, an event of *communion*, and that is why it cannot be realized as the achievement of an *individual*, but only as an *ecclesial* fact.[20] Nevertheless, there is a pressing need to relate the Church as the bride of Christ, as mystery and prophetic sign and instrument to the empirical reality of the Church.[21]

Humans as fallen[22]

You can't discern the Imago Dei empirically, by observation. In a fallen, sinful world it is hidden, obscured, radically distorted. Human selfishness, arrogance, insensitivity, lust, exploitation, violence, legalism, manipulation – all obscure the image of God and demonstrate the brokenness of the human condition.

An emphasis on human beings as sinners has been particularly strong and important in theologies that have been deeply influenced by the Augustinian tradition of thought. There have, of course, been disputes in the course of time about the pervasiveness of sin, with the

Calvinists teaching a doctrine of 'total depravity', and others taking a less gloomy view of the human condition. In modern theological anthropology, sin is commonly seen as primarily a matter of broken relationships, or the replacement of what ought to be relationships of love, justice and care for one another with aggression, exploitation, manipulation and violence.

The American theologian, Reinhold Niebuhr, developed an account of sin as essentially pride, particularly in his *The Nature and Destiny of Man* (1941 and 1943). Niebuhr based his Gifford Lectures on the 'conviction that there are resources in the Christian faith for an understanding of human nature which have been lost in modern culture'.[23] Niebuhr's anthropology was, and is, amazingly influential in certain areas of secular social thinking, particularly in international relations theory. Niebuhr was convinced that a Christian anthropology which took the measure of the *misère* and the *grandeur* of human beings was more true than any of the alternatives on offer and, for a time at least, many people seemed to agree with him, and saw Christian anthropology as closely corresponding to the observed human realities, collective as well as individual.

An emphasis on sin in theological anthropology helps to protect against two dangers: first, an inclination to suggest that the Christian view of human beings stresses their inherent and basic goodness – a view strongly reinforced in modern times by certain types of liberalism; secondly, a tendency to believe that an understanding of true humanity can in any sense be read off empirical realities or the observation of actual human beings, even people of extraordinary holiness. It is worth remembering that saints tend to be people who have an unusually vivid sense of their own sinfulness and dependence on grace. For an adequate account of the actuality and potentiality of human nature we must turn, not to psychology, sociology or the human sciences, but to the created order, to the eschatological reality, and above all to the incarnate one, Jesus Christ.

Sin and the brokenness of the human condition need healing and forgiveness. And the message of the gospel is that God has forgiven sin; we are healed and redeemed to be a chosen people, a holy nation, a kingdom of priests.

Human nature redeemed and glorified

A new interest in the place of eschatology and hope in theological anthropology arose in part out of the dialogue between Marxism and

Christianity, most notably, perhaps, in the response of Jürgen Moltmann and his associates to the thought of Ernst Bloch. Hope, destiny and providence provided interlocking themes here, and as well as a rediscovery of the significance of the themes of hope and eschatology there was a need to take the measure of competing secular hopes, and commend and expound the Christian hope.

Today's problem may be much different, if Habermas is right to speak of 'an exhaustion of utopian energies' today.[24] And I think he is. Could it be that a major responsibility of theological anthropology in this generation is the rekindling of an eschatological hope shaped and sustained by Christian faith, both challenging other, more limited and selfish hopes, and confronting what the American economist, J. W. Galbraith, calls 'the culture of contentment'?

Moltmann's words make my final point far better than I can:

> 'Hope' is often writ large today, but what is meant by it is often optimism, or bravery to order: 'to hope and not despair'. In reality hope is a rare gift. In effective hope man does not flee from the unbearable pressure of the present into a consoling, better future, but draws the other, human future into the present, and lives already by it. This does not make the present any more bearable, but often rather more unbearable, in any case richer in conflict. In hope man opens himself to the future which has been promised him, and leaves the cocoon of his life, and of his society. If hope is directed at the human reign of the Son of Man, it brings the one who hopes into conflict with the inhumanities which he sees... The Christian hope, in so far as it is Christian, is the hope of those who have no future. It is therefore a hope in contradiction of self-satisfied optimists and of equally self-satisfied pessimists...
>
> Life in hope means being able to love, and being able to love in particular the life which is unloved and rejected. But what does love mean other than to allow for the unawakened possibilities of the other?[25]

And the last word I will leave to William Blake, who speaks so persuasively and profoundly:

The Divine Image

To Mercy, Pity, Peace, and Love
All pray in their distress;
And to these virtues of delight
Return their thankfulness.

For Mercy, Pity, Peace, and Love
Is God, our father dear,
And Mercy, Pity, Peace, and Love
Is Man, his child and care.

For Mercy has a human heart,
Pity a human face,
And Love, the human form divine,
And Peace, the human dress.

Then every man, of every clime,
That prays in his distress,
Prays to the human form divine,
Love, Mercy, Pity, Peace.

And all must love the human form,
In heathen, Turk, or Jew;
Where Mercy, Love and Pity dwell
There God is dwelling too.

3

Good and gay?[1]

'Lord, make my spirit good and gay' – George MacDonald could not
have anticipated how these words from his wonderful morning hymn,
'O Lord of life, thy quickening voice awakes my morning song', would
be heard and understood today. It is the contention of this chapter that
gay can be good, and that gay people may have a specific vocation or
calling, a special service they may render to the Church and to the
broader community. We can all learn from gay people about the
importance of friendship, about how to keep on loving even when one
is subjected to contempt, prejudice and derision, about keeping one's
integrity when one is abused and feared.

The whole discussion of sexuality in the Churches is highly charged
emotionally. And nothing arouses so much irrational feeling and
intense prejudice as the question of homosexuality, or rather the place,
if any, for gay people and gay ministers in the Church of Jesus Christ.
My purpose in this chapter is not to investigate the sources of the
passions aroused by the mere mention of the topic, or to challenge and
dissect the irrational prejudice which dominates so many Christians'
thinking on the matter. I want simply, by way of introduction, to note
how easily the Christian tradition has been distorted and misunderstood in order to buttress a basically unChristian homophobia. Only
when we have brought into the open the subtle ways in which theology
may be used, or rather abused, to legitimate conventional prejudices,
are we in a position to venture statements which may be more authentically Christian, and firmly rooted in the Gospel rather than our own
society's nervous values and prejudices.

Christians' understanding of the nature of human sexuality is, and
has for decades been, in a state of flux, as traditional formulations are
increasingly questioned and account is taken of modern developments
in theology and biblical studies, and of new knowledge coming from

the human sciences. This is *not* to say that the tradition is being, or ought to be, jettisoned. Indeed my own view is almost the opposite of this: that despite distortion and abuse, the Christian tradition preserves an understanding of human sexuality of unequalled profundity and perennial relevance. But the tradition has to be re-examined, reviewed, tested, reformulated; accretions and misunderstandings have to be removed, if it is to commend itself as a relevant and challenging contribution to modern people's self-understanding.

'The mastery of sex'

I would like to mention three sources of distortion which have deeply, and harmfully, influenced the Christian understanding of sexuality.

First, from certain strands in Greek philosophy there came a deep suspicion of the emotional life, of the Dionysian element in life. Sexuality, so necessarily united with the emotions, was seen as something dangerous, threatening, requiring to be controlled, curbed, channelled, if it is not to be demonic. Sexuality involves, according to the preamble to *The Book of Common Prayer*'s marriage service, people having 'carnal lusts and appetites like brute beasts that have no understanding'. These are to be controlled and restrained, usually in marriage, which is to be entered into (again, according to *The Book of Common Prayer*) 'as a remedy against sin and to avoid fornication, that such persons as have not the gift of continency may marry and keep themselves undefiled members of Christ's body'. A not dissimilar attitude was shown by the title – and much of the contents – of a book on sexuality by Leslie Weatherhead which was still popular in my student days, *The Mastery of Sex*.

This sense of sex as a dangerous enemy that is to be feared and mastered is not, I believe, authentically Christian, but it has penetrated deeply into the Christian tradition, making it hard to affirm the goodness of sexuality and giving much sexual ethics an extraordinarily repressive skew. According to this view, sexuality is not something to be celebrated and enjoyed, a vital dimension of all worthwhile and lasting relationships. It has become rather a frightening force that must be restrained within as narrow a compass as possible because it cannot be eliminated. When such attitudes become influential, it is hardly surprising if minority forms of sexuality attract particularly vigorous condemnation. Such condemnation highlights the negative and sub-Christian attitude towards sexuality as a whole which has been so influential, and so harmful, within the Christian tradition.

What is natural?

The second distortion is most clearly evidenced in natural law thinking, but it is by no means confined there. If we ask what is the nature of sexuality, what it is there for, what good it is intended to achieve, we clearly do not have a simple question capable of a simple answer. But unfortunately, rather glib and superficial answers have only too often been given to this question. For instance, it has repeatedly been affirmed that sexuality is for procreation, or primarily for procreation; it is that part or aspect of human nature which is devoted to the propagation of the species. It follows that any use of sex which does not have procreation primarily in view is illegitimate and unnatural.

This may make some kind of biological sense, but it wholly neglects the fact that human beings are more than biological entities. Humans are complex creatures, and human sexuality performs a range of functions. I think it was Berdyaev who long ago lamented that so many Christian books on sex read like treatises on cattle breeding; they leave out the personal dimension, the integration of sexuality into the understanding of love and of relationships, the central core of what it means to be human. Sexuality is, of course, necessarily involved in procreation, even in an age of IVF and the possibility of reproductive cloning, but that is not all that sexuality is about; and to suggest that it is involves a drastic impoverishment of the whole understanding of sexuality, and indeed a dehumanizing of human sexuality. Sexuality is concerned with love and relationships primarily; and only if this is recognized very clearly is the procreative and nurturing role of sexuality put in its proper context.

There is another trap into which natural law thinking about sex can very easily fall. It is this: to allow, consciously or unconsciously, the conventional view of the time to define what is, and what is not, 'natural' behaviour. The danger here is of what purports to be an objective approach to ethics becoming simply an expression of the prejudices of the age. Not uncommonly, the claim that homosexuality is 'unnatural' boils down either to a belief that behaviour that differs from that of the majority, or the opinions of an influential minority, must be wrong. But in either case all that is happening is that the prejudices of many are being passed on and reinforced without serious critical examination. If we choose to speak in terms of natural law, it is good to be aware of how easily it may be manipulated and misused for the buttressing of unthinking prejudice.

The Bible and sexuality

Similar dangers lurk in the use of the Bible, 'the supreme rule of life and doctrine'. It is easy to fall into the trap of reading the Bible in such a way that it simply reflects back to us our own prejudices and assumptions, confirming opinions that were not in any real sense derived from Scripture. The danger of the spirit of the age controlling the interpretation is particularly liable to occur when the Bible is used as a quarry of proof-texts deployed in an argument without regard to their context or original meaning. I would go along with Henry Morton's rejoinder to the extreme Covenanters in Walter Scott's novel, *Old Mortality*:

> I revere the Scriptures as deeply as you or any Christian can do. I look into them with humble hope of extracting a rule of conduct and a law of salvation. But I expect to find this by their general tenor, and of the spirit which they uniformly breathe, and not by wresting particular passages from their context, or by the application of scriptural phrases to circumstances and events with which they have often very slender relations.[2]

Yet again and again Christian opinions on homosexuality have been based on proof-texts which turn out on examination to have little if any bearing on the issue. It is, for example, blatantly absurd to base a blanket condemnation of homosexuality on passages in the Old Testament which condemn sexual assault or cultic prostitution. Such a way of proceeding is to take neither the Bible nor people with adequate seriousness.

A second danger is that of regarding the Bible as primarily a rule book. There *are* rules in the Bible, it is true, some of them time-bound but others of apparently universal validity. The exegete has to attempt to distinguish between the two sorts of rules, and to see even in antique structures of law what cannot and must not be applied today, matters of perennial significance. But always the Christian must remember that the Bible is primarily gospel, good news, promise, and only secondarily and derivatively, law. The gospel is prior to the law. It is about love, forgiveness, new beginnings, grace, fulfilment, abundant life, rather than about condemnation, rejection, repression and the meticulous observance of a battery of rules.

We should never forget that in the New Testament sexual sins are quite systematically treated as of themselves of much less importance than other sorts of sins: pride, callousness, oppressing the poor, and so on. There is very little in the Bible about homosexuality; and any Christian and biblical understanding of homosexuality must pay attention not only to these passages, peripheral as they are, but also the far more significant, central and plentiful things that the Bible has to say about love and relationships, and the place of sexuality in loving relationships. A Christian understanding of homosexuality must be rooted in 'the general tenor' of Scripture; it must arise out of real dialogue, a mutual questioning between Scripture and our modern understandings and assumptions. The Christian gospel questions not only our assumptions, but also *us*, particularly if we feel ourselves to be righteous, good, 'all right'.

Persons in love

In attempting to outline a Christian understanding of humanity, the necessary starting point is that there is no such being as the isolated individual; persons are to be understood in relation. The Triune God is united in the loving dance of *perichoresis*. Our relationships – to God, mother, father, siblings, peers, spouse, children – not only show what kind of people we are, but they make us, shape us, form us. Sin, the theological term to indicate the human predicament, the problematic side of human existence, the flaw in the human condition, is primarily a matter of broken relationships, of fear of relationships at depth, and, consequently, of incapacity for relationships. Sin was aptly described by Augustine and Luther as the condition of being *incurvatus in se*, turned in on oneself, and consequently turned away from one's neighbour. C. S. Lewis, in his autobiography, *Surprised by Joy*, tells how before his conversion he was obsessed with himself and with his own inner working. His experience of becoming a Christian involved liberation from being obsessed with himself and a new free and spontaneous openness to others. Thus free and confident relatedness to the neighbour is a central component in the Christian understanding of humanity. It is not good for a human being to be alone, for destiny, maturity and completeness involve fellowship.

Human beings' capacity for relationship is founded upon the fact that we are beings loved by God, loved so much that God sent his Son to show God's love, ultimately in dying for those who loved him not. God's love is mediated to us in all sorts of ways, some normal, even mundane; others extraordinary or even miraculous – through the love of parents, brothers, sisters, friends, spouses, partners. The experience of being loved is absolutely necessary for growth, maturity, confidence, indeed for sanity. The Christian tradition has all along known well the teaching of modern psychology, that in being loved we learn to love: 'We love because he loved us first' (1 John 4.19). And the Christian faith goes further, and affirms that in loving we come to know God – there is no other way to knowledge of him – and to enter into the mystery of God's own being, for God is love: 'Beloved, let us love one another; because love is of God; everyone who loves is born of God and knows God. Whoever does not love does not know God, for God is love' (1 John 4.7–8).

Let me take the discussion a bit further by looking at three New Testament passages:

1 Corinthians 13 is as familiar as it is profound and challenging. It tells us that love is patient, love is kind; love is not envious or boastful or arrogant or rude. Love doesn't take offence. It is not conditional, something that we earn. It is the greatest of the three things that last for ever – faith, hope and love. Love and fidelity, love and faithfulness, are inseparable. Love is constancy – utterly reliable. It cannot be predatory, or exploitative or episodic.

1 John 4.7–21 is a passage full of amazing statements. God is love; love flows from God. In Jesus we see the full reality of God's love. God loves us first, and this sets us free to love, to obey the strange and wonderful command: 'Beloved, let us love one another, because love is from God'. And then the amazing words: '*everyone* who loves is born of God and knows God'. Yes, *everyone*. People who love know God, even if they don't recognize it. People who love are in touch with the very mystery of God's own being. And people who don't love, however disciplined, however hardworking, however good at keeping the rules, however much they may be pillars of the Kirk, don't know God.

In Luke 7.36–50 we find the familiar story of the woman with the alabaster box of ointment, who gatecrashed a dinner given for Jesus, and washed and anointed his feet. Embarrassing! Everyone knew she was a prostitute, a woman who made her living from sex, not a respectable person, someone who was universally despised and shunned, in public at least. She bursts into the party and in an impulsive act of love and generosity she pours the expensive ointment over Jesus' feet, and washes them with her tears, drying them with her hair. We don't like, any more than the Pharisees of long ago, public displays of emotion, of love, especially from such a woman. Jesus should have known what kind of a woman she was. He should have been very cautious and judgemental in all his dealings with her.

There is a problem in the text, over which the translators have fretted. Towards the end of the passage Jesus says, 'her sins, which are many, are forgiven, for she loved much'. FOR SHE LOVED MUCH. That's pretty strong. It suggests that in all the uncertainties and the degradations of the life of a whore, this woman had tried to love, and had learned to love. Her great love had often been distorted, and oftener, no doubt, exploited. But Jesus recognized it as love, a love more real than the love of the Pharisee and his kind. And so her sins are forgiven, and she can go in peace.

All this is rather much for some translators, who add some words to the text and say that her love *to Jesus* shows that her sins are forgiven (Phillips), or that 'her great love *proves* that her many sins have been forgiven' (NEB), or 'her sins, which are many, have been forgiven, *hence* she has shown great love' (NRSV). Anything to avoid the suggestion that her loving has brought her close to God in Jesus, sitting at the table. Anything to avoid the suggestion that Jesus accepted this whore without qualification, and proclaimed that her sins were forgiven because she loved so much. Anything to avoid what John says so clearly: 'Everyone who loves is born of God and knows God.'

Love, then, is completely central and definitive for the Christian understanding of human beings. Indeed I think it could be quite acceptable to define human beings as creatures who are loved and are accordingly capable of loving. This would at least be better than the common obsession with sin and human incapacity, and consequently with the need for restraint and coercion. Love, of course, exists in various modes, as C. S. Lewis reminds us in his book, *The Four Loves*. And so I make three affirmations about love:

1 Love, in any of its modes, excludes using the other as a means to one's own ends. Loving relationships are non-exploitative, non-manipulative, equal. They involve self-giving, *kenosis*, and are quite incompatible with using the other for one's own gratification, or as a tool for one's own purposes.

2 Fundamental relationships (for example, to God, parent, child, spouse or partner) have a necessary quality of exclusiveness, so that when they are threatened, jealousy is naturally engendered.

3 Fidelity is the condition for growth in love; God's fidelity is absolute – so should be the fidelity of those who truly love.

People are sexual beings, with varying sexual drives, orientations and appetites. Sexuality is an integral dimension of what it means to be a person. These sexual drives and orientations are in themselves morally neutral; their goodness or badness depends on how they are mobilized and used, and how effectively they are integrated into the personality.

Christian confusions

We have already seen how the Christian tradition has been deeply infected with a pagan fear of sexuality, which joined hands with a more genuinely Christian rejection of the idolatry of sex. In combination, these two elements made it hard for Christians to give sexuality its proper place in their understanding of human life. Only too often sex was seen as something to be repressed, controlled, or ashamed of. Virginity and celibacy were given a quite exaggeratedly high status in comparison with all forms of active sexuality. Sex was regarded as allowable because necessary for procreation, but not as something to be enjoyed or celebrated, let alone as a channel or strengthening of love. Prudery and guilt and embarrassed silence have only too often been substitutes for a serious attempt at a Christian consideration of the placing of sexuality.

And the failure of the Church has been to a large extent responsible for what I call the modern sexual heresy. This involves the reduction of love to sexual intercourse, the identification of sexual fulfilment and human fulfilment, understood in rather crude terms as the widest possible variety and intensity of sexual experience. We have here as total a separation between sex and procreation as the alliance between the two in the older Christian tradition. Sexual expression is artificially separated from loving, reliable relationships, and these become strangely idealistically considered.

At this point something must be said about the Christian placing of sexuality. Where does it belong in the understanding of personality? How are we to regard it? St Francis used to refer to his body as 'Brother Ass' – a useful reminder, perhaps, that we should not be over solemn or pretentious in matters affecting our bodies or our sexuality. Sex is often funny, an inability to be light-hearted about sex suggests we have made sex our god. People are more than sexual beings, and labelling people in terms of their sexual orientation can be a very dangerous thing, reducing, freezing, limiting, dehumanizing. One of the oldest games a society plays is to label a feared, or subtly attractive, minority in such a way as to degrade and humiliate it, and draw clear and tight frontiers around the minority, insulating it from the rest of society. I understand why oppressed and threatened minorities feel they must affirm their group identity by strengthening solidarity among themselves. But this should not be more than a stage toward the acceptance of the one true label – a person, or child of God – and the comprehensive solidarity of humankind.

Before addressing directly the question of homosexuality, let me tell you two true stories about homosexual people, who like everyone else are made to love and to be loved. These two events deeply affected my thinking on these matters, and questioned some of my prejudices.

Some years ago I was involved in a group of Christians discussing sexuality. One middle-aged woman called Pat said – and it was heartfelt – 'The very idea of homosexuality disgusts me'. She wasn't the only one who thought that. Then someone else asked her: 'Pat, if your son or your daughter came to you and said, "Mum, I'm gay and I have a partner whom I love dearly", would you reply, "Johnny, or Helen, you disgust me."' Pat thought for a moment, and then she said 'Of course not. You see, I love them, and as a mother and as a Christian I couldn't say that. I need to love them as they are, to love them in their difference, and to trust that their love is faithful and generous and lasting.' She really believed, you see, that 'Everyone who loves is born of God and knows God'.

My second story is an experience which profoundly challenged and changed some of my prejudices. It is this. Years ago I was chaplain at a university in England. One day I was called in and told that a middle-aged woman from the school of education had died. I went immediately, of course, to call at the home. When I got there I found a woman who had been in a lesbian relationship with the dead woman for many years. The dead woman's friend and partner was in deep grief. As I spoke with her, I learned of their constant, reliable, loving relationship over some 15 years. I heard of the rich gifts and experiences they had shared over many years, of the problems they had faced together, of the way their love had grown through times of difficulty and times of joy, of how they had supported and encouraged one another. And, of course, she spoke of her grief, of how she had tended her partner through her long and painful illness. Like almost everyone else who has been bereaved, she wanted to tell the stories of her loved one, and their relationship. She wanted to share her grief. But to her partner's family she was an embarrassment. They wanted her to be forgotten, excluded, her very existence denied. Neither in the law nor in her partner's family circle did she, her grief, or her love have a place.

As I listened to this woman, almost despite myself, I had to recognize that the love that she and her partner had shared was not different from the love that unites my wife, Margaret and me. The words of 1 John came into my mind: 'Everyone who loves is born of God and knows God.' And I was heartsore that, whereas the love that Margaret and I have for one another and for our children is recognized, supported and encouraged by Church and society, the love of these two women is still to many an embarrassment and an offence. It gets neither recognition nor support. It is still for many people dismissed as disgusting and wrong.

Ethics for gay people?

Years ago I accepted an invitation to speak at a conference about 'ethics for gay people'. But the more I reflected on the subject I had been given, the more I became convinced that there wasn't such a thing as an ethics for heterosexual people, and another ethics for gay people, any more than there is an ethics for English people and a different ethics for Scots! Even the ethics that Jesus taught his disciples claimed to have a universal bearing, to be, potentially at least, an ethics for everyone.

I feel it makes no sense whatever for a Christian to condemn, or for that matter, to commend, a homosexual orientation. It is not that sort of thing. For most people their sexual orientation is part of the *givenness* of their personal situation, and a Christian should regard this as a vocation or indeed a talent to be used to God's glory, and for the good of God's children.

Some who would accept what I have just said about orientation would nevertheless draw a sharp distinction between orientation and behaviour, and affirm that homosexual genital behaviour is inherently wrong. Accordingly, the homosexual should be a lifelong celibate. Now it is fashionable to speak a good deal of nonsense about celibacy. Many people seem to believe that celibacy is impossible as well as undesirable. The celibate, they feel, cannot be a full, satisfied and mature person. This is, not to spin things out, complete nonsense. Some people of all types of sexual orientation have a vocation to celibacy and find it a high, wonderful and fulfilling vocation. Some of the celibates I know are the most vital, complete and loving of people.

But celibacy is a *special* calling; it must be something freely chosen, not imposed from outside. It is a destructive state of life unless it is chosen, embraced and lived in from conviction. While I accept that some people find the eschewing of any particular sexual attachment is, for them, the way to a wider, and richer, loving directed towards God and their neighbours, I also believe that for most people their ability to love is rooted in the basic primary relationships. If these relationships are reliable, consistent, honest and accepting, a confident openness towards others results. I do not believe that all homosexuals are called to celibacy, although some undoubtedly are.

But perhaps, as many like the former Moderator of the General Assembly of the Church of Scotland, my friend Professor Ian Torrance, suggest, gay people and gay ministers are fine as long as they are celibate. And certainly some people are called by God to be celibates. For others, imposed celibacy is an impossible burden and a well of loneliness. Most of us continue to learn how to love, and grow in love, in the context of faithful, exclusive, loving relationships.

And I don't believe that what happens, or doesn't happen, in the bedroom is nearly as important as some people suggest. Love is communicated in many ways – physical, emotional, material, spiritual. Gay people, like the rest of us, are made to love and to be loved. We can often learn from them about friendship, love and fidelity. What matters for gay and straight, single and married, parents and children is love. For those who love much are, like the woman with the alabaster box of ointment, forgiven and accepted and loved by God, and 'Everyone who loves is born of God and knows God.'

In what I have said about celibacy, I have not suggested that continence and sexual restraint are either impossible or undesirable. I happen to believe that continence before marriage is a good thing, and even within a heterosexual marriage there are times when sexual intercourse is inappropriate or undesirable. In a good and growing relationship sexual expression and its place should be sensitively explored; and sensitivity sometimes involves continence and restraint. Christian marriage is not a licence to rape one's partner – would that all talk of 'conjugal rights' were forgotten, and people realized that there is a wrong use of sex within marriage as well as without.

What are the conditions within which homosexual acts may be regarded as legitimate and good? Very simply, I would suggest that these are precisely the same as for heterosexual acts. In other words, they should be expressions of love rather than exploitation, and they should be concerned for the deepening of a relationship of care and self-giving. They should confirm and strengthen a relationship that is reliable – and this means as far as I can see permanent, honest and exclusive, that is non-promiscuous. Such a relationship is, to my mind, chaste and faithful.

I am, of course, commending the pattern of monogamous heterosexual marriage. But in doing so, some difficulties need to be faced. First, while for heterosexuals, there are still strong, sometimes too strong, confirmations for monogamy, precisely the opposite is true for homosexuals. Homosexual unions have neither social nor religious nor legal recognition; and such social pressures as there are still encourage furtiveness, promiscuity and instability in relationships. Indeed, society goes a long way in encouraging the kind of behaviour among homosexuals which it then denounces as vices characteristic of the gay condition. Putting the same point another way: the lack of social support for homosexual partnerships makes it even easier for them to come unstuck through the difficulty in keeping together in times of tension.

I believe that the Church should help by affirming the Christian worth of homosexual unions, and providing support, recognition, counselling and blessing to help gay couples to grow in love through difficulties as well as joys. There is also a pressing need on the part of the Churches for the provision of more sensitive and honest pastoral help when a union is broken through death or otherwise.

One final point: because homosexual unions are not procreative, and because for homosexual people sex is a vehicle of love, relationship, tenderness, caring, but is not usually capable of producing children, we all have, I believe, things to learn from the gay experience in an age when heterosexual sex is more commonly a way of communicating love than a way of producing children. We have things to learn about sexuality apart from procreative intent; about tenderness, care, self-giving, reciprocity. We all need to learn from one another, and ultimately from God, about love. But this is only possible if we recognize that Christ on his cross has broken down the walls of suspicion, hostility and distrust among people; only if we have the courage to live and to love in the freedom Christ has given us.

II

Public theology

4

Divinity in use and practice[1]

'Divinity', said Martin Luther, 'consists in use and practice, not in speculation and meditation. Everyone that deals in speculations, either in household affairs or in temporal government, without practice, is lost and worth nothing.'[2] And elsewhere, more strongly: 'true theology is practical ... speculative theology belongs with the devil in hell'.[3] But *can* theology be *practical*? The conventional stereotype of theology in the modern world is as the most impractical of all disciplines, the very epitome of irrelevance. The friendly banter we sometimes receive from secular colleagues who regard the title 'practical theology' as a contradiction in terms demands some kind of apologia which goes beyond a nervous reminder that there are still religious professionals who require training for the fulfilment of their duties. After all, we claim that theology has a relevance and a significance far beyond the shaping of ministerial activity.

It is not just the intellectual credentials of the particular discipline of practical theology, but the right of theology to a place in the academy, and indeed the proper bearing of matters of theory and principle on the life of action which are at issue. The former British Prime Minister, Harold Wilson, was voicing the pragmatic prejudices of his generation when he denounced with derision attempts to discuss political principles as just 'theology' – in other words, an unproductive luxury which is a distraction from the serious business of seeking efficiency, success, economic growth and all the unexamined and often conflicting values of today.

In the 1980s, the Thatcher era, in Britain and elsewhere an even more alarming edge was added to the popular use of the term 'theology', as doctrinaire adherence to economic theories, which seemed capable of no form of confirmation or refutation, and in application had the most grievous social consequences, was described as a 'theological stance'. With the arrival of the New Right we entered a new era, the age of 'conviction politics'. No one any longer proclaimed 'the death of ideology' (Daniel Bell); it was clearly alive and well. But in 'conviction politics' policies were not based on open discussion and the attempt to achieve some general agreement about the goals of society, or on careful attention to the facts of the case. Neither empirical evidence nor informed but contrary opinions were allowed to challenge conclusions which sprang from invulnerable dogmas about human beings, and society, and the way things are and how they ought to be.

When efforts were made to root these dogmas in the Christian gospel, as was done very explicitly in Mrs Thatcher's speech to the General Assembly of the Church of Scotland in 1988, not only was a dangerously oversimplified view of the relation of beliefs and policies presented, but the very integrity of the gospel was at stake.[4] Critical and responsible theology had to ask whether it was a true or a false gospel which was being proclaimed, and protest against the ideological use of theology. There was a crisis and a challenge to theology when the gospel was reduced to slogans or weapons which the prosperous and powerful used to defend their privilege against the weak and poor.

The issue is essentially one of truth. It was Pilate, sitting in judgment upon Jesus who, according to John's Gospel, asked the question, 'What is truth?' only to brush it aside in order to proceed to actions which could not but have been deeply affected had he pursued his question until it received an answer. To have continued the discussion, he may have felt, would have been a political luxury which might have led him into a morass of profitless verbal polemics; certainly it would inhibit him from the immediate and decisive action for which the people were clamouring and to which expediency counselled him. As only too commonly, the refusal to take the question of truth with ultimate seriousness leads to practice which is ill-considered and dangerously responsive to the pressures of the powerful and of the moment. And so we may start with the suggestion that practical theology is *that branch of theology which is concerned with questions of truth in relation to action*. This points to a deep reciprocity between theory and practice, whereby theological understanding not only leads to action, but also arises out of practice, involvement in the life of the world: 'He who does what is true comes to the light' (John 3.21). Practical theology is therefore concerned with the doing of the truth, and with the encounter with truth in action, with what the French philosopher Roger Garaudy called 'the active nature of knowledge'.[5]

Much of our thinking in this area has been dominated, not entirely helpfully, by the Greek duality between the *vita activa* and the *vita contemplativa,* and by the corresponding distinction between the practical and theoretical sciences. The Greek understanding of the nature of the two lifestyles and the relation between them was not uniform. Plato exalted the contemplative life so far above the life of action that his Guardians, who had been illumined by a training in contemplation, had to be induced unwillingly to engage in the only kind of practice which possessed real significance, that is, ruling. Their task was to bring down from heaven, as it were, a blueprint of the ideal state and soul, and impose this on an infinitely malleable society and its individual citizens. The Guardians' wisdom did not arise out of their experience of ruling, but was brought to it from their comprehension of the form of the Good. Practice must conform to theory; it is not itself in any way constitutive of truth. And as for the practices of the lower orders – indeed almost all practice apart from ruling – these were of little interest and related to nothing that could be dignified as wisdom or science. Aristotle, on the other hand, emphasized something which he called *phronesis,* or practical wisdom, which relates directly to action. Yet despite his more positive view of practice, when pressed, Aristotle, hardly less than Plato, asserts the superiority of the *vita contemplativa* over the *vita activa,* of *theoria* over *praxis.*

Closely related to this duality, indeed in many ways an alternative formulation of it, is another which may be indicated by the contrast between Dionysus and Apollo. Dionysus represents the affective life, the emotions and the passions – joy, fear, pain, delight, love, anger, and so on. Dionysus stands for the feelings as a central part of what it means to be human. Apollo, on the other hand, stands for reason, for the claim of the head to rule over the heart. The main philosophic tradition was strongly Apollonian, and looked askance at all that Dionysus signified. Emotions might need some outlet, even among educated and enlightened people, hence the festivals of sexuality in Plato's *Republic.* But emotions are seen as dangerous, unpredictable, subhuman, irrational; they must be controlled if they are not to be disruptive of social order, of rationality, of wisdom. Hence Socrates dies without fear or regret, secure in the knowledge that such events do not matter, and that it is unseemly for a philosopher to be emotional. And by way of Stoicism a heavy emphasis on the need to control, to curb, to master the emotions has penetrated deep into the Christian tradition. The reference to Apollo and Dionysus reminds us that this duality reflects two contrary ideas of God: the god of the philosophers is apathetic, impassible, detached, uninvolved and the philosopher should model himself on him. Dionysus is pure emotion, uncontrolled, unpredictable, spontaneous, shown best in ecstasy or orgy. His followers imitate him, taking as their slogan David Hume's reversal of the Stoics' wisdom: 'Reason is, and ought to be, the slave of the passions.'

The Christian theologian nurtures a distinctive unease with this kind of dualistic thought. He cannot accept the philosophers' depreciation of action which runs so deep, nor the suspicion of emotion. On the other hand, the theologian does not reverse the classical priorities; rather he must transcend the duality. For he knows that understanding and doing, theory and practice, contemplation and action, reason and emotion – and especially loving and knowing – are integrally related and interdependent. Above all, perhaps, he is mindful that the wisdom of God became incarnate in a man, who wrought our salvation through his active and passive obedience to the Father. The Logos – that term for the rational principle of the universe beloved of the Stoics – acts. He goes, like Dionysus, to a wedding party. His prayers and his teaching, his deeds and his suffering make a strange unity such that one cannot allocate him either to the active or to the contemplative role. He belongs to both, or to neither, for he draws the two into a harmony.

It is not simply that theology accords to practice a greater significance than did the Greeks; it has a far broader and more complex notion of the nature of practice. The practice with which the theologian is concerned ranges from the world-transforming political praxis which figures so largely in the important and challenging work of the liberation theologians to the practical faithfulness and love of the simple believer in work and relationships; and it must encompass passion in both its senses, as suffering and, more generally, as emotion.

Luther suggests that the *via crucis* is a third way, and the specifically Christian way, which embraces and transcends both the *vita contemplativa* and the *vita activa*: 'We must beware,' he writes, 'that the active life with its work and the contemplative life with its speculations do not lead us astray. Both are very attractive and peaceful, but for that reason also dangerous, until they are tempered by the cross and disturbed by adversaries. But the cross is the safest of all.'[6]

Furthermore, if theology is compelled to choose between regarding itself as a 'pure' theoretical science in the Greek sense or a practical science (and it would do well to resist the terms in which the choice is posed), it cannot but opt for the latter. For theology is not a detached, dispassionate endeavour to understand the things of God, but the coming to know God in striving to do God's will: it 'consists in use and practice'. An immediate implication of this, of course, is that theology, and particularly Practical Theology, must pursue its task in the closest dialogue with the other practical social sciences, open to their insights and ready to contribute its own. To mention but one instance of the profitability of such an enterprise from modern times: it is hardly possible to exaggerate the contribution of Reinhold Niebuhr, operating strictly as a theologian, to the secular study, and practice, of politics and international relations between the 1930s and the 1970s.

Much of what has been said so far relates to theology as a whole; but within theology there has perforce to be a division of labour, although not such that the various theological disciplines neglect dialogue with each other or refuse to cultivate the fascinating border-lands between specific branches of theology, and between theological and secular studies. The peculiar responsibilities of Practical Theology involve acting as a bridge between theology and the social sciences and reflecting critically upon, learning from, and endeavouring to renew, reform and strengthen practice and, in particular, Christian practice.

Practical Theology is not 'applied theology', if that term implies that the practical theologian receives ready-made the results fed in by the biblical and systematic theologians and considers, as the practical theologian's part, how these conclusions may be put to work. If this rather platonic account were accurate, the subject would merit the title sometimes given it in Scotland in the past by irreverent students by the addition of two letters: 'practically theology': ancillary to the other subjects, but hardly a theological discipline in its own right. In dealing with communication – and specifically with homiletics – , for example, the practical theologian is concerned, as are all theologians, with the content of the message no less than with the techniques of putting it across. As a theologian, not a sophist or public relations specialist teaching students how to make friends and influence people, the practical theologian's distinctive contribution arises from a special concern with the contemporary context, relevance, and relation to practice of the message preached.

Wolfhart Pannenberg has pointed out that 'any fundamental consideration of the meaning and function of practical theology must clarify the concept of practice which gives it its name'.[7] It is not enough, I would suggest, to confine the practice with which the practical theologian is concerned with the traditional subdivisions of homiletics, liturgics, catechetics, pastoralia and ethics. We need a broader understanding of practice within which the traditional subdivisions may be studied in their proper perspective. We are also reminded forcefully by the political theologians of the Third World that Christian practice is not adequately regarded as either the fulfilment by clergy of a traditional, accepted role within an unquestioned ecclesiastical established order of things. Rather, they say, it has at its centre world-transforming political activity. This should be received as a friendly corrective to much of our timidity and narrowness. The fact that so many Christians in various lands have come to see the path of obedience to Christ as necessarily involving political commitment to radical change, and a positive identification with the oppressed and exploited, must come as a challenge to our sometimes very conventional and parochial undertakings of Christian practice and of theology.

Within such a context, practical theologians concern themselves with what in other traditions is labelled 'priestly formation', and in the Churches of the Reformation, the practical training of the ministry, but we cannot do this without looking to the priestly formation of the whole *laos*, the equipping of all the saints for the work of ministry. Furthermore, our concern is with reformation rather than formation, for increasingly the call of God is to do the unprecedented, and traditional forms of Christian practice are subjected these days to a questioning which is a fundamental challenge to renewal. Within such a context we strive to prepare a ministry committed to the Lord, sensitive to the needs of the age, and imbued with a vision of the Church which is ecumenical and world-wide. Practical theology today cannot, and must not, provide an induction into a fully recognized, secure and sheltered pattern of ministerial practice. This is partly because there is in church and society so much exhilarating and liberating uncertainty about the role of the minister, but more significantly because ministerial practice is *semper reformandum* and must be constantly scrutinized in the light of new theological insights, and deeper knowledge of contemporary society.

I have said enough to make it clear that Practical Theology is, in my opinion, a churchly discipline. But this does not imply that it accepts without question the validity of the existing practice of the Churches. It is involved rather in a dialectical interaction between the practice of the Churches and theology, which must both be understood within the horizon of the Kingdom into which men and women of every tribe and tongue and people and nation are at the last to be gathered.[8] That is why missiology is so important in Practical Theology, and why all fruitful Practical Theology must today be profoundly ecumenical.

Practical Theology strives to engage with questions of truth in relation to practice in general, to Christian practice, and to ministerial practice. It bases its work on the conviction that there is a unity of theory and practice. And the final objective of its enquiries is nothing less than the equipment of pilgrims for the use and practice of their true homeland.

5

The pastoral significance of Mary: a Protestant perspective[1]

One who, like me, would label himself a Reformed Evangelical Catholic Christian, or just a Christian, if one is in a hurry, must welcome dialogue among Christians. It is not only an indispensable way towards the fuller visible unity in truth and holiness which is our common Lord's will for his followers; it is also stimulus and nourishment for that inner dialogue which marks our growth towards Christian maturity.

The dialogue of Christians demands honesty about what we affirm with confidence, and what we are not sure about. It must have frankness not just about the areas of agreement, but also, and probably especially, about things in which we differ. In dialogue we need to be open to the possibility that we might change our minds – we must be willing not only to review our position but to put it at risk. Dialogue between those who are, or pretend to be, totally like-minded is tedious and unproductive. But dialogue between those who bombard the opposition with missiles from entrenched positions from which they will not budge only too often confirms error and inhibits growth in truth. It is when both sides are on the move, when both are eager to reform their beliefs, theological formulations and practices, that dialogue catches fire. And the best of dialogues is when all parties recognize the others as fellow pilgrims being led into truth by the Spirit, and on the way we can speak the truth in love to one another.

For myself I must acknowledge how deeply I have been influenced and enriched by friendship and dialogue with Roman Catholics since Vatican II. It is not easy to imagine now what relations were like before that Council. There was so much misunderstanding, suspicion and lack of warmth between Roman and Reformed Christians, so little sense of sharing the same faith, so few opportunities of praying together, so much irrational fear of one another. As a theological student I don't think I was ever encouraged to read any work of modern Roman Catholic theology; it was assumed, not without some justice, that they and we were living and working in different worlds. Now, thank God, all that has changed or is changing, even in Scotland, where old suspicions die hard and obsessive memories of the past linger long. The new sense of belonging together, a fruit very largely of the openness, confidence and reformation engendered by Vatican II, encourages a new frankness and seriousness in dialogue among Christians. So I am emboldened to say that I am deeply concerned about the future dialogue between Roman and Reformed Christians as I see the brakes so firmly and authoritatively applied on the Roman side to the movement of convergence in theology, in worship, in Christian practice. I share to the full the worry expressed by many Reformed theologians and church leaders and by the World Council of Churches about the ecumenical implications of the proceedings against prominent Roman Catholic theologians, at the untimely and emphatic reaffirmation of doctrinal and ethical positions which are peculiarly divisive, the forbidding of practices in worship which Reformed Christians regard as thoroughly evangelical, and the patronage of forms of popular piety which are deeply disturbing to all serious Reformed theologians. However, if I feel hurt, as I do, by these things, and distressed that they cannot but make dialogue and its great goal of growing together in Christ more difficult, we must not despair, or allow those who have discovered their unity in Christ at the deepest level to be driven apart once more. Dialogue is more difficult today than it was in the quite recent past; but it is not impossible.

Nor is the Blessed Virgin Mary the easiest subject for dialogue. In other, and more central, areas of Christian faith we have far more in common than we have here. But dialogue must not avoid the difficult areas if it is to produce a way forward: 'Can there be any reunion in Christ', asks Hans Küng, 'which would leave the mystery of Mary to one side? Do we not here again need the undiminished Gospel given its undiminished value and brought out into the full light of day? ... It is only reform from both sides that can help us.'[2]

Reformed theologians do understand themselves as standing with the generations which 'Call her blessed'; they are happy to name her the Mother of God, and believe a correct and biblical understanding of Mary to be a necessary, if minor, element in Christology. But it is not for nothing that Reformed Christians are called Protestants and have so consistently in the past and present protested against the growth of Mariological doctrine and the popular profusion of the cult of Mary. Indeed Roman Catholic extravagances in this field have not infrequently frightened Protestants away from any serious consideration of the person and role of Mary. Yet it is also true that responsible Reformed theologians, such as Karl Barth, who have concerned themselves with the place of Mary, have been no less emphatic in their rejection of the Marian dogmas and much of the popular Marian piety.

Protestants on the whole are more sensitive than Roman Catholics to the dangers and ambiguities involved in the phenomena of religion and pious subjectivity and in particular the temptations of assimilating Christian faith to folk religion so that its distinctiveness is obscured or lost. The extravagances of popular piety – whether Roman Catholic or Protestant – must be looked at with not a little scepticism, and it is impossible for a Reformed theologian to see much in the development of Marian doctrine and devotion as other than an accommodation of a dangerous sort to a florid and inadequately controlled popular piety.

Protestant extravagances lie in a different direction, but are no more admissible. It is necessary, I think, to ask why Roman Catholic piety has taken this particular direction, what it finds here of which it is starved in what one might call the 'main-line' life and teaching of the Church. If there is substance to the suspicion that Mary is seen as complementary to Jesus, Mariology parallel to Christology, the cult of Mary as the 'gentle road' to Jesus, then there is indeed ground for concern that the understanding of Christ and his place has been dangerously narrowed, the remedy making more extreme the malady it seeks to cure. However, let us not fall into the common trap of allowing the extravagances of Marian devotion and doctrine to frighten us off from a serious consideration of the place of Mary.

Jesus, Mary and gender roles

The incarnation, the *assumptio carnis*, involves a necessary but to some people offensive or disturbing particularity. The Word of God became flesh at a particular time at the start of the Christian era, in a particular place – Bethlehem in Palestine – in a child of a particular despised race – a Jew – of a particular gender – a male. But while affirming the particularity, and the significance of this particularity, we also believe that God assumed humanity as such. The particularity is not a limitation, so that we could say that only Jews, or Palestinians, or people of the first century, or males are redeemed in Christ. The patristic saying, 'The unassumed is the unhealed', is not to be interpreted in an exclusive sense; God in Christ assumed *humanity* and that means that the healing wrought by Christ is for *all*.

For present purposes I want to concentrate on the matter of gender; how significant is it that Christ was of the masculine gender? Clearly it is not unimportant, any more than his Jewishness or his birth in Bethlehem are unimportant; but it is surely not to be understood as a limitation, as if God in Christ assumed maleness, which is thereby healed, but did not assume femaleness, which is therefore still unhealed, or only healed through male mediation. When we say that the Word became flesh we mean that God assumed humanity in both its genders. This has an immediate bearing on the issue of women in the priesthood. To say, as some do, that since Jesus was male, only males can represent him as a priest is not very different from suggesting that since Jesus was a Jew, only Jews can be priests. An argument of this sort when applied to the only Christian priesthood other than that of Christ known to the New Testament, the royal priesthood of the faithful, has implications which would be alarming if they were not so comic.

When Pilate pointed to Jesus he said, 'Behold the Man', – *anthrōpos* – he did not use the terms for male – *anēr, arsēn, arrēn* – but the word that means *human being*. Here is *the* human being, the one in whose life and sufferings humanity reaches its perfection. The problem with us Christians is that we have consistently found difficulty in seeing Jesus Christ as *the human being*, and have allowed our understanding of him to be influenced, limited and distorted by the gender stereotypes of our age. This is, it seems to me, precisely what has happened: as Jesus has been understood increasingly as a dominant, authoritative male he has been felt by many Christians to be a frightening figure, so 'male' as to be hardly human, a judge rather than one who shares our lot. Consequently the need has been urgently felt for an alternative, more feminine focus of gentleness and grace to mediate between people and this exaggeratedly male image of Jesus. This distorted understanding of Jesus as the stern and wrathful divine judge, and Mary as the gentle and understanding woman who intercedes as a mother for her children, is open to strictly theological objection in so far as it so stresses the divinity and masculinity of Christ as to require a complementary human and feminine figure, and thus effectively denies the hypostatic union of the two natures of Christ. There is also a process going on, I believe, in which stereotypes of masculinity and femininity which are in fact culturally defined are allowed an inordinate influence in our theological thinking, and are in their turn reinforced and given an aura of sanctity by the theological images of

Jesus and of Mary. The distortions involved are well illustrated in this medieval parable: 'A certain brother Leo saw in a vision two ladders, the one red the other white. On the upper end of the red ladder stood Jesus and on the other stood His Holy Mother. The brother saw that some tried to climb the red ladder but scarcely had they mounted some rungs when they fell back; they tried again, but with no better success. Then they were advised to try the white ladder and to their surprise they succeeded, for the Blessed Virgin stretched out her hand and with her aid they reached Heaven.'[3]

My point here is excellently put by Schillebeeckx:

> One of the commonest errors is to think that the man Jesus is rather remote from us and that the gulf is, as it were, bridged by Mary. To regard Mary in this way as the link between ourselves and distant Christ is to totally misconstrue the deepest meaning of the incarnation – the fact that Christ became our fellow – a [hu]man like us. This in turn inevitably leads to a fundamental falsification of the central Christian vision of life – the significance for us of Christ's sacred *humanity* as the divine organ instituted by God for our salvation. God was born of Mary. Because of this, He is emphatically one of us. He was brought *close to us* by Mary. The relationship between Christ and ourselves is ... direct. He alone is the Mediator between God and mankind, and this is so by virtue of the fact that He was born as a God-Man of Mary. Everything comes to us from Christ.[4]

Even in a theologian of the stature of Newman there seems to be something of this over-emphasis on the divinity conjoined with the masculinity of Jesus Christ, so that his humanity is obscured and the Virgin Mary is introduced not in her proper role as recognized in Scripture and the early Church, but as a necessary human and feminine complement to the distorted image of Jesus. Newman defends devotion to the Blessed Virgin Mary as a protection against a 'specious Humanitarianism' – a term I think he would apply to most contemporary Christology, and especially that of Küng and Schillebeeckx. He wishes to distinguish the 'supreme and true worship paid to the Almighty', which is 'severe, profound, awful as well as tender, confiding and beautiful' from the devotional language directed towards Mary which is 'affectionate and ardent ... though subdued'. What I miss in his discussion is a clear recognition of the humanity of God, and that through Christ and Christ alone we may approach the Father with confidence and joy, in the company of Mary and all the saints.[5]

It is not hard to appreciate why in the Judaeo-Christian tradition God is normally spoken of as male rather than female or neuter. An understanding of God as personal, or of personality in God, demands that we speak of God as male or female, or as male *and* female; but we must beware of gratuitous and unnecessary sexism in our God-talk, lest this encourage culturally induced misunderstanding, and result in an increasing number of people experiencing alienation from our fellowship of communication. If Gandhi could be regarded, and freely spoken of, as mother as well as father of his disciples, we must not be afraid to use feminine as well as masculine language about God and Jesus Christ. Besides we know that any healthy individual will have a mixture of traits labelled 'masculine' and 'feminine' and that the models of the ideal man and the ideal woman produced by our society must not be allowed to dominate our theological thinking. Nor is what I am advocating in any way alien to the tradition. Julian of Norwich rejoiced to speak of 'God all-wise, our kindly Mother', of motherhood as an attribute of the blessed Trinity, and of Jesus Christ as being in a special sense our Mother: 'Jesus Christ ... is our real Mother. We owe our being to Him – and this is the essence of motherhood! – and all the delightful, loving protection which ever follows'.[6]

For Anselm too, motherhood is primarily a dimension of Christology:

'And you, Jesus, are you not also a Mother?
Are you not the mother who, like a hen,
Gathers her chickens under her wings?

Truly, Lord, you are a Mother;
For both they who are in labour
And they who are brought forth
Are accepted by you.

You have died more than they, that they may labour to bear.
It is by your death that they have been born,
For if you had not been in labour,
You could not have borne death;

And if you had not died, you would not have brought forth.
For, longing to bear sons into life,
You tasted of death,
And by dying you begot them.'[7]

All this goes to show the importance of a Mariology which is not parallel to Christology, or complementary to it, but an ancillary part of Christology and no more.[8] A proper understanding of Mary must enrich rather than impoverish the understanding of Jesus Christ.

Mary, Jesus and the idea of the Christian family

There has been a tendency in Churches of all traditions to paint an ideal and highly selective picture of the family of Jesus and in particular of the relations between Jesus and his mother. The resultant model of the holy family often reflects many characteristics of the contemporary family and is used to buttress the contemporary family and preserve it from criticism. The holy family and the relation between Jesus and Mary are used as norms for Christian family life and for the relations between children and parents, and Christians who find their experience of family life destructive and threatening, or who have tensions with their parents (and who does not?) are made to feel guilty and ashamed. We live in an age when patterns of family life are increasingly questioned, when relationships are under peculiar pressure and when it is clear large numbers of people are being deeply hurt both by family breakdowns and by the bitterness, hostility and aggression that many people experience in families which may outwardly seem models of Christian family life.

If the Christian response to people who are critical of family life as they see it, or who have been deeply hurt by family life, or who as a result of childhood experiences are frightened of family life, is to point to an idyllic, Botticelli-style image of the holy family as an ideal to emulate, the response is adequate neither to the problem expressed nor to the testimony of Scripture. The gospels present a variegated and it may seem rather contradictory (but no more contradictory than many relationships in real life) picture of the relation of Jesus and his mother, a picture which in its diversity and its realism can speak far more convincingly to people today than the sunny and smooth image commonly presented.

In the Gospel of Mark, the oldest gospel, we find a disturbing account of the relations of Jesus and his family emerging. His family – his mother and his brothers – seem to share the belief that Jesus' behaviour shows that he is off his head; they do not understand him, they set out to seize him. They come to the house where he is speaking to a throng, and send a message asking for him. Jesus' response is abrupt and disconcerting: 'Who are my mother and my brothers?' and then, turning to his hearers, 'Here are my mother and my brothers! Whoever does the will of God is my brother and sister and mother' (Mark 3.20–35). This negative view of his family is strengthened in 6.4 when Jesus complains that a prophet is not without honour except in his own country, *among his own relatives and in his own house.*

Although the parallels in Matthew and Luke soften the incident somewhat, it is clear that in Mark, at this stage at any rate, Mary and the brothers are regarded as outside Jesus' eschatological family, and neither understand nor support his mission.[9] Furthermore, Jesus here rejects his mother and brothers in order to affirm that he belongs to a different family, the fellowship of believers.

I mention this passage for various reasons. First of all, because only too often in discussions of Mary and the Christian family it is totally disregarded, as are of the passages which speak of Jesus as having come to bring division to the family (Luke 12.53 and 11.5) and, hardest of all: 'If anyone comes to me and does not hate his own father and mother and wife and children and brothers and sisters, yea, even his own life, he cannot be my disciple' (Luke 14.26). Secondly, because we are reminded that for Jesus there had to be at times a distancing from his mother and family and a clear distinction had to be affirmed between the natural family and the family of faith. It follows that Christians must do more than affirm the goodness of family life, and put all their energies to its defence. They have to look at the family with a critical eye, be sensitive to its inadequacies and dangers, and open to the possibility that some of the critics of family life today may be saying things that are both true and Christian. And in distinguishing that family of faith from the natural family we are also affirming that the household of faith in which the glorious liberty of the sons of God is enjoyed is the model for the natural family. The distinction is not a final one, for at the end the human family, transformed and renewed, is to be received back (Mark 10.29–31 and John 19.26–27).

The Magnificat faith: the political significance of Mary

In the chapter on Mary in the Dogmatic Constitution on the Church (*Lumen Gentium*) of Vatican II we read this: 'She stands out among the lowly and the Lord's poor who have confident hope of salvation at his hands, and who receive it.' (para. 55). She is, in other words, the representative, and in the Magnificat the mouthpiece as well, of the *Anawim*, the poor, the humble, the afflicted and the downtrodden. The *Anawim* were not simply those who were economically poor although they were that, but those who did not trust in their own strength. God is said in the OT (especially in the Psalms) to be specially concerned to protect, defend, rescue and save the *Anawim*.[10] In the Magnificat, Mary is proleptically the preacher *to* them of the gospel which reverses the standards and values and ranking of this world, and simultaneously she speaks *for* them. Her own exaltation from humiliation to blessedness is in itself a sign of the new order which is to open out for all the *Anawim*, the people of God in the sense of the people for whom God cares.

As George Caird wrote in his commentary:

> If the Magnificat had been preserved as a separate psalm outside of its present context we might have taken it to be the manifesto of a political and economic revolution ... 'The poor' had become almost a technical term for the faithful adherents of the Law, who trusted to God alone for their ultimate deliverance and vindication. Jesus was to take up this hope for the reversal of human fortunes and rid it of its limitation of nationalism and self-righteousness, so that it could become the basis of a more profound revolution than the Jews had ever bargained for.[11]

Over-familiarity has deafened us to the message of the Magnificat, and the Mary of the Magnificat seems almost unknown today – at least in the Churches of the West. It would be good for us to sit with the peasants in Solentiname to encounter the Magnificat anew through their eyes and see how they interpret it in the light of their experience. This could well be the beginning of a new encounter with the Mary of the Magnificat, the Mary who is with the oppressed as one of them and a sign of hope and liberation for them. Here is Ernesto Cardenal's account of such a Bible study:

> I asked what they thought Herod would have said if he had known that a woman of the people had sung that God had pulled down the mighty and raised up the humble, filled the hungry with good things and left the rich with nothing.
>   NATALIA laughed and said: 'He'd say she was crazy'. ROSITA: 'That she was a communist'. LAUREANO: 'The point isn't that they would just say the Virgin was a communist. She was a communist'. 'And what would they say in Nicaragua if they heard what we're saying here in Solentiname?' Several voices: 'That we're communists'. Someone asked: 'That part about filling the hungry with good things?' A young man answered: 'The hungry are going to eat'. And another: 'The Revolution'. LAUREANO: 'That is the Revolution. The rich person or the mighty is brought down and the poor person, the one who was down, is raised up'. Still another: 'If God is against the mighty, then he has to be on the side of the poor'. ANDREA, Oscar's wife, asked: 'That promise that the poor would have those good things, was it for then, for Mary's time, or would it happen in our time? I ask because I don't know'. One of the young people answered: 'She spoke for the future, it seems to me, because we are just barely beginning to see the liberation she announces'.[12]

Mary, in other words, is not herself the liberator, but is a pointer to the liberation wrought by her Son, for women and for all the poor and oppressed, the whole *Anawim* of God. Achieved, but not yet fully realized. This is the understanding of Mary which is, I believe, of the most pressing relevance today.

6

Biblical interpretation and cultural relativism[1]

Most children brought up, as I was, in a Christian home, encounter the Bible long before they can read it for themselves. I heard it read in church and at home. I had Bible stories read to me; a great deal of biblical language flowed over my head and eddied around my awakening consciousness before I was given my first simplified book of Bible stories and, somewhat later, a blue-bound Authorized Version in bold print so that I should not strain my eyes. Cumulatively all this gave me the impression that the Bible was different from other books, the most important of all books, the one book that the child and his parents, and grandparents, and all sorts of people had in common. Like the stories from the Bible, my parents told me or read me the stories of Goldilocks, and Beauty and the Beast, but I was conscious that even if they enjoyed reading fairy stories to me they did not read them themselves, and that although I might savour Rumpelstiltskin, grown-ups were not really interested in discussing *that* story, but would happily talk with me about Joseph, or the marriage at Cana of Galilee. It seemed that the adults with whom I was in most immediate contact felt that they were still exploring the meaning of a book I was just starting to discover for myself; and felt that meaning to be important to me as to them, for unlike almost all the other books they read and then put back on the shelves, this one was constantly thumbed and divided into portions to be wrestled with day by day.

Every child knows that good stories may be, indeed must be, told over and over again; Bible stories are not peculiar in this regard. I remember, for instance, pestering my mother almost every day as we passed a certain old house on our way to the shops to tell me the story of Willie Douglas, who once, many years before, had lived there – or so we believed. As a boy, Willie Douglas had been page to Mary Queen of Scots, and had attended her while she was imprisoned in

Loch Leven castle. It was he who had stolen the key from the Governor while he was in his cups, and ushered the Queen out to the waiting boat, throwing the key to the depths of the loch, from which it had been dredged up centuries later. Why did I insist on this story being told to me so constantly that it must have driven my mother, imaginative story teller though she was, half demented? The answer, I think, looking back, is quite simple: it answered my questions, Who am I? Where do I belong? Where do I come from? In dramatic and vivid fashion, it gave me a history in a way Beauty and the Beast, for all the profundity of its meaning never could. And the same is true of Bible stories when told or read in this kind of context, which is as it were the natural setting for a sacred book, in which the text and the reader enter into a particular kind of urgent, if repetitive, dialogue.

Repetition is, of course, a prominent characteristic of ritual, and I am suggesting that when the Bible is read within the believing community we have a ritual way of reading which is a special kind of dialogue between the reader and the text. This is made unusually explicit in the Passover Haggada within Judaism, in which, soon after the start of the rite, the youngest child present asks four questions:

> Why does this night differ from all other nights? For on all other nights we eat either leavened or unleavened bread; why on this night only unleavened bread?
> On all other nights we eat all kinds of herbs; why on this night only bitter herbs?
> On all other nights we need not dip our herbs even once; why on this night must we dip them twice?
> On all other nights we eat either sitting or reclining; why on this night do we all recline?

To which the response is:

> We were Pharoah's slaves in Egypt, and the Lord our God brought us forth with a mighty hand and an outstretched arm. And if the Holy One, Blessed be he, had not brought our forefathers forth from Egypt, then we, our children, and our children's children would still be slaves in Egypt.
> So, even though all of us were wise, all of us full of understanding, all of us elders, all of us knowing the Torah, we should still be under the commandment to tell the story of the departure from Egypt. And the more one tells the story of the departure from Egypt the more praiseworthy he is.[2]

And then they do just that – reading and discussing passages of the Bible and all sorts of rabbinical stories which have a bearing upon the liberation from bondage, from which gradually emerge answers to the child's questions, which are also the perennial questions of the adults present.

I have dwelt upon the Passover ritual for a variety of reasons, It illustrates the point I made earlier that biblical stories have a bearing, sometimes oblique, sometimes direct, upon fundamental questions of identity, and their repetition within the believing community confirms and strengthens the answers to these questions. But the context within which the stories are told and told again is a ritual context, that is, things are done as well as said, and the whole is charged with a depth of symbolic meaning. The context generates the questions, shapes the answers, and gives plausibility to the whole way of reading. This may most clearly be obvious in the Passover or in the Lord's Supper, but my point is that biblical stories told within the believing community can never be totally detached from the representation of the central acts of salvation in ritual. This means that the believing community is affirming in the strongest possible way that these stories are *their* history, that they understand themselves in the light of them; but also that they are *present* now, in their re-enactment: *we* experience deliverance from bondage in Egypt, the Lord makes himself known to us, now, in the breaking of the bread. The story of Willie Douglas was important to me because it was about a boy, because it was history, my history, however highly embroidered, because the house in which he had lived was there, close by the house in which I lived. Willie Douglas and I belonged together within the same community, constant in place and continuous over time, and I felt no insuperable difficulty in entering into his experience any more than encountering Jesus in story and in ritual.

All of this, of course, bristles with problems, some of which we will return to later. There is a perhaps terribly naïve confidence in the possibility not only of communicating across vast periods of time, but even of making the past present today, which simply sidesteps the difficulty of historical understanding. There is a singular lack of interest in drawing any hard and fast distinction between history and myth. There is a breathtaking confidence in the continuity and sameness of the believing community across the ages. There is a conviction that history, stories, are the heart of the Bible, to which the myths and parables and ethics and doctrine and poetry and proverbs are all in a sense ancillary. And binding all these presuppositions together is the conviction that the Bible is the *Holy* Bible, different from, and more important than, all other books.

As a student I encountered a different sort of book, and was trained in reading philosophical texts such as Plato's *Republic*. A book such as this was presented for our study over many weeks on the assumption, made perfectly explicit to us, that this was a work of genius, with a subtlety and profundity of meaning which made it difficult to understand, but ultimately worth the intellectual effort required. The problem was not essentially that it had been written many centuries ago and that ancient Athens was clearly a very different kind of community from St Andrews; it was that the mind of a genius moved on a higher plane: it was hard for us to understand Plato because we were not geniuses rather than because we were twentieth-century undergraduates. The techniques of interpretation, it is true, were of more general application, but this particular text had been chosen for us not just as the focus for a new way of reading, but because its matter was assumed to have some perennial relevance and importance, although just how this might be the case was left to us to discover. It was dinned into us that it was hard, but not impossible, to understand the *Republic*, and we were encouraged to apply ourselves in detail to Plato's words, if possible in the original Greek. We were advised to beware of commentaries and secondary works, and were given the minimum of contextual material, probably lest the effort to understand might be frustrated by glib attempts to explain a superficial account of Plato's teaching as a reflection of class conflicts in ancient Athens, or the psychological quirks of the author's personality. We were warned not to neglect the possibility that there might be some perennial teaching in the book by interpreting it as a tract for the times and nothing more.

Above all, we were taught to be modest in our approach to the text: because Plato wrote many centuries before, we cannot assume that his thought has been superseded. Modesty involved setting aside as far as possible one's own presuppositions and untutored questions, and in particular struggling to make sure that one understood what Plato was saying, and why, and how it all hung together before one dared to criticize or ask questions about relevance. And we were given the impression that few, if any, among us would ever be in a position actually to enter into dialogue with Plato; it was enough, for the present, if we penetrated to an understanding of what the text was saying. The modesty before the text with which we were inculcated was no doubt excessive, but to a degree it was necessary if the reader were to be properly open to the text with an awareness that it must be read in a different way from an Agatha Christie detective story, and it was not *toto coelo* different from the reverence with which I had learned to approach Scripture. Neither modesty nor reverence, unless taken to ridiculous extremes, impedes a scholarly reading.

Neither for the Bible nor for the *Republic* was there felt to be any basic problem involved in lifting a text from one century and reading it in a very different setting; in both cases the reading of the text was seen as presenting the possibility of a critical stance towards the spirit of one's own age – by no means a bad thing, if it can be achieved. The two books belonged in different communities: the *Republic* was a book for the mature and for an intellectual elite, for Guardians, an intellectual text; the Bible was a book for everyone, even for children, a book to be made available for all, a book which must not be confined to the Academy or withheld from the masses. Each had shaped a community, and if only for that reason, merited attention.

But the Bible had, and has, a place, if a rather strange and problematic one, in the Academy as well as in the Church, as I was to discover when I proceeded to read theology. Here we found the Bible presented to us as an authoritative text much as Plato's *Republic* had been, rather than a book presupposed to be sacred. The distinction may be a hard one to maintain, for, as I have suggested, modesty, even reverence, in one's approach to an authoritative text need not inhibit scholarship, and indeed may be the condition for a proper reading. Reverence is not incompatible with scholarly rigour. But the student who was already familiar with the Bible as a sacred text, who had been brought up in an atmosphere saturated with the Bible, who had in all probability memorized a variety of passages, read the Bible daily, and used it in his prayers, now had to learn a new way of reading a well-known text. He had to learn to address a different sort of question to the text, suspending as far as he was able his earlier conclusions about what the Bible says in order to read it afresh, as if it were a new and unfamiliar book. This process often enough resulted in confusion and dismay; certainly the transition in ways of reading was frequently profoundly unsettling, as it was realized that there were profound discrepancies between the old reading and the new.

The situation was further complicated by problems of motivation. Most students who study Plato's *Republic* do so because they have to, or because they find the book interesting and stimulating; few I imagine, read it as a key to how to become a successful politician, or as a relevant blueprint for social and political reform today; they read it to sharpen their wits rather than their political skills. But although there are those in universities who study the Bible because of its intrinsic interest or its literary and cultural significance, most students still come to it as 'the supreme rule of life and doctrine', a book on which to build their prayers, their preaching and their lives – in other words, a sacred book, the Holy Bible. And such students often find that the older type of exegesis which was clearly a function of the community of faith and dealt with Scripture unashamedly as a holy book is more congenial by far than the newer biblical criticism which seems to them 'academic' (in the bad sense, as being detached from and irrelevant to real life), and sometimes positively subversive to faith. There is a real dilemma here: the modern biblical scholar may respond to his students' unease by saying that faithfulness to the text is destructive only of belief which is based on a naïve view of Scripture, to which the students are entitled to reply that it is strange that only now, after 2000 years, do we possess the critical techniques necessary for a correct reading of the Bible; and if these techniques have made redundant the exegesis of all earlier commentators, perhaps they have destroyed or questioned the very features of the text which make it significant enough to justify so much study.

Our problems are beginning clearly to emerge. There is, at least potentially, a conflict between the study of the Bible as a holy book within the Church, and the study of the Bible as an important ancient text within the university. There are significant differences in approach, techniques and motives for study, as well as in the uses to which the results of study are put. The contrast is a real one, although I have undoubtedly simplified the issues in order to present a clear polarity. It is no part of my present concern to enquire which way of reading is the better, the more useful, or the more faithful to the text. I do not wish to take sides with Kierkegaard in attacking biblical scholarship (although I must admit to a certain sympathy with him) when he argues:

> Suppose that in the New Testament it were written, for example (a thing which we can at least suppose), that every man should have $100,000...do you believe that there would then be any question of a commentary? – or not rather that every one would say: That is easy enough to understand, there is absolutely no need of a commentary, for God's sake, let us be delivered from any commentary...
>
> But what actually is written in the New Testament (about the narrow way, about dying to the world) is not a bit more difficult to understand than that about the $100,000. The difficulty lies elsewhere, in the fact that it is not to our liking – and therefore, therefore [*sic*] we must have commentaries and professors and commentaries.
>
> It is to get rid of doing God's will that we have invented learning...we shield ourselves by hiding behind tomes.[3]

Kierkegaard certainly had a point, but his presupposition that there is a simple, faithful, and responsive way of reading the Bible, which gives immediate access to the meaning of the text, cannot be accepted as it stands. On the other hand, the assumption that only now has academic study rescued the Bible from churchly obscurantism so that its true meaning may for the first time be dredged up from beneath the pious imaginings with which it has been overlaid carries little conviction. My real sympathies are with the Jewish student training to be a rabbi who had great problems with his first encounter with modern biblical criticism, but eventually won through to a conviction that this kind of study provided positive help to him in his reading of the Bible. And going from university to study in a Yeshiva in Jerusalem, where the students devoted themselves entirely to the traditional rabbinical study of the Torah as the law in which their whole being delighted, he found there a different, but no less useful and illuminating, way of studying the Bible.

What is of primary interest to us in this essay is the fact that the two ways of reading the Bible arise in different social contexts, the university and the believing community, and that to a large extent it is the social context that determines the questions which are posed and the general approach to the text. But if it is admitted that the social context influences the way a text is read, three issues call out for clarification: first, what we mean by a social context; secondly, how the social context influences the reading of a text; and finally, what the relation is between various ways of reading arising from different social contexts. Is there any way of judging between different ways of reading, or are we in a realm of total relativity, in which even the words of the text themselves provide no objective criterion for rival inter-pretations?

The two social contexts we have already distinguished have, of course, an area of overlap, and both are set within the broader social and cultural context of the modern West. Thus there are those who belong both to the university and to the believing community, and see no fundamental incompatibility in the ways of reading and inter-preting the Bible characteristic of the pulpit and the lecture room. But perhaps this is simply because they are twentieth-century people whose exposition in Church and Academy is more influenced by the basic presuppositions of modern Western culture than by anything else. Of course, this simply pushes the problem of what we mean by a social and cultural context to a different level. Dennis Nineham borrows from Troeltsch and other German thinkers the concept of 'cultural totalities', by which he means unified and coherent complexes, any aspect of which can only be understood in relation to the whole.[4] He is primarily (indeed, I suspect, exclusively) interested in totalities which occur in different ages rather than in totalities which exist simultaneously, like the contexts of Church and university which we have just discussed. These also serve to remind us of the facts of interaction and overlap which make it impossible for us to speak of Church and university as self-contained totalities, or even to regard modern Western culture as a totality since it has such complex and fascinating contacts with other modern cultures and with its own past. Nineham's over-hasty acceptance of the concept of totality, and his emphatic insistence upon the difficulty of communicating between one age and another, lead him to a rather despairing picture of modern man as encapsulated within his age, incapable of questioning the underlying assumptions of his contemporaries, or communicating in any real sense with those of other ages or cultures. This view of people as isolated within their own age and culture naturally leads on to regarding the thought-forms of our age – our old friend, the *Zeitgeist* – as in some sense absolute, the peak of human achievement. The modern age, together with the ways of reading the Bible which it has developed, is placed beyond question.

It is not, however, necessary to go to such an extreme in order to make a proper allowance for the influence of the social and cultural context, in all its fascinating diversity, upon the way in which a text is read and interpreted. Communication, between one context and another very different one, is no doubt difficult and bristles with problems, but it is a counsel of despair to assume that it is virtually impossible, precisely because this assumes an absolutizing of one's own culture and the dominant forms of understanding and interpretation in that culture. Nineham's book is haunted by a shadowy 'visiting anthropologist' who is never formally introduced to the reader, and remains anonymous; which is just as well, for no serious anthropologist of whom I am aware would countenance Nineham's gloomy conclusions about the inaccessibility of other cultures, or support his neat escape from total relativism by absolutizing the present moment. The anthropologist appears also as the typical modern man, since his function is to present 'the strange world of the Bible' which Karl Barth discovered to be so exciting that it forced modernity into crisis, as not only infinitely strange, but quaint, naïve and impenetrable by the modern mind. The language of Canaan cannot be translated into modern speech; it is a code beyond our power to break. Collingwood may have been rather too optimistic about the ability of the careful historian to enter into the mind of Julius Caesar as he hesitated on the bank of the Rubicon, but he was surely quite realistic in believing that, given effort, eagerness and sympathy, one may understand a radically different cultural context and learn from it. It is not helpful to reify 'cultural totalities' after the style of German Romanticism, and then voluntarily imprison oneself in one's own.

Our second question, concerning the influence of a cultural context on the reading of a text, we have already touched upon. Particular questions arise from the context, and are addressed to the text; and here as elsewhere, the questions you ask largely determine the answers you get. A text is used in different ways, depending on the context. The Bible is perhaps pre-eminently a book which questions the reader, and often rejects or reshapes the questions she brings to her reading, putting her and her context into question. It relativizes the relativizer, in other words, thereby inducing a proper modesty before the text. It is no escape from this to say that there are two ways of reading, the one seeking as objective as possible an understanding of what the writer really meant, the other concerning itself with the application of the teaching of an authoritative text to a fresh situation. Karl Popper's account of the *Republic* as the foundation document of totalitarian oppression was not simply a criticism of the modern *use* of the *Republic*, but a fresh reading of the meaning and intention of the text itself. He did not argue that the book was being misused or wrongly understood, but that its teaching was objectively malignant and morally repulsive. Modern totalitarianism had underlined the true, and dangerous, meaning of the text. In a not dissimilar way, Nineham cannot but recognize that the Bible is the foundation document of the Church. But he argues that 'modern man' (that elusive figure with whom some contemporary theologians have such intimate acquaintance, and to whose conjectural opinions they accord such authority) can no longer read the Bible as a sacred book.[5] This is so, because Nineham believes there is no longer a slot within our cultural totality for sacred books, so that the whole concept does not make sense. Closely allied to this is his rejection of the canon, leaving the Christian free to seek illumination where she will – from other books, from sermons, and from the liturgy, provided sermons and liturgy are freed from 'what has rightly been called "the curse of the canon"'.[6] Precisely why it is no longer appropriate or possible to read the Bible as a sacred text is nowhere spelled out, and we are left to conjecture that it is simply because the majority of people do not regard it as such. What is, of course, abundantly clear is that if Nineham and his like won the day the Bible would soon lose its strange capacity to question the reader and relativize modern preconceptions, and could never merit a Popperian onslaught since biblical scholars would be seen as having lost confidence in its authority, relevance and indeed intelligibility.

Our third problem concerns the possibility of discriminating between various ways of reading the Bible. Traditional exegesis has, as we know, distinguished various types of meaning in biblical passages – literal, spiritual, allegorical, and so on – and has often sought to arrange them in some kind of hierarchy of meanings, under the ultimate control of the text itself. The modern scholar is also aware of diversities of meaning and interpretation, and relates many of them not unilluminatingly to variable social and cultural circumstances. Whereas the traditional exegete tried (with what measure of success is immaterial to present purposes) to test interpretations against the text, the modern scholar of the school of Nineham judges an interpretation by its compatibility or otherwise with 'modernity', rather loosely defined. It is rather like the student who demands immediate relevance in everything she studies. Christians of past ages may have been rather naïve in their belief that they had direct access to the world of the Bible, and could draw directly from the Scriptures perennially relevant patterns of faith and behaviour; but at least they did not feel themselves imprisoned in the present moment, and drew from the Bible tools for the refashioning of themselves, their Church, and their society. If the choice is between absolutizing the Bible or absolutizing modernity we are indeed in a sorry state. But the dilemma is false. Other possibilities are before us.

'Day unto day uttereth speech, and night unto night sheweth knowledge': Nineham has provoked us into giving perhaps excessive attention to matters concerning interpretation across time. There are problems and possibilities relating to interpretation from one contemporary culture to another, one social context to another, which are of no less interest and which have the capability of enriching and deepening ways of reading the Bible, and teaching a proper modesty through relativizing the relativizers. The process of translation, dialogue – and sometimes conflict – between those who read the Bible in different ways relating to their varying cultural background can be most illuminating as well as frustrating.

My initial contact with India helped me immediately to understand certain biblical passages more clearly. Seeing daily flocks of indistinguishable sheep and goats running together, and gradually discovering that the only reliable differentiating sign was that the sheep's tails hung down, while the goats' pointed heavenwards, helped me to understand why the separation of sheep and goats was regarded as not altogether a simple operation in the Bible. In studying the gospels with students who had come straight from the villages I found my rather tortuous attempts to explain, or rather explain away, the miracle stories met with amazed incredulity; miracles as such were not problematic for them as they were for me, since many of them had seen people possessed by demons healed through prayer and the laying on of hands, and accordingly found my scepticism quite implausible prejudice – which perhaps it was. Virtually all my friends and students had a clear idea of what a sacred text was, and well-defined notions of how best it should be read, which were in many respects far different from mine. Hindu students opted to take courses on the Bible in large numbers not just because it is an important work of literature but because they and their parents, while remaining Hindus, regarded the Bible as a holy book, from which they derived spiritual nourishment. They brought, of course, their own presuppositions to the reading of the text. The more philosophically inclined among them, for instance, would interpret the New Testament – John's Gospel in particular – in a monist way, centring their reading on sayings such as 'I and the Father are one' and the high priestly prayer 'that they may all be one; even as thou, Father, art in me, and I in thee, that they also may be in us... that they may become perfectly one'. Such encounters forced me to re-examine and explain, and sometimes modify, my own reading of some passages, and made others which I had found virtually unintelligible spring vividly to life.

The whole process of translation and communication from one culture to another can provide extraordinary illumination of the text. I am intrigued, for instance, at the way in which Protestant missionaries in India throughout the nineteenth century read the New Testament as a charter of equality, so that their converts had to renounce caste and demonstrate their willingness to accept as brothers and sisters those who were, within the caste system, regarded as irremediably polluting. But when these converts argued that the same New Testament passages raised question marks against denominational barriers among Christians, put class as well as caste under judgement, and disallowed the practice of racial superiority, these same missionaries were horrified and commonly found their converts' way of reading the Bible quite unacceptable.

There is a story, which I hope is true, of a group of Buddhists and Christians who decided they would study the Bible together. They started, appropriately enough, with John's Gospel. 'In the beginning was the Word', was read out, and immediately an aged Buddhist monk groaned, 'Even in the very beginning was there no silence in your religion?' The story does not relate how the Christians talked themselves out of that one; but I am sure the effort to explain in itself enriched their reading of the text. I remember once preparing to preach on the passage in Romans 8 about the whole creation groaning in travail together until it will be set free from its bondage to decay and obtain the glorious liberty of the children of God. I consulted, as I have been trained to do, a number of commentaries. All save one seemed highly embarrassed by Paul's talk of cosmic redemption and treated it as a kind of spiritualized picture of the salvation of individuals which had little to do with the material universe. Only the commentary by F. F. Bruce, a conservative biblical scholar, seemed to take what Paul was clearly saying about nature seriously, and thereby highlighted deficiencies in the liberal scholarly reading of the other commentators.

I have consciously kept from discussing the politics of differing ways of reading the Bible although a political dimension has been latent in much of what I have said. I have done this partly because the political hermeneutic which is coming today mainly from Latin America is, in my opinion, so important that it deserves more extensive treatment than I can afford here; but also because it should be obvious that every social and cultural context which affects reading is also a political context. Kierkegaard is surely right in suggesting that we are reluctant to read, or unable to understand, what we do not want to know in a text; we are unwilling often enough to be questioned by a book. We interpret away or tone down the unacceptable parts, or become deaf to their significance through constant reiteration. I remember in the early years of my ministry sometimes having a horror in the middle of reading the Bible in Church either because the passage seemed to call in question the person who was reading so blandly and authoritatively, or because I felt it so offensive to the congregation that they must surely walk out. But they never did, and I now rarely find it threatening to read the Bible aloud. Which suggests, I believe, that ritual repetition and over-familiarity can distance one from the meaning even as one delights in the words. It would be good for those of us who, in our comfortable and rather self-indulgent society enjoy – among other things – chanting the Magnificat, if we could sit with the peasants in Solentiname, studying the same passage, as recounted by Ernesto Cardenal.

I, for one, find it impossible to deny that this represents a way of reading the Magnificat from which we can easily be excluded if we become imprisoned in our own immediate context. But if we are truly open to a plurality of ways of reading it can liberate us for a new and better understanding of the Bible. What I am saying cannot be better summed up than in the words of Pastor John Robinson in 1620 as he bade farewell to those of his congregation in Leiden who were joining the Pilgrim Fathers to sail in the *Mayflower* from one context, seeking another that was new and free for the faithful reading of the Bible:

> He charged us, before God and his blessed angels, to follow him no further than he followed Christ; and if God should reveal anything to us by any other instrument of his to be as ready to receive it, as ever we were to receive any truth by his ministry. For he was very confident that the Lord had more truth and light yet to break forth out of his Holy Word.[7]

7

The Church and the concentration camp: some reflections on moral community[1]

We were returning home from holiday in Austria with our children some years ago. After Munich we began to notice road signs pointing to Dachau. These signs and that word brought back for Margaret and me a host of dark memories – of the news of the concentration camps that became public in the latter years of the Second World War, of the films of the liberation of the camps that were shown in British cinemas for a time after the war, 'Lest We Forget'; of the stories that were told to us by a German Jewish family that stayed with us in St Andrews in 1939 before going to safety in the States. That road-sign brought back old feelings of anger, shock and dismay that human beings could be so wicked, that evil of a cataclysmic sort should flourish in 'civilized' and 'Christian' Europe, that such awfulness should come to pass in the twentieth century after an epoch of what we had believed was progress.

As we drove past a section of the perimeter fence and glanced at the ominous huts and edifices preserved intact inside the boundary, our children seemed to sense that something was wrong, that their parents were distressed, that this place stood for something that seemed to inspire horror. They asked, as children do, the obvious, but often profound, questions: What is this place? What happened there? Why did it take place? Couldn't good people have stopped it?

We told them as honestly as we could about the concentration camps, about Nazism, about the Holocaust, about what happened there. We always felt that it is important to tell truth to children, not to shield them from reality, even if that reality is appalling evil and ugly. We always tried to answer their questions directly, to ensure that they received from their parents the truthfulness they are entitled to expect.

But this time it was peculiarly difficult to be truthful. Dachau and Auschwitz and the other camps were and are a problem not just for sunny, over-optimistic liberals who have a cheery confidence in moral progress, but for everyone, and particularly for Christian believers. We did the best we could to respond to our children's questions and explain how it all happened, and why it wasn't nipped in the bud, and how many ordinary people like us knowingly or unknowingly colluded in what was going on. We described what went on in the camps in relation to Jews, and gays, and gypsies, and Christians, and communists. We talked particularly about anti-Semitism, and we were at pains to pass on a lesson that we had learned in Christian homes during the war, that one mustn't blame the German people as a whole, and we must honour those who courageously stood against the evil. We tried not to disguise the horror of it all. And I think we made clear that we felt that ultimately the only response possible to the horror of Dachau was a war of liberation, despite all the reservations and all the unease that Christians must have about violence.

The children picked up our unease. Somehow it didn't all add up, theologically or ethically. There were no satisfactory explanations for the horror. None of the responses seemed to be adequate. In some way we felt ourselves to be implicated. The evidence coming from the only part of the United Kingdom to be occupied, the Channel Islands, suggested that had Britain been occupied it would have been no different here. Many would have been willing collaborators with the Nazis. As we responded to their questions, the children knew us to be in turmoil.

The next day we drove across the plains of northern France. Here the unavoidable theme for discussion with the children was the significance of the acre upon acre of First World War military graveyards. Somewhere there, amidst the tens of thousands of tombstones and the vast number of unmarked graves, lay the body of the uncle after whom I am named, killed aged nineteen in a vastly destructive, horrifying and muddy trench battle and now lying in a nameless grave. Once again, the children asked questions. They wanted to know what that war had been about; they wanted an explanation for this huge orgy of destruction and violence. I have a history degree. I have studied the origins of the First World War. I know about the assassination in Sarajevo of the Archduke Ferdinand of Austria. I tried explaining all this historical 'wisdom' to the children. But as I spoke, I knew it didn't add up to an explanation, let alone a justification of this vast orgy of destruction, violence and death. It certainly didn't make any *Christian* sense. And the children, aware of our embarrassment, must have wondered in what sort of world they were to grow up.

A few years later, we took the children to the only extermination camp the Nazis established in France, near Strasbourg. After seeing the barracks, the gas chamber, the ovens for cremating the bodies, the villa of the governor with its rose garden, fertilized with the ashes from the ovens, where the prisoners' orchestra played Mozart to entertain the governor's guests, our daughter was physically sick, and remained distressed for days. Our son bombarded us with questions: How could this happen? Who was responsible? Why did God allow it? After tortuous and inadequate attempts on our part to make sense of all this, we had to say, quite simply, that Hitler and his associates were very evil men. What would *you* do about him? Does God love Hitler? Ought we to love him? – the questions poured out. And wrestling with such questions is what serious theological ethics is all about, for the questions of children more commonly go straight to the heart of the matter than do the convoluted and pretentious questions of adults, and particularly perhaps of academics.

Outside the camp…with Jesus?

Driving past Dachau, our children did not seem to notice what was glaringly obtrusive and problematic for Margaret and me: just outside the perimeter wire there stood a graceful little eighteenth-century church, freshly painted and with a typical central European onion dome on the top of its tower. It was probably Roman Catholic, but it might possibly have been Evangelical; that really didn't matter. Here was a Christian church, almost certainly regularly used for worship, standing less than a hundred yards from the fence, visible to anyone moving about inside the camp.

Perhaps it was significant that it stood *outside* the camp. In most Western prisons the chapel is inside, signifying a religious involvement in what goes on in prison. That is the Christendom locale for a chapel, for in Christendom the Christian faith is involved in the discipline of the society, and often enough the prison was run by a troika of governor, chaplain and doctor. Perhaps it is healthier in normal circumstances for the location of the church to be *outside* the camp, a standing reminder of the impermanence of the camp, and the need to seek the city that is to come. After all, that place, outside the camp, was where Jesus bore the stigma and suffered for the sake of the life of the camp, of the city (Hebrews 13.12–14). But these Nazi days were no normal circumstances, and inevitably we had to ask what went on in that little church outside the camp when the camp behind the wire was active in its death-dealing ways of destruction.

Some things are almost certain. The Bible would have been read, Sunday by Sunday, or day by day. There would, at least from time to time, have been preaching, expounding and application of the message of Scripture. Bread would have been broken in the Lord's Supper, the Eucharist, the Mass, with the people receiving the Body and Blood of the Lord. From time to time children and even adults would have been received into the household of faith in baptism. God's praise would have been sung, and prayers offered for the Church and the world. All the ordinary central activities of a congregation of God's people within a hundred yards of the Dachau concentration camp! And through the wire all the comings and goings of congregation and of concentration camp visible to one another, paraded before one another! But sometimes, of course, for a variety of reasons, people cannot see, or chose not to see what lies before them.

Here, presumably, was a congregation which had all 'the marks of the true Church', as the dogmaticians say, existing within a hundred yards of the concentration camp. Was the worship of that little congregation timeless, allowing the worshippers to step, or believe that they stepped, into a different reality in which the Dachau concentration camp no longer existed? Did that church provide an escape from the awful reality so close by? Or did it engage in prayer, in protest, in action with what was going on, which could be seen and heard and smelled, and could have been touched had there not been a wire and a guard tower in between?

Who, I wonder, attended that church? Local villagers, no doubt, and probably older ones, for the young people would be away fighting the war. Did SS or Gestapo men ever happen to come into the little church? Did members of the staff of the camp, or their families worship there? Perhaps a doctor carrying out experiments on inmates, or even the governor might happen by. What would the worship and the life of that church say to them? Would it give them solace, allowing them to carry on their activities with a quiet mind? Would it transport them to a different world, enabling them to evade responsibility for what they did in this world? Would they receive beneath that onion dome a premature and illusory forgiveness, cheap grace that makes no demands, at a knock-down price?

We will never know the answer to these questions. But what we do know without a shadow of doubt is that people engaged in unspeakably evil courses of action often find solace in religion. General Pinochet, throughout the torture and repression of innocent people by his government, was regular in his attendance at Mass. Frantz Fanon, in a different but not unconnected realm, found himself, as a psychiatrist in Algeria, expected to treat and 'heal' government torturers who were suffering from remorse so that they could return with an equable mind to the torture of the innocent.

Did the congregation meeting in that little church in the shadow of Dachau raise up prophets who dared to denounce the system and confront the evil? Almost certainly the answer to that is no, as there is so little evidence of dissident voices from within the Churches requiring to be silenced. Or was the Dachau church a quiet school of virtue and faithfulness, like the little congregation under Pastor Trocmé in the village of Chambon-sur-Lignon in the Cévennes, where, when a Jewish woman knocked on the door late at night and asked if she could come in, Madame Trocmé totally unselfconsciously answered, 'Yes'. And that, as is well known, started an escape route for several hundred Jews into safety in Switzerland – discipleship spontaneously in action. But that kind of faithfulness may perhaps not be possible, cheek by jowl with Dachau.

Or did the little church outside the wire proclaim an apocalyptic faith, denouncing Dachau as Babylon the great whore, and confidently foreseeing its destruction and the vindication of its victims? Or did it even sustain its people on apocalyptic imagery striving to be reborn, or come alive in courageous critique of the camp and all it stood for? Was the congregation a peaceable community which by its very existence and walk presented an alternative to the violence being unleashed behind the fence? I wonder, and I hesitate to press my questions towards an answer because I fear the truth about that little church would not be as I might wish it to be. In all probability it was just a quiet little congregation meeting in a much loved building, and carrying on as if nothing unusual was happening behind the wire close by.

Let us press our speculations one step further. Suppose the prisoners in the camp could see the people coming and going around that little church; perhaps through an open door or window they could see a little of what was going on, hear part of a chorale, perhaps on the wind catch phrases of a sermon or a prayer. Was it possible that they might glimpse the expression on people's faces as they came to church, and see whether it was changed or the same when they left? The prisoners would notice without a doubt whether the worshippers glanced towards the camp or kept their gaze averted. They would take the measure of the expression on their faces. Do they care about the camp, and us, and what goes on here? the prisoners would ask each other, I have no doubt.

And what would the prisoners make of all this? We have no evidence, apart from the wire and the watchtower and the little church, and the knowledge that there must have been prisoners, and guards, and worshippers, and pastors around these places when the camp was operating. What was the impact of all this on the prisoners? Was it in any sense a sign of hope to them? Did it affirm or destroy any faith they might have? Did it in any way lift up their hearts and minds to a coming day, which would be a day of judgement as well as of vindication? In its compromised mundane ordinariness did the life of that congregation suggest that the camp lacked ultimacy, and despite everything was doomed to destruction? Did its existence raise a question mark against the existence of the camp? Or was it a sign to the prisoners of sheer irrelevance?

We will never be able to answer these questions, but we have to ask them. For that church outside the perimeter fence at Dachau stands in a sense for every church although its locale is apparently so much more extreme and demanding. And if it is a church which neither has nor is a social ethic, its existence, and the existence of many another church just like it, raises awkward questions about one of Stanley Hauerwas's most suggestive and problematic epigrams: 'The church does not have, but is a social ethic.'

Inside the camp...with Jesus?

Dachau was the first concentration camp to be established by the Nazis, almost immediately upon their gaining power in 1933. It was not at the beginning an extermination camp – that came somewhat later, but as a logical development of the purposes for which Dachau was established. Churchill proclaimed during a debate about the rebuilding of the House of Commons after it had been destroyed in the Blitz, when some people were advocating moving from the traditional and rather adversarial layout to the more common semicircular legislature layout, 'We shape our buildings, and then our buildings shape us'. He was right. I taught for eight years in India in a Christian college, the premises of which had been carefully designed in 1938 to enable and encourage the development of well-integrated and diverse community life, and good relations between staff and students. These buildings served their community-building purpose remarkably well.

Dachau was designed and built to make a very different statement, and to be the prototype of a ruthless instrument for carrying through the grand design of the Nazis. The camp, Goldhagen says, 'was the first major distinctively new institution that Nazism founded after Hitler's accession to power'.[2] It symbolized and enabled a regime that depended on division, hatred and contempt to carry out its evil work, and it demanded that whole sections of the population, most notably the Jews, should be first systematically excluded, degraded and intimidated, and then eliminated in the 'final solution' in the extermination camps.

From 9 March 1933 at Dachau, in Martin Gilbert's words, 'terror found a hidden base behind barbed wire'. But the purpose was not that it should remain hidden; it was important that terror should spread from the camps throughout the population like ripples from a stone thrown into a pool. The fence was, as it were, calculated to enable outsiders to see a little of what went on inside, and to give inmates a tantalizing glimpse of the outside world. The local SS, with a reputation for savagery, established the camp in a set of empty huts in a gravel pit. Within a month, the camp had expanded to house 5000 prisoners, Jews, gypsies, gays and critics of the regime. The camp started as a kind of crystallization and intensification of the terror that was ruling the streets, and in a subtle way it conferred legitimacy on the terror and encouraged brutality outside.[3]

In October 1933 a new code of discipline and punishment was introduced to make Dachau a model of what was to become the central distinctive institution of the Nazi state. Absolute obedience to orders was ensured by the strictest of sanctions; 'agitators' were to be hung.[4] Large numbers of prisoners were killed through summary executions, erratic outbreaks of violence on the part of guards, or simply through exhaustion, sickness and overwork. The purpose of the camp from the beginning was degradation, destruction and death, all as an expression of the ideology of the Nazi regime. A Jewish prisoner who survived described the camp in February 1938:

> The Jewish prisoners worked in special detachments and received the hardest tasks. They were beaten at every opportunity – for instance, if the space between the barrows with which they had to walk or even to run over loose flints was not correctly kept. They were overwhelmed with abusive epithets such as 'Sow Jew', 'Filth Jew' and 'Stink Jew'. During the working period the non-Jewish prisoners were issued with one piece of bread at breakfast – the Jews with nothing. But the Jews were always paraded with the others to see the bread ration issued... In February, March and April there were a number of 'suicides' and shootings 'during attempted escape'. The Jew Lowenberg was horribly beaten during a works' task, and committed suicide that night. In March two men were 'shot while attempting escape'. The Jew

Lowy was shot dead for approaching closer than the regulation six metres to a sentry who had called him up. Another was ordered by a sentry again and again to approach until he stepped on the forbidden 'neutral zone' outside the barbed wire, whereupon he was shot dead.[5]

Goldhagen saw the camp as having four crucial features which are of relevance to our discussion:

1 It was a place of violence, where extreme violence was regarded as a laudable and necessary means of reaching goals.

2 It was a place where Germans could act as masters without 'the bourgeois restraints which Nazism was rapidly superseding with a new anti-Christian morality'.

3 In the camps the victims were refashioned to confirm the Nazi world-view and their hatred and contempt for their victims.

4 It was a new world, the harbinger of the Nazi hope, 'in which the social trans-formation and value transmutation that were at the heart of Nazism's program were being most assiduously implemented'.[6]

Thus Dachau and the other camps not only had, but exemplified and embodied, a social ethic, albeit an ethic of almost unbelievable evil. In an essay, 'A Century of Camps?' in which he considers the camps as an appalling exemplar of a modernist project, Zygmunt Bauman examines the camps as an extreme case of a perverse desire to have mastery over human nature, craving and needs. The camps in this context had their own 'sinister rationality', and were intended to fulfil three functions:

They were laboratories where the new unheard-of volumes of domination and control were explored and tested. They were schools in which the unheard-of readiness to commit cruelty in formerly ordinary human beings was trained. And they were swords held over the heads of those remaining on the other side of the barbed-wire fence, so that they would learn not only that their dissent would not be tolerated but also that their consent was not called for, and that pretty little depends on their choice between protest and acclaim. The camps were distillations of an essence diluted elsewhere, condensations of totalitarian domination and its corollary, the superfluity of man, in a pure form difficult or impossible to achieve elsewhere. The camps were patterns and blueprints for the totalitarian society, that modern dream of total order, domination and mastery run wild, cleansed of the last vestiges of that wayward and unpredictable human freedom, spontaneity and predictability that held it back. The camps were testing grounds for societies run as concentration camps.[7]

So here, in Dachau and the other camps, we have, I cannot say a community or a society, but a structure for people to live and die together. The camps had and were a perverse social ethic, which expresses, exemplifies and promotes an understanding of human beings, of the world and of God or the ultimate reality which recognizes itself as being radically at odds with Christian and Jewish faith. And just as when I was meditating on the Church, and in particular the little church close to the Dachau perimeter fence, I noted that there is often a jarring dissonance between the ethic that the Church proclaims and what the Church in a particular context actually stands for and how Christians behave, so here also we have to enquire about moral life within the camps, and the effectiveness of the camps in promoting evil and vice. This I intend to do through a discussion of Tzvetan Todorov's amazing book, *Facing the Extreme: Moral Life in the Concentration Camps.*[8]

Inside the camps there was a regime of degradation and death, the reversal of all decent and humane values, an unveiling of the heart of darkness. It was explicitly intended to destroy self-respect, integrity, honour, responsibility and affection among the prisoners, and to train and encourage the guards and administrators in the ways of evil. The concentration camp was planned to be a school of dehumanizing vice. Here structural evil reigned without check. And yet, even here, goodness and love were found to be present, surviving and even flourishing in a hostile climate.

Where keeping the prisoners at the edge of starvation was a matter of calculated policy, partly in the hope that hunger would turn prisoner against prisoner, and one would steal the other's food, there was to be found from time to time a virtually sacramental sharing of bread, which expressed just that basic human solidarity that the Nazis were determined to destroy. Robert Antelme, who survived Buchenwald, remembered 'the hungry old man who'd steal in front of his son, so that the son could eat. Father and son…hungry together, offering their bread to each other with hungry eyes'.[9]

Eugenia Ginzburg remembered discovering some cranberries growing: 'I ate the first two clusters all by myself; only on finding a third one did I remember my fellow creatures'. She also remembered an old prisoner bringing her some oat jelly he had prepared but would not eat himself; he was simply happy to watch her enjoyment. After recounting a number of such instances of caring and sharing, Todorov concludes, 'In the end, there is not a single prisoner, male or female, who does not remember being cared for, counselled, or protected at least once by someone else'.[10] These were essentially expressions of solidarity, of responsibility for one another, of accountability to one another, or perhaps in some cases of accountability to God.

There was, however, the issue of particular solidarities conflicting with the universal claims of the neighbour. In Auschwitz, we are told, the Poles would share among themselves but refuse to share with the French. The French, when they received food parcels, drove the hungry Russians away with clubs and blows. Christians cared for fellow Christians. Jews tended to share among themselves but were commonly shunned by the others – so far had the system worked, in setting group against group in a hierarchy of degradation and competition for meagre resources. Such solidarities with those like us, defined in antagonism to the other, are simply, of course, collective self-interest, what Primo Levi calls 'we-ism', the selfishness of a group. Yet Todorov concludes, rather optimistically perhaps, that 'people will generally help those whose need is greatest, whether or not they are of the same nationality'.[11]

Todorov makes an interesting and important distinction between caring and solidarity:

> Caring...differs from solidarity in that those who receive care cannot automatically count on it; they are, after all, individuals, not members of a group. Caring cannot include everyone, not everyone in the world or even everyone in the same camp. The choice is made according to criteria other than nationality, profession or political persuasion; each person who is cared for is deserving in and of himself or herself. Yet here, too, having a common language is important – how does one discern the individuality of a person one cannot understand?
>
> There is a second boundary that should also be defined, that between caring and *charity* (or any of its synonyms). Unlike solidarity, charity makes no distinctions; it excludes no one. The recipient of charity need only be suffering or be somehow in jeopardy. With charity, there is no danger of its being turned to the advantage of any particular group. It is incontestably a moral act. Charity differs from caring, then, precisely in its being directed toward everyone rather than toward particular individuals.[12]

Yet again and again there was the discovery that caring for others, even in the camp, brings its own rewards and is a way of caring for oneself as well.

Todorov has important things to say about believers in the camps as prisoners, and even Christians themselves involved in the process of extirpation of Jews and others. We need to ponder, awful as it is, the story of the *Einsatzkommando* operating within Russia that was ordered to kill 3000 Jews and gypsies before Christmas so that they could celebrate the birth of Christ in peace. And when Christmas came, their leader preached to them a moving sermon about the incarnation.[13]

Within the camps among the inmates, Christians and other believers in a religious system or a political ideology such as communism provided the largest numbers of martyrs, people willing to die for a cause, which gave some kind of meaning to their dying and their life. Todorov suggests that the true believer 'can so love God (or Communism…) that he or she forgets to love people'. Love of God, it seems, does not translate in any simple and direct way into love of one's fellows. Jehovah's Witnesses, for example, refused to do any work which might aid the war effort because they believed Hitler to be the devil; but they had no interest either in helping their fellow prisoners who were not Witnesses.[14] For most inmates who gave their lives as martyrs, the dying was a heroic witness rather than an act of care for others:

> Father Kolbe gave his life to save that of another man. But more than that…it was to proclaim his faith in God; it scarcely mattered to him who in particular it was whose life he saved. The mothers, daughters, fathers and sons who went to their deaths with those they loved acted in a very different spirit. Their attraction to the specific individuals whom they cared about was stronger than their desire to live. In a sense, these people are more selfish; they do not want to die so that the other may live; they would prefer that both survive, so that they can continue to enjoy each other. Since that is impossible, they accept death – with the other, and not in his or her stead.[15]

Thus Grossman may be right in characterizing kindness, unqualified attention to the other, as involving an absence of doctrine. And evil is the mindless following of rules.[16]

Varlam Shalamov, a prisoner in the Soviet gulag for 25 years, declared, 'The camp was a great test of our moral strength, of our everyday morality, and 99% of us failed it'. And that included a multitude who bore the name of Christ. Yet even in such ultimately dehumanizing conditions some could resist the ultimate demoralization and degradation and leave a memory as heroes, saints or martyrs.

Remembering is important, and telling the story gives significance to the lives of those who have suffered and provides a warning lest the same things should happen again. In the camps telling the story became a main reason for staying alive. At the top of his manuscript, a prisoner, Zalmen Gradowski, wrote:

> Dear discoverer of these writings! I have a request of you: this is the real reason I write, that my doomed life may attain some meaning, that my hellish days and hopeless tomorrows may find a purpose in the future.[17]

Anamnesis is at the core not just of sacramental life and faith, but gives significance to our lives, even in the hellish camps, and holds out hope for the future. The story must be told, and possessed and handed on, if we are to have dignity and expectation. Especially for Christians the anamnesis of the Holocaust and the camps is important, for as Stephen Bonner has said: 'The holocaust manifests the *latent potential* of their history and reconfigures it. The holocaust is *their story* and "working through" the past is necessary for all of them, not just the Germans. *They* must lift the holocaust beyond the relative, beyond other atrocities, in order to understand themselves and what their civilisation made possible.'[18]

On being the Church

There are interesting, and indeed alarming, similarities between the Church and the concentration camp, between Dachau and the onion-domed church just outside its perimeter fence. John Milbank makes a neat contrast between world and Church, the world represented by Aristotle's *polis*, ultimately founded on violence, and the Church as the *civitas Dei*, the abode of peace. But when we turn to the world in which we live this contrast is shown to be dangerously facile. The little church outside the camp has a highly ambiguous relationship to the violence that is concentrated in the camp, and to the peaceableness of the gospel. In some alarming ways it possibly gives tacit, but nonetheless effective, support to the violence of the camp. In the camp with all its awfulness, faith, hope and charity somehow manage to survive, perhaps in purer, truer form than within the church outside the fence. Sam Wells argues that, for Hauerwas, the model of virtue was the martyr or the saint, as against the classical tradition which accorded primacy to the hero; the Church was to be a school of saints and martyrs.[19] And yet in our scenario it is in the camp rather than the Church that the saints, martyrs and heroes are in all probability to be found; and it is not quite convincing to suggest that they can be so only because they have been nurtured for such a time as this within the church or synagogue.

'What makes the Church the church', we learn from Stanley Hauerwas, 'is its faithful manifestation of the peaceable Kingdom.'[20] The camp, on the other hand, stands for the triumph of unbridled violence, the Kingdom of Darkness, if you prefer such terminology. Each is intended to be both a school and an instrument. And each was in certain ways strikingly unsuccessful in the fulfilment of its task. The only peace that the little onion-domed church offered was a temporary refuge from the violence of its context. In the concentration camp, despite an evil panoply of means to degrade, demoralize and reduce to despair, there still occurred caring, generosity, courage, nobility and hope. And in 1945 the concentration camps were abolished, and some decades later the gulag disappeared – although there still remain around the world foci of genocidal violence, and techniques of oppression developed in the camps have been copied elsewhere.

Hauerwas's epigram that the Church does not have but is a social ethic appears in many places in his writings. It is a very attractive notion, suggesting that Christian ethics must be embodied in the life of a community, that ethics is not a possession of the Church but the gift to the Church which constitutes it as Church. The Church, for Hauerwas, is a social ethic in as far as it is a 'faithful manifestation of the peaceable Kingdom in the world'.[21] Its first task is to be the Church, a community which can clearly be distinguished from the world.[22] It is shaped by a story which is sharply different from the world's story. Its most important social function is *to be itself*.[23] It is called to be a community of the cross, and an alternative to the hostilities and divisions to be found elsewhere.

This is all heady stuff to which one is tempted to say that the church and the camp at Dachau provide an empirical refutation: that church is not like the Church of which Hauerwas speaks, and paradoxically the virtues that he sees as central to the Christian community are exemplified in costly ways within the camp, far from the orbit of the church. And yet the tense and mood of Hauerwas's adage are perhaps part of my trouble with it. He writes in the present rather than the future eschatological tense, and in the indicative rather than imperative mood. And so it is easy to suggest the epigram does not correspond, is not relevant, to the Church as we know it, or the church near the Dachau wire. But is he not perhaps in fact discussing the *calling* of the Church today? And is Hauerwas not perfectly aware that that calling can differ in various contexts, and that the actual visible Church to which we belong falls far short of living up to its calling? If that is so, the Church must be a community of forgiven sinners who have learned to live by grace rather than a fellowship of moral heroes and virtuous achievers. Let Stanley speak for himself:

> I suspect that theologically today the most vital form of Christian social ethics must actually be a concern about the kind of community that Christians form among themselves. In other words, the church will serve the world best as it serves its Lord through the depth of its doctrinal affirmations, its liturgical experience, and the kind of moral concern the members of the church share with one another. If it does this well the church cannot be content with its institutional affairs as an end in themselves,

for the content of its doctrine, liturgy and communal form will not let it forget that it exists only as a mission to the world.[24]

In other words – and here, I think, is the nub of Stanley's epigram – the Church is called to be the Church in different ways in different contexts. We attend to the Dachau concentration camp and the little church outside, and to the complex and often terrible story of the Church down the ages, and above all to Scripture, not to find there some universally valid pattern of being the Church, but rather to learn from the failures and the triumphs of the past how God is calling us to be the Church, a fellowship of disciples, today, and in relation to today's opportunities and problems. And in this conversation we are seeking above all to attend to the Church's Lord who calls the Church to be a manifestation not so much of goodness as of grace, of achievement as of faithfulness.

III
Understanding worship

8

Lex orandi, lex credendi[1]

At the heart of Christian practice there stands worship – the strange, distinctive and characteristic activity of the people of God. In worship God is glorified and enjoyed, the mystery of God's purposes is glimpsed, however faintly, and God's people are united with their Lord and nourished for life in God's service. There is, of course, an awesome provisionality and incompleteness in our practice of worship: all earthly worship is necessarily partial and imperfect, a looking forward and anticipation of the joyful and glorious praise of heaven, where worship finds its fulfilment and perfection. But it is also true that God can and does use for his glory and the good of humankind our frail and stumbling efforts to worship God.

To affirm the centrality of worship within Christian practice is to suggest not only that worship is an indispensable component of Christian practice, but that it is the centre without which all else falls apart, the point from which one may extrapolate the other dimensions of Christian practice, the part that sustains and clarifies all the rest. Such an affirmation would not be universally acceptable. For example, the liberation theologian José P. Miranda in his *Marx and the Bible*[2] argues that in the Bible there is a consistent teaching that doing justice is the only true service of God, and the cult is regarded either as an irrelevance, or as a cloak for oppression. Miranda overstates his case. But it *is* true that in both testaments there is plentiful criticism of worship when it becomes a substitute for doing justice, or worship which has become separated from life and ethics – an autonomous self-contained sphere, as it were. And this reminds us of the truth that worship segregated from the rest of life in fact becomes false worship. True worship must infect and reflect the whole of practice, as it is an offering of the wholeness of life to God, and recognizes God's concern with every aspect of worldly existence.

A second group of people who would challenge our statement about the centrality of worship are those Protestants who so stress the import-ance of preaching that worship becomes little more than the 'prelim-inaries' to the sermon, or the setting for the proclamation of the Word. This generates an extremely didactic understanding of worship. It is to do with words and ideas rather than activity. The people become recipi-ents, 'hearers' (to use the old Scots term for churchgoers), essentially passive. But although this view fails to retain a proper balance and complementarity between Word and Sacrament and impoverishes the practice of worship, it also reminds us that the Word must have a crucial place in Christian worship, and that worship is not only our activity but the place where God has graciously promised to be present with his people to nourish, encourage and teach them.

In a memorable passage, Michael Polanyi, scientist, philosopher and seminal Christian thinker, says this of Christian worship:

> It resembles not the dwelling within a great theory of which we enjoy the complete understanding, nor an immersion in the pattern of a musical masterpiece, but the heuristic upsurge which strives to break through the accepted frameworks of thought, guided by intimations of discoveries still beyond our horizons. Christian worship sustains, as it were, an eternal, never to be consummated hunch; a heuristic vision which is accepted for the sake of its irresolvable tension. It is like an obsession with a problem known to be insoluble, which yet follows against reason, unswervingly, the heuristic command, 'Look at the Unknown!' Christianity sedulously fosters, and in a sense permanently satisfies, man's cravings for mental dissatisfaction by offering him the comfort of a crucified God.[3]

Worship stimulates, provokes and encourages enquiry; it points towards the truth and sustains seekers of truth; but it only indicates in paradoxical and fragmentary ways the nature of the truth which 'we see in a mirror dimly' until at the last we encounter the truth 'face to face' (1 Cor. 13.12). Polanyi's concern is with the relation between worship and enquiry in general, but he believes in a close organic relationship between theology and other sciences: all are nourished, kept to their task, and pointed steadily towards the truth by worship. Our concern in this chapter is the exploration of the relation of worship and theology, the ways in which worship guides theology and points towards its content, and the ways in which theology may purify, enrich and shape worship. We have here a kind of case study in the relation of theology and practice, and an issue which has attracted interest and controversy down the ages.

We will not here go into the origins or the complicated history of the epigram *lex orandi, lex credendi*, law of praying, law of believing.[4] 'The old saying', wrote Karl Barth, 'lex orandi lex credendi, far from being a pious statement, is one of the most profound descriptions of the theological method'.[5] Yet, for all that, it has been used in a bewildering variety of ways and is capable of numerous and often conflicting interpretations.

First, let us explore some of the possibilities which flow from understanding the adage as saying that the law of prayer, or how we worship, is normative for how and what we ought to believe – more or less the position Polanyi was proposing. This suggests that in some sense worship and prayer are sources of theological truth; or perhaps that theology is explication of what we do and say in worship, reflection on worship and the God we encounter in worship. It would follow that in cases where there is a clear discrepancy between what is done and said in worship and what is believed and taught in theology, it is theology which is to be brought into line with worship. 'Tell me how you pray', runs the proverb, 'and I will tell you how you *ought* to believe.' Worship here provides a source, data and norms for doing theology; and it becomes easy to regard theology as quite simply an aspect or dimension of worship. Theology is not simply prayerful discussion or meditative reflection in the presence of God, but itself *doxology*, the praise of God. In their different ways the meditations of St Anselm and the hymns of Charles Wesley are splendid examples of theology as worship, and worship as theology.

This approach is exemplified in much of the early history of dogma.[6] Orthodox Christology and the doctrine of the Trinity, for instance, cannot simply be read off scriptural texts. What we know of the earliest Christian worship suggest that this generated questions to which doctrinal formulation attempted to provide answers and interpretations. The New Testament, for example, offers abundant evidence that the worship of the Church involved ascribing divine titles, particularly *kyrios*, to Jesus from the earliest times.[7] We might note, for instance, the use of the Aramaic *maranatha* ('Come, Lord'), a liturgical prayer addressed to Jesus, in 1 Cor. 16.22, together with passages such as Phil. 2.10–11: 'That at the name of Jesus every knee should bow, in heaven and on earth and under the earth, and every tongue confess that Jesus Christ is Lord to the glory of God the Father.' Extracanonical evidence suggests that in the early Church worship was offered to Jesus as divine, even if official liturgies, when they began to appear, preferred that prayer should be offered to the Father *through* the Son. But this did not, of course, imply any questioning of the divinity of the Son, or of the appropriateness of offering him divine honours. Indeed one of the commonest objections to the Arians was that they worshipped a Jesus whom they believed to be a creature, less than divine. A major motive for Christological formulation was therefore explaining and legitimating how Christians could be monotheists and yet offer divine honour to Jesus; Christology arises as a necessary explanation of how Christians worship. The experience of worship demands theological explication.

The development of the doctrine of the Spirit follows not dissimilar lines. The fact that baptism was in the threefold name was used by Athanasius, Basil and other Fathers as evidence for the divinity of the Spirit as a distinct *hypostasis*, a dogma which it was widely recognized could not be established from Scripture alone. And as a consequence we must recognize that the doctrine of the Trinity has its tap-root in Christian worship: only thus were Christians able to make more or less coherent sense of the varied and often inconclusive evidence of Scripture together with their experience of God in the practice of worship. What was said and done in worship was a major factor in the development of doctrine.

Few Protestants would be in any way uneasy about regarding the Lord's Prayer as a model of prayer, and indeed as a source for our understanding of God. It is, after all, in the Bible! Cyprian spoke of it as the *lex orandi*, and the Churches of the Reformation not only use it in their worship but commonly base the teaching on prayer in their catechisms and confessions on the clauses of the Our Father. But matters become more controversial if we talk of articulating the theology implicit in the action of the Lord's Supper, drawing theological and ethical conclusions from what we say and do in the central act of Christian worship. Paul shared many times with his fellow believers in the Lord's Supper before he recalled the Corinthian Church to the authentic practice which he had received from the Lord and delivered to them (1 Cor. 11.23). Paul in this passage is explaining, theologizing and correcting a practice which was already in existence. And he is drawing out ethical implications from the practice; showing that the gluttony of the rich and their humiliation of the poor are so radical a denial of the authenticity of the rite that 'it is not the Lord's Supper that you eat' (1 Cor. 11.20).

Is it then legitimate for us to derive from the action of the Lord's Supper theological and ethical positions which are not to be found explicitly in the New Testament? Consider, for example, this passage by a left-wing British Roman Catholic:

The liturgy is radically egalitarian in its basic conceptions. And in this sense it is a scandal in the eyes of a world which is dedicated to quite other social structures – a world based on differences of 'intelligence', 'ability', 'attainment', 'class', 'wealth', 'status', 'rank', or even 'race' and 'religion'. Inevitably then the problem of the liturgy is a problem of creating the Christian community in a condition of tension with the world. That is, quite clearly and obviously, a political problem. For it is a question of achieving a radically egalitarian society, with nothing but functional differentiation in it, against the grain of what is experienced elsewhere. This is the basic reason why a genuine understanding of the theology of liturgy must involve, in a general sense, a socialist commitment.[8]

In this passage we find an assumption that the Eucharist is a constant manifestation of the true nature of Christian *koinonia* which is sharply at variance with the way the world is structured. This seems quite unexceptionable. Nor in principle is the effort to extract from the Lord's Supper ethical implications different from what Paul does in First Corinthians 11 and elsewhere, except that Paul seems concerned primarily for the ordering of the inner life of the Christian community while Wicker draws conclusions for the social and political orders and suggests that the Eucharist points towards a specific ideological orientation in politics. But unless we think of church and world as two totally separate spheres – and this is certainly not Paul's view – it seems inevitable that efforts are made to spell out the secular social and political commitments that participation in the Lord's Supper involves. The Johannine saying, 'The bread which I shall give *for the life of the world* is my flesh', surely implies that the body broken on the cross and the bread broken and shared among believers are both for the life of the world. To share that bread involves quite specific commitments to the hungry neighbour and to the needs of the world. We would then suggest that it is not only legitimate but necessary to explore the theology and the ethics implicit in what happens in the central and perennial acts of Christian worship.

But does that mean that we can derive new theological insights from the development of Christian worship and devotion? Protestants find this a particularly acute problem in relation to Roman Catholic Mariology. Historically it would seem that the cult of Mary in popular devotion developed well in advance of its various stages receiving official endorsement, theological articulation or dogmatic definition. Both Bernard of Clairvaux and Thomas Aquinas, for example, used the fact that the Church observed a feast of Mary's nativity as a kind of proof or confirmation of her sanctification before her birth.[9] And in the definitions of the Immaculate Conception (1854) and the Assumption (1950) the widespread and prolonged expression of these beliefs in worship is used as a major argument, although care is taken to suggest, misleadingly, that popular piety was in fact always under the careful control of the *magisterium*.[10]

Protestants traditionally have considerable reserve about this whole mode of theological argumentation, because they see popular piety as a thoroughly ambiguous phenomenon, by no means consistently reflecting the Holy Spirit's leading into all truth. They characteristically resist any suggestion that the development of forms of worship on its own is capable of producing new truths. This suspicion is however perfectly compatible with accepting that the universal and central thrusts, symbols and emphases of Christian worship have some normative role in theology, helping with the clarification, confirmation and development of doctrine rather than producing new truths. Worship does not create new doctrine *ex nihilo*, as it were.

Protestants are coming to recognize that the relation between theology and worship is a more complex and dynamic one than their traditional insistence that theology must control, inform and determine Christian worship might suggest. This is indeed how Protestants have tended to understand the epigram *lex orandi, lex credendi*: the law of believing, or theology, is the law of praying or worship. This, our second interpretation, is of course the contrary of the first, and represents a characteristically, but not exclusively, Protestant view. The Reformation's desired return to the purity and simplicity of the worship of the early Church is in one sense, of course, impossible to achieve – the practice of one age and culture cannot be transferred without modification to another. The Reformation did indeed make a notable effort to reform worship, stripping away mediaeval accretion and pious elaborations to make the significance and structure of Christian worship more clear than it had been for many centuries, and attempting to produce patterns of worship which were authentically Christian and free of adulteration of folk piety.

There were, it is true, important differences in the approaches adopted by the Lutherans and the Calvinists. Here, as elsewhere, the Calvinists were more radical, advocating and carrying through a transformation of worship based on the conviction that only that explicitly commanded in Scripture, or for which there was explicit biblical precedent, was to be permitted. The Lutherans were less thorough-going, seeing Scripture as providing general guidelines, and excluding certain things, but leaving a large area of freedom, so that more could be taken over consciously from the mediaeval tradition than was allowable in Calvinist circles. One instance is the case of hymnody. For long Calvinists insisted that only psalms or Scripture paraphrases might be sung in church. Only very gradually – in Scotland hardly before the nineteenth century – were 'hymns of human composition' admitted to public worship. From the beginning, in contrast, the Lutheran Churches, like the Wesleyans, fostered a lively, prolific and rich tradition of hymnody, which in modern times has been shared with all the Churches of the *oikumene*. Neither Lutheran nor Calvinist was as successful as they hoped in sloughing off mediaevalism in worship. But for our present purposes the important point is to note how clearly and unambiguously the Reformation affirmed that the Bible and doctrine must control the worship of the Church. It was not only important that true doctrine should be preached; it must also be expressed in the approved ways of worship and in particular in the administration of the sacraments.

The tendency of some Protestant Churches to give their service books almost the status of confessions of faith is more than an indication that the *lex orandi* is effectively controlled by the *lex credendi*. Here the form and content of worship is not the choice of congregation or clergy, but is authoritatively laid down so that it expresses the official theology. Service books are used to conserve orthodoxy, so that eventually the service book itself comes to be used as a theological *locus*. The same is true in some Churches of the hymnal. The situation is more confused in Churches which emphatically affirm the need for theological control over worship but have no mandatory liturgy or service book. The result is that theological control exists in name only, and the form and content of worship is left almost entirely to the whim of the minister or the conservatism of the congregation.

It is not without interest to note the multitudinous similarities between what the Reformation did and attempted (for achievement often fell far short of what was desired, in the establishment of weekly communion, for instance) and the impact of the modern liturgical movement. The project of the liturgical movement which now so deeply affects the worship of Churches of every tradition gives to the Bible and the primitive Church a normative status. But the liturgical movement is not an attempt simply to restore the primitive; nor is it the endeavour to adapt worship to the modern world, marrying liturgy and the Spirit of the Age, as it were. Rather it is the endeavour to renew worship in the light of enlarged and deepened biblical and theological understanding in the conviction that this will also involve a fresh relevance to the needs and issues of the day. The law of believing here is to be the law of worship and of prayer.

We have said enough of the two contrary interpretations of *lex orandi, lex credendi*, that worship should shape theology or that theology should control worship, to make it clear that neither is without its serious problems. But that does not mean that we are obliged to dismiss the epigram as valueless. Other, more lively and fruitful relations are possible between theology and worship, theory and practice. The interaction between them may be likened to an ongoing dialectic, or perhaps to a hermeneutic circle. One could well argue that Christian theology must be rooted in worship and should flow into doxology, the giving of praise to God. Suggestions such as that language affirming or presupposing the incarnation and the divinity of Christ is acceptable in worship, but is no longer tenable in theology, separate worship and doctrine in an intolerable way which would prove destructive to the integrity of each. It is surely a central responsibility of theology to monitor as a loving critic the worship, prayer and preaching of the Church. Barth was quite correct in affirming this relationship as necessary if theology is to be Christian. A theology which refuses to accept this responsibility may for a time have significance in the academy but it has lost its churchly relevance. This does not mean that there can be or ought to be total and constant harmony between worship and theology. Each is an exploration into the ultimate mysteries, and at times they will be out of step with one another. We may rejoice to join 'with angels and archangels and all the company of heaven' in praising God even as we agonize about the problems of whether an angelology is possible and our difficulty in articulating what we mean by heaven. But if we believe that the existence of angels must be stoutly denied and heaven is a fruit of false consciousness, integrity would demand that we attempt to excise the angels and archangels and all such language from our orders of worship. But to move between worship and theology convinced that both are orientations towards the same mysteries is exhilarating and challenging in both areas. It is also true that worship provides some important tests of theological positions – can they be prayed or preached? Do they lead into worship? Do they engage reverently as well as rigorously with mysteries which are to be adored, explored and lived out?

Lex orandi, lex credendi affirms very simply and directly the truth that worship and theology must be held together in an ongoing inter-action for the good of each. Christian worship is a form of practice which sustains and stimulates and challenges the theological enterprise, and serves as a constant demonstration that the truth of God is to be encountered in life, in praise and in prayer as well as in reflection.

9

The liberation of worship[1]

The title I have chosen for this chapter is intentionally ambiguous. It refers first to worship as liberating, the freedom to which Christian worship points us, into which in part we enter in worship, of which worship is the sign. And, in the second place, it refers to the freeing of worship so that it may be authentically Christian, and therefore liberating, an expression of the freedom of the Spirit.

Worship as liberating

Come with me to the remote little village of Muthialapad in the Andhra country of South India. There is as yet no motorable road, and we must approach either on foot or by bullock-cart, a sign that this is far from being a prosperous part of the country. The little Christian community is entirely composed of converts, one or two generations back, from an Untouchable caste, the Malas. Poverty-stricken, oppressed, and despised for centuries, the change of religion has brought little visible change in the social and economic condition of the community. Their ramshackle huts are crowded together in a damp hollow a little distance from where the high-caste people live. And there, totally incongruous, stands a tidy little gothic church. The building, and – far more important – the worship which takes place within it are of profound significance for that little group of poor and oppressed people. To us at first this comes as something of a surprise. The building has no architectural or artistic merit, and it jars with its cultural and physical setting; but to the Muthialapad Christians it is a constant visible reminder that the God and Father of our Lord Jesus Christ dwells with them, and that they have here no abiding city. No outsider would think of calling their worship glorious, rather it is on the surface at least rather humdrum and too Westernized in form; but to these Christians, despised by their neighbours as irremediably polluting, ostracized and subject to daily indignities, petty or more severe, worship is a constant assurance that they are the beloved children of God, forgiven and endowed with dignity and regarded as of infinite worth by the God who is no respecter of persons.

Until 35 years ago, the Christians of Muthialapad were compelled to perform the traditional role of the Malas in the annual village festival. When the buffalo had been sacrificed, its entrails were draped around the necks of the Christian Malas who, thus attired, had to go on procession, dancing and playing drums and tambourines, through the main streets of the village. Here was worship which confirmed their degradation, which legitimized the social order of the village, which expressed a totally different message from that of the worship in the little Mala church. Under duress they had to continue to participate in this repulsive idolatry, until a teenage boy, now a leading Christian academic and a dear friend of mine, led the Mala Christians in refusing to take part in the traditional Hindu festival. The Christians' huts were burnt, there was violence; the police had to be called in to maintain a fragile peace. But finally the point was won. Henceforward it must be recognized that there were two kinds of worship in Muthialapad. The one sanctified injustice and oppression, confirmed the social order of the village, and condemned many to bondage and degradation. The other was the worship of free men and women, who found in it a human dignity denied to them in village society, and a vision of justice and liberty.

Now we change continents, going to North America to listen to James Cone speaking of the significance of worship for American Blacks:

The eschatological significance of the black community is found in the people believing that the Spirit of Jesus is coming to visit them in the worship service each time two or three are gathered in his name, and to bestow upon them a new vision of their future humanity. This eschatological revolution is ... a change in the people's identity, wherein they are no longer named by the world but named by the Spirit of Jesus. ... The Holy Spirit's presence with the people is a liberating experience. Black people who have been humiliated and oppressed by the structures of white society six days of the week, gather together each Sunday morning in order to experience a new definition of their humanity. The transition from Saturday to Sunday is not just a chronological change from the seventh to the first day of the week. It is rather a rupture in time ... which produces a radical transformation in the people's identity. The janitor becomes the chairperson of the Deacon Board; the maid becomes the president of Stewardess Board Number 1. Everyone becomes Mr and Mrs, or Brother and Sister. The last becomes first, making a radical change of self and one's calling in the society. Every person becomes somebody, and one can see the people's recognition of their new found identity by the way they walk and talk and 'carry themselves'. They walk with a rhythm of an assurance that they know where they are going, and they talk as if they know the truth about which they speak. It is this experience of being radically transformed by the power of the Spirit that defines the primary style of black worship. This transformation is found not only in the titles of Deacons, Stewardesses, Trustees and Ushers, but also in the excitement of the entire congregation at worship. To be at the end of time where one has been given a new name requires a passionate response with the felt power of the Spirit in one's heart.[2]

All around the world, in all sorts of contexts, one finds this exhilarating experience of Christian worship as liberating. Polish shipyard workers, striking for free trade unions and free expression in an authoritarian society, were sustained in their search for liberty by daily celebrations of the Mass in the yards. Groups of the victims of dictatorship in South Korea found that their thirst for freedom and justice was totally dependent on regular meetings together for prayer – and for those who are in prison, the knowledge that their brothers and sisters are praying for them gives them new courage.[3] In Latin America even traditional forms of piety, such as the stations of the cross, have often come to be regarded as protests against oppressive regimes which deny liberty to the people. As the sufferings of Christ are remembered, the words 'As you did it to one of the least of these my brethren, you did it to me', come to mind.[4] That Archbishop Romero was murdered while presiding over the worship of the people of God was no accident, for he and the Church he led had often shown that worship was central to their concern for the oppressed, at the same time a protest against oppression and the nourishing of a thirst for liberty.

Enough has been said to show that in our day there has been a remarkable recovery of the experience of Christian worship as liberating. But one must enquire as to the authenticity of this understanding of worship. Is it, perhaps, that people turn to worship for the stimulant or tranquilizer most in demand at any given time, and in an age of liberation movements fighting for political emancipation, of women's liberation, and gay liberation, and so on and so forth, they naturally seek liberation in and through worship? Are we in danger of speaking not of worship in the Spirit, but of worship in the *Zeitgeist*? The question is a real one, but the answer is quite clear: what has happened is in fact the recovery of a central emphasis of Christian worship which has in the past often been all but lost. It is not, of course, as if worship as such, in isolation as it were, is liberating. Christian worship is the re-presentation of God's mighty deliverance of His people, the recapitulation of salvation history, in which the people of God appropriate and enter into the salvation or liberation wrought by God, express their gratitude and delight in freedom, are nourished to work for liberty and stimulated to yearn for freedom's final consummation. It is God who is the liberator; in worship we respond to his act, enter into the freedom he has given us and are nourished to share in his continuing work of deliverance. As the psalmist puts it:

> When the Lord delivered Sion from bondage,
> it seemed like a dream.
> Then was our mouth filled with laughter,
> on our lips there were songs.
>
> The heathens themselves said: 'What marvels
> the Lord worked for them!'
> What marvels the Lord worked for us!
> Indeed we were glad.
>
> Deliver us, O Lord, from our bondage
> as streams in dry land.[5]

Passover above all was the celebration of God's liberation of his people. The rite expressed, and continues to express, the present liberty of God's people, reclining as free men and women around the table, as totally dependent on God's gracious act of deliverance. Had God not acted, the Jews would still be in bondage, not yet a People (*laos*), without name or dignity. The rite repeats and re-enacts the story, reminding the people of their roots, of their dependence upon God, of their dignity, and celebrating the liberty they have been given. And it does more than represent a past deliverance: it gives resources for living as free men and women now, and provides an appetiser and a foretaste of the joys of the fully consummated liberty that is to come. Each Passover points forward – 'Next year in Jerusalem' – and beyond that to the messianic banquet.

It is hardly surprising that Passover became a time when a peculiarly intense thirst for liberty was commonly in the air, a time when Jews were usually liable to protest or revolt against contemporary oppression, being nourished at the feast of liberty. And it was this rite that Jesus took, reshaped, and attached for ever to the 'exodus' that he was to accomplish in Jerusalem. In the Lord's Supper, at the centre of Christian worship, there is accordingly this inescapable focusing on liberation. We remember, recapitulate, and participate in the liberty won and given to us by Christ. Here we receive food for living as free men and women, and a thirst for the banquet in the Kingdom of heaven when many will come from north and south and east and west and sit down with Abraham and Isaac and Jacob. And in this Supper not only do we receive liberty and a thirst for liberty, but our understanding of liberty is clarified and refined, our vision enlarged and our hope stimulated.

Authentic Christian worship, then, cannot be separated from a concern for liberation, for this would be to detach it from its rooting in the mighty acts of the God who delivers his people from bondage. For freedom Christ has set us free; in worship we appreciate, enjoy, proclaim and express this freedom; and the freedom celebrated in the cult must infect the life and structures of society if we are to avoid a quite blasphemous separation between the sacred and the secular.

Freeing worship

'What,' asked the history teacher, 'were the Four Freedoms?' Promptly the boy replied: 'Freedom from want, Freedom from fear, Freedom from thought, and Freedom from religion'. His answer, although wrong, was revealing, for many people, particularly in the secular West, see religion and worship as the opposite of emancipating. They are held to be things that bind, that limit, that enslave – the opium of the people. Freedom and maturity alike involve freedom from religion, leaving worship behind as something childish and enslaving, unworthy of an emancipated adult. Worship, many people believe, is outgrown, like playing with dolls or Hornby trains.

We may well point out that modern people, having proclaimed that they have no need for worship, invent a multitude of surrogates, and devote a remarkable amount of time and energy to the worship of strange gods – the pomp of civic religion, the ritual of the demonstration or the football match, the fertility cult that is denounced as pornography, and countless other substitute forms of worship. We may go on to say that false worship is indeed an opiate of the people; that it often disguises strong yet subtle forms of social control; that it discourages the asking of awkward questions; that it frequently conceals injustice and exploitation under a pall of sanctimoniousness. But when we have said such things we still have to face the problem that many people, including many Christian and intelligent people, find what passes as Christian worship dull, irrelevant, and totally remote from the great issues of freedom and human dignity with which we found Christian worship to be properly and necessarily linked all round the world.

Those who have dealings with young people these days must have become sadly accustomed to young Christians, brought up in good Christian homes, who abandon the public worship of God and put all their enthusiasm, commitment and concern into the work of Amnesty International, Anti-Apartheid, or the like. If you talk with them you quickly discover that they have been unable to find any connection between the worship which they have experienced and the great causes and concerns of justice and liberty. They have come to feel, as Reinhold Niebuhr did, that if the Churches were realistic about their own worship they would remove the crosses from their buildings and put instead on the holy table the three little monkeys, who hear no evil, see no evil, and speak no evil. Is it possible for our worship to recover what once it had, when every conventicle on the hillsides was an act of protest, an affirmation of the crown rights of the Redeemer, and a laying hold of the freedom with which Christ makes us free? Could the day come again when people could say of Christian worship in Scotland something like this comment of a Latin American theologian: 'Every truthful and consciously celebrated Eucharist can be regarded as the most radical act of protest,' proclaiming and showing forth the rule of Christ, 'the only saviour and liberator, the only Lord of history and of man. ... His rule excludes every other rule which seeks to dominate man and ... in him all men are made free. ... By celebrating the Eucharist, we commit ourselves to the work of removing all forms of political, social and ideological oppression that are incompatible with what we have proclaimed'.[6]

But first, our worship must be freed from the distortions and limitations which make it so much less than Christian worship ought to be. Worship must be freed, if it is itself to be liberating.

How easy it is for worship to become domesticated and tamed within a particular culture, an expression of the national spirit, a custodian of one people's ethos – and nothing more. There is, of course, a sense in which Christian worship must find itself at home in every age and culture, just as the language of worship should be language understood by the people. There is no case at all for worship being entirely uniform in every age and place. But Christian worship may be tamed if it is confined too closely within a particular culture and society, and ceases to be aware of itself as a specific expression of the constant worship of heaven and of every age and nation upon earth. Sometimes worship, which should be catholic in the truest sense, seems instead to have been imprisoned in the kailyard, incapable of seeing over the fence or sharing in the worship of the whole Church of God. The integrity of worship demands its liberation from provincialism and ethnic captivity, together with the realization that Christian worship is a challenge, a questioning, a disturbance to all cultures and all social orders. For it points to, and is already the anticipation of, the Kingdom of God.

Our problem is not simply that so often in worship the kailyard triumphs over the catholic; it is also that, within Scotland worship is so often seen as a middle-class activity; so that there is a kind of 'bourgeois captivity' of worship. John Miller, an experienced minister in a great housing estate and at one time Moderator, said this: 'The mass of Protestant working people do not believe that the Church is on their side. ... It is obvious to the working class community that the Church does not belong among them, and that it is not in solidarity with them in their lives. It is always a visitor from the outside.'[7]

In one sense, of course, the Church and her worship must always be a 'visitor from outside'; or, to put the point more clearly, the Church is a pilgrim people, exiles and strangers seeking their true homeland, and worship is nourishment and direction for the way. But if worship is to speak of Christian freedom to the working class it must be nourishment for *their* pilgrimage; it must relate to *their* hopes and fears, to *their* condition rather as Christian worship relates to the Mala Christians of Muthialapad. The remarkable renewal of the Church in Latin America in recent decades arose largely from the discovery that it was impossible to worship God in the horrendous slums without sharing at the deepest level in the hopes and despair of the poor and the oppressed. Christian worship lost its integrity if it became either isolated from the realities of life, or an escape from the implications of oppression. It is impossible to keep company with Christ if we refuse to accept the company he has chosen to keep. Following the patristic principle *ubi Christus ibi ecclesia* (where Christ is, there is the Church), it is necessary to go to find Christ and therefore the Church among the poor he loves, to listen to them, and to learn afresh from them how to worship God in Spirit and in truth. If we were to realize this in Scotland, it could well ignite a revival of the Church and a new vitality in worship.

Our worship needs to be freed from its obsessive wordiness if it is to recover a vital awareness of the Word of God which is living and active. Only too often the Reformers' insistence on the complementarity of the Word and Sacrament, so that each interprets and confirms the other, has been lost. Instead we have unease about symbols, signs, actions, movement, silence and indeed all forms of non-verbal communication and expression. Sacraments become regarded as little more than visual aids, and worship sinks into a dry didactic exercise reminiscent of school classrooms prior to the advent of modern pedagogical method, with its emphasis on participation and learning by doing. There is more truth than we might care to admit in the words of the great Scottish Christian poet, Edwin Muir, writing of his motherland. In his remarkable poem, 'The Incarnate One',[8] Muir writes that the incarnate Word is 'made word again' in modern Scotland, but now as a word of arrogance and ostentation. The emphasis has become unbalanced in the direction of judgement and the fear of an angry God, while the true mystery of the incarnation is 'impaled and bent', to serve purely ideological purposes.

From this there flows the extraordinary passivity of the people in worship. We cannot expect to have an active, living Church which lives out its royal priesthood in responsible involvement in the life of the world, if in worship, the throbbing heart of Christian love and care, the people of God are taught to be passive. In much of our worship the priestly activity of the People of God is hardly in evidence; instead the minister does and says practically everything. The symbolism is powerful – and terrifying. It runs directly counter to the doctrine of the corporate priesthood of believers and confirms a disastrously inade-quate understanding of the nature and mission of the Church. We need to recover the sense of worship as an activity in which the whole People of God participates, and which involves the whole person, not just the eyes, or ears, or brain. And in doing so we will also find a truer understanding of the wondrous mystery of God and of Christ in our neighbour, a mystery which must be worshipped, loved and served, which must not be 'impaled and bent into an ideological instrument'; a mystery which spills over constantly into common life, calling into being fellowship, sharing, justice and hope.

Worship separated from the great issues of liberty and justice has become idolatry, an instrument of ideological manipulation, a way of hiding from God rather than encountering Him. The prophets teach that it is not acceptable to God:

> 'What are your endless sacrifices to me?'
> says Yahweh.
> 'I am sick of holocausts of rams
> and the fat of calves.
> The blood of bulls and of goats revolts me.
> When you come to present yourselves before me,
> who asked you to trample over my courts?
> Bring me your worthless offerings no more,

the smoke of them fills me with disgust.
New Moons, sabbaths, assemblies –
I cannot endure festival and solemnity,
Your New Moons and your pilgrimages
I hate with all my soul.
They lie heavy on me,
I am tired of bearing them.
When you stretch out your hands
I turn my eyes away.
You may multiply your prayers,
I shall not listen.
Your hands are covered with blood,
wash, make yourselves clean.
Take your wrong-doing out of my sight.
Cease to do evil.
Learn to do good,
search for justice,
help the oppressed,
be just to the orphan,
plead for the widow.[9]

'My grandfather,' a rabbi in one of Martin Buber's writings relates, 'was paralysed. One day he was asked to tell about something that happened with his teacher – the great Baalshem. Then he told how the saintly Baalshem used to leap about and dance while he was at his prayers. As he went on with the story, my grandfather stood up; he was so carried away that he had to show how the master had done it, and started to caper about and dance. From that moment he was cured.'[10] That is an apt parable of the way in which Christian worship, the ritual re-presentation of the story of God's liberation of his people, must be the authentic source of ongoing participation in the liberating activity of God himself.

Worship in Spirit and in truth is an encounter with the God who cares so deeply for justice and for those in bondage that he sent his Son in order that we might be free. And the joy of freedom which we find in the worship of the one true God is something which must flow out into the world, sustaining and clarifying the passion for liberty.

10

The end of sacraments?: sacramental action and discipleship[1]

As a young graduate student of politics at the University of Chicago, fresh from an arts degree at St Andrews, I was introduced one day to a visiting German theologian. He turned out to be Professor Markus Barth, son of the great Karl, and himself a New Testament scholar of distinction. His work on baptism in the New Testament had persuaded his father to change his mind, and resolve that baptism was not a sacrament. On hearing that I came from Scotland, and was, as they used to say, 'intending the ministry', Markus Barth looked me straight in the eye, and said, 'Beware the Scottish sacramentalists'.

At the time I didn't really know what Markus Barth was talking about, or what a sacramentalist might be. To this day my word processor puts a wiggly red line beneath the term every time I use it. Despite the limitations of my computer's dictionary, I think I have in the intervening decades discovered what sacramentalism is, and who the sacramentalists are. I suppose I am now myself one of them, and indeed honoured to be the President of what some believe to be a society of sacramentalists!

But why should I *beware* of the Scottish sacramentalists? I wondered and I still wonder. Under the initial impetus of his son's exegetical writings, Karl Barth progressively distanced himself in his later theological writing from an understanding of baptism and the Lord's Supper as sacraments. But this by no means meant that he favoured abandoning the practice of baptism and the celebration of the Lord's Supper, like the Quakers, the Salvation Army and some other sects. The truth is rather to the contrary: baptism and the Lord's Supper are very much the culmination of his theology, and close to the heart of his whole theological project. On the face of it, this may appear strange, but I would argue that Barth's position here is a perfectly coherent and challenging expression of some of his most basic theological insights.

His critique of sacramentality, if properly attended to, could be a considerable help towards a recovery and renewal of the worship of the Church.

The critique of sacramentality

Søren Kierkegaard accurately anticipated the gist of Barth's unease with the sacraments when he declared:

> Nothing is truer than the statement of Pascal, the most accurate ever uttered on Christendom; that Christendom is a society of people who, with the help of a few sacraments, escape the desire to love God.[2]

Baptism, particularly infant baptism, according to Kierkegaard, suggests objective inclusion in the people of God, independently of discipleship: 'So the following of Christ', he writes, 'has been completely abolished.'[3] The Lord's Supper 'is calculated to set one at rest – objectively and rapidly – in relation to the matter of eternity, and then we live our own lives, enjoying existence, multiplying and filling the earth'.[4] For Kierkegaard the sacraments have become disjoined from discipleship and from ethics, and this is a characteristic, almost a prerequisite, for the existence of 'Christendom'.

Barth, writing a century and more later, is convinced that the Christendom that Kierkegaard attacked so vigorously has now disintegrated. That development, he believes, gives urgency to the critique of the sacraments, especially, perhaps, to the critique of infant baptism. Sacramental practices that could go unquestioned during the centuries of Christendom must now be radically re-examined, and rejected or reformed if they are found to be wanting. In the new situation, Barth believed that 'the community must accept the fact that it will always be a small minority'.[5] And the ethics and lifestyle of that minority are of the greatest importance as a practical witness to the broader community.

Barth, in his later works, explicitly rejects the idea of the sacraments:

> Baptism and the Lord's Supper are not events, institutions, mediations, or extensions, nor indeed guarantees and seals of the work and word of God; nor are they instruments, vehicles, channels, or means of God's reconciling grace. They are not what they have been called since the first century, namely, mysteries or sacraments.[6]

Instead, 'Baptism and the Lord's Supper belong to *ethics*, and especially to ethics as it is to be worked out in the special light of God's reconciling action'.[7] Just as Barth argues elsewhere that dogmatics is ethics, and any dogmatics which claims to be 'scientific' and purified of ethical content is spurious, so now he sees a major threat to Christian faith in an understanding of baptism and the Lord's Supper which is not through and through ethical. Ethics, in a real sense, is the culmination of Barth's theology, and a way of talking about discipleship, which is peculiarly apt after the end of Christendom.[8]

There was huge interest in the theology and practice of baptism in the Church of Scotland in the 1950s, culminating in the reports of the Commission on Baptism, and leading to significant changes in the regulations concerning baptism, which deeply affected the practice of baptism in the Church. A great deal of this was sparked off by the disturbing fact that the great guru of Scottish theology in the 1940s and 50s, Karl Barth himself, had increasingly emphatically rejected the practice of infant baptism, and was already questioning whether baptism as such should be considered as a sacrament. That period of turmoil and debate about baptism deserves a study in its own right, but will not concern me here, save for noting a couple of points.

In the first place, Barth believed, and his experience from the 1930s onwards confirmed, that Christendom was dead. In Scotland, on the other hand, in the 1950s, Christendom at least appeared to be flourishing. There was a heady sense in the 1950s that, with the diverse leadership of George MacLeod, Tom Allan and Billy Graham we were engaged in mopping up the not yet Christian fringes left in a basically Christian Scotland. Christendom was alive and well; in a sense the Second World War had been a vindication of Christendom. In that context the baptism of infants made some kind of sociological sense, which needed to be reinforced by a theology which rejected at this point the teaching of the master. The situation today is radically different, and no responsible person could say that Christendom now survives intact in our land.

In the second place, there was at that time, and even today in Scotland, very little controversy about the Lord's Supper. We were pretty confident that we were maintaining a classical tradition going back through Robert Bruce, John Knox, and Calvin's Geneva to the early Church. The remnants of the old communion season still flourished, even in the cities. And Barth's critique of the Lord's Supper had not yet clearly emerged. It was only in the last huge 'fragments' of the *Church Dogmatics*, IV/4, that Barth made clear both that he did not regard the Lord's Supper any more than baptism as a sacrament, and yet that the Lord's Supper would be the 'conclusion and crown' of his whole treatment of the Christian life, itself the culmination of his whole theological project.[9] That treatment of the Lord's Supper never appeared and was not in fact written.

What I want to do in this essay is, not to presume to complete Barth's project for him, but to explore some ethical aspects of the Lord's Supper, and see if this deepens and enlarges our understanding of the Supper and its place in Christian life and faith in today's post-Christendom Church.

The action of actions

As we have seen, Barth progressively distanced himself from a sacramental understanding, first of baptism and then of the Lord's Supper. Essentially this was a critique of ritualism, of sacraments separated from discipleship and from ethics. For Barth the Lord's Supper is not a sacrament, but it is the 'action of actions', and the crown of his ethics.[10] He constantly insists that it should be celebrated every Sunday in every congregation. The only true sacrament is Jesus Christ,[11] but as 'the action of actions' the Lord's Supper celebrates the community's union with Christ, presenting a model of the lifestyle of disciples, so that holy living should flow from the grace, forgiveness and fellowship encountered and received in the Supper.

In the Supper, divine and human action come together. *The* Action (note the definite article in the use of a term for the Lord's Supper which is deeply entrenched in the Scottish Presbyterian tradition) is the model of all true and faithful action, the type or template or foundation of the life of discipleship. The rite is exemplary as well as challenging. 'It is', according to Cochrane, 'an ethical response to God's one justifying and saving work in the death of Christ and to the outpouring of the Holy Spirit'.[12] And in the Supper we find resources for the life of discipleship.

But the affirmation that the Lord's Supper is in some sense the crown of ethics, or the action of actions, is worlds apart from the moralism and the sharp distinction of the sacred and the profane which have so deeply and so calamitously deformed the practice and understanding of the Lord's Supper in Scotland, with these awful fencings of the Table, and the suggestion that one has to be good or holy before one takes part in the Supper. 'Rabbi Duncan' had the right response when, from the pulpit of St Giles, the High Kirk of Edinburgh, seeing an old woman in a shawl obviously unwilling to approach the Table, he shouted to her – and to all the congregation,

'Tak' it, woman, it's for sinners'. Holy, ethical living is not a *qualification* for admission to the Supper; rather it flows out of sharing in the breaking of bread as forgiveness, fellowship and grace.

Last Supper, cross and resurrection

The Last Supper, the cross and the resurrection belong together at the heart of our redemption. The meal that Jesus shared with his disciples in the upper room and the action of God in the cross and resurrection interpret one another. Whether or not that meal was a Passover meal is not important for present purposes; certainly it was a *meal*, and a real meal, around Passover time and thus suffused with the imagery of the Passover. This made it inevitable that the cross and resurrection should be interpreted as 'the exodus which he [Jesus] accomplished in Jerusalem', that Christ should be seen as the true paschal lamb, that the theme of deliverance from bondage and from slavery should be at the forefront of any interpretation of the events of Good Friday and Easter day. When Jesus took the bread and broke it and said, 'This is my body which is for you. Do this in *anamnesis* of me', and when he took the cup and said, 'This cup is the new covenant in my blood. Do this, as often as you drink it, in *anamnesis* of me', he was tying together for ever the action of the Supper and the action of cross and resurrection, radically reinterpreting the Passover and also interpreting the conviction and execution of the innocent One, and the mysterious events of Easter day.

The meal, the Action, that is to be repeated by disciples is pregnant with imperatives. Disciples are to break the bread and take the cup, and eat and drink, and so proclaim, or placard, the Lord's death until his coming. And this meal of thanksgiving for God's actions in the past, the present and the future is in *anamnesis* of Jesus. That is, of course, far more than simply the remembrance of a dead Lord; it is the assurance, in the words of Knox's Genevan Service Book, that 'by hym alone, we haue entrance to the throne of thy grace; that by hym alone, we are possessed in our spirituall kingedome, to eate and drinke at his table'.[13] But this raising up into the spiritual kingdom does not separate us from responsibilities in the world. Indeed, it gives us an experiential measure of what we mean when we pray that 'Your will be done on earth as it is in heaven', and it sharpens the imperatives that are involved in participation in the Supper.

And there is more that we could and should recover from the Passover for the renewal of our celebrations of the Lord's Supper, and the strengthening of our faith and our discipleship. Passover was and is, as we all know, a family feast at the common table. But it was also an occasion for hospitality towards the stranger, and a welcome to the messiah whenever he may come. Children are present by right, and indeed have a central role in asking the key question, 'What does all this mean?', to which the response is the renewed telling of the story, which comes alive ever anew to a fresh generation, and is normative as well as descriptive.

I envy the celebratory informality of the Passover. Participants are not constantly on edge, determined that every detail should be correct. But they are aware that the meal confirms their identity and strengthens their vocation and their hope: 'Next year, in Jerusalem!' The celebration is relaxed and friendly, and moves quite naturally from the majesty of the story of salvation symbolically re-enacted, to lively and entirely secular folksongs. People enjoy the Passover; it is a celebration, even in face of suffering, uncertainty and danger. It does not have the accoutrements of a wake for a dead God – black ties and dark suits, as for a funeral, solemn silence, children and the young excluded.

It was not ever thus in Scotland. Think of the great 'Holy Fairs' that marked the old communion seasons; note the huge quantity of wine that is on record as having sometimes been consumed.[14] Surely we should be thinking very seriously today of ways of making the Lord's Supper again a real *festive* meal, giving thanks for the deliverance wrought for us in Christ, and celebrating his abiding presence with us.

Passover and Last Supper were clearly real meals, even if eaten in haste with sandals on the feet and the loins girt, nourishing people for a journey and for the challenges of discipleship. The link between these meals and the common daily table, even the 'fast food' of modern times, was obvious and unavoidable. For disciples the Lord's Table made the table of everyday holy; thanksgiving flowed from the Eucharist to encompass our daily eating and drinking, to enable a lifestyle that was indeed eucharistic and lived in the presence of the Lord. But the Church down the ages has renewed the barrier between the sacred and profane and separated the holy table from the table of everyday in such a way as to convince the people of today, even many churchgoers, that the Lord's Supper is irrelevant to ordinary life. It is not good to have tasteless wafers or cubes of tired bread and little phials of sickly juice – things that no one would choose to eat and drink at a celebration, or for nourishment. There should be real eating and drinking at the Lord's Supper, an eating and drinking which is exemplary for all our eating and all our drinking. It should be a real feast, not a symbolic fast, a meal at which people can say, as did a woman with Downs Syndrome on drinking from the cup: 'That tastes good. I like it.' Thus Cochrane is right when he suggests that 'The Lord's Supper is the model and criterion of all meals...all eating and drinking is to be eucharistic.'[15]

The Lord's Supper clearly draws on the imagery of the Passover, and is intended as a repetition of the Last Supper of Jesus and his disciples in the upper room. That is central. But other associations are also important for the proper understanding of the Supper, in particular the rich and varied material in the New Testament about Jesus' practices of eating and drinking. The first disciples had plenty of experience of eating and drinking with Jesus before they gathered in the upper room for the Last Supper, which was in fact to be the first of a multitude of celebrations down the ages and in every land.

To an amazing extent their experience of the presence of the Lord, before and after the resurrection, involved eating and drinking with him and with others. The Church of South India liturgy, for example, draws upon the story of the Emmaus road where the Stranger unfolds the Scriptures so that the disciples' hearts burn within them, and is then 'made known to them in the breaking of the bread'. The liturgy contains a wonderful prayer immediately before the Great Thanksgiving:

> Be present, be present, Jesus, good High Priest, as you were with your disciples, and make yourself known to us in the breaking of the bread.

This is a real, if seldom recognized, *anamnesis*: we experience the presence of the Lord at the table as did the first disciples. The Supper should be a place where we can discern the presence of the Lord with us, calling us to discipleship. But precisely at this point there is a danger, identified by Trevor Huddleston, that we become so concerned with the presence of Christ in the Supper that we neglect his presence in the needy neighbour, and in the challenges of daily living. The real presence of the Lord in the Supper should enable us to discern the Lord where he is, especially in the needy, the confused, the oppressed and the poor. And that same Lord who is present with us calls us to serve the needy of our day and of our world.

Supper and unity

There is also much to suggest that other accounts of Jesus' eating and drinking, the narratives of his feeding miracles, and the stories he told about feasts, deeply influenced the understanding of the Supper in various ways. His welcoming to his table all sorts of people, including notorious rogues and women of the streets, caused scandal among the religious leaders of the day, who are like those bidden to the great feast in the parable. They invent all sorts of excuses for not attending, so that their places are taken by the people from the highways and the byways, the folk for whom Jesus had a special care. He did not break bread only with the respectable, the successful, or the pious. To the contrary, he was denounced for eating and drinking with sinners. These are the people he still invites and welcomes to his table. At the table Jesus broke through ritual and real barriers of purity, suspicion, fear and hostility. And at the table he still breaks down these barriers to establish fellowship and unity. And I have become more and more convinced as I have meditated on Jesus' hospitality that the Churches are not, and never have been, in fact entitled to overrule and limit his generous invitation. Only his open invitation can be a sign and expression of reconciliation and healing in a broken world.

The Lord's Supper as challenge

The Last Supper was an action of God which evoked, involved and demanded human action. The disciples responded with denial, betrayal or desertion; the authorities, Roman and Jewish, with condemnation and execution; the crowds who had cried 'Hosannah' on the Sunday, cried 'Crucify Him' on Thursday. The Lord's Supper also is an action which evokes, involves and demands a response from disciples, a response which taken as a whole can be considered as a eucharistic lifestyle, or the way of discipleship.

First of all, as Jesus gave himself and gives himself to us, so we are called to share with one another. When we share the bread and the cup with one another we are all as the royal priesthood serving one another, ministering to one another. There is no guzzling while others go hungry and thirsty – St Paul declared that when that happens it is not in fact the Lord's Supper.[16] And the sharing in the Supper is not an isolated, self-contained event; it involves a commitment to sharing with the hungry and the needy neighbours whether they be close at hand or far away. The bread that is given and shared is not simply for disciples, but as Jesus said, 'the bread of God is that which comes down from heaven and gives life to the world' and 'the bread that I will give for the life of the world is my own flesh'.[17] Disciples receive the bread in order that they may share it with the hungry, the needy, the lost, the oppressed and the forgotten.

Another way in which the Supper is exemplary is the emphasis on the necessity of service, emphasized particularly in the Johannine account of the foot-washing at the Supper, which we often ritually re-enact on Maundy Thursday. Jesus declares to his disciples: 'I have set you an example, that you also should do as I have done to you'.[18] This is not simply a call to serve other disciples; it is an affirmation that our commitment to God demands a commitment to the neighbour and to the needs of the world. It calls disciples to humble service.

Eating and drinking with Jesus was often life-transforming, for instance in the case of Zacchaeus. And it often is still today. But all the evidence also suggests that disciples who failed to obey the commands involved in the meal could still find at Jesus' table forgiveness and the grace of a new beginning.

The Lord's Supper also manifests, or makes, a very special sort of fellowship in which the infinite and equal worth of each is affirmed and celebrated along with an affirmation of the value of difference and particularity. Where else can the wise and the foolish, the rich and the poor, the weak and the powerful, the failures and the successful, the young and the old meet together as equals, and attend to one another and serve one another and bring their diverse lifestyles and abilities into God's presence and under God's judgement? The Church is most fully manifested when it gathers at the Lord's table. What it receives, and does and says there involves a commitment – a *sacramentum* – that reaches far beyond the particular moment or the specific believing community. It is at one and the same time a prefiguring of the Reign of God and a sign of hope set amidst the injustices and oppressions of the world, the world God loves so much that he sent his Son, the world in which disciples live and serve and hope and pray.

If part of the ethical content of the Supper calls for and expresses the just sharing of bread and wine and all that is necessary for a decent human life, it is also true that the Supper enacts a proper and responsible use and delight in the good gifts of creation. The bread 'which earth has given and human hands have made', and 'the fruit of the vine and work of human hands' are treated with reverence not only because they are for us the bread of life and our spiritual drink, but because they are representative of God's good gifts to us and to everyone in his wonderful creation. Our use and sharing of them involve a commitment to the proper delight and respectful use and sharing of the gifts of creation.

But the Lord's Supper must be, and is, far more than exemplary and challenging to the lovelessness and injustices of the world. It nourishes holiness and right action. In it we find the presence of God and our neighbour, forgiveness, grace, solidarity and peace. The lifestyle of disciples that flows from the Lord's Supper is not a matter of anxious ethical striving, or the earning of merit. It has rather to do with the nourishing of disciples, and setting them free to allow grace to flow through them to the world. The Supper frees us from obsession with ourselves to give our loving, unselfconscious attention to God, our neighbours and the needs of the world. For holiness is a matter of delight rather than of effort.

* * *

I doubt if Karl Barth would agree with my ethical interpretation of the Lord's Supper, or consider it an adequate response to the challenge he threw out. But my intention has simply been to restore a balance which has, I feel, sometimes been lost, and reaffirm the importance and centrality of the Lord's Supper in the modern age. But we must always remember that it is food – fast food! – for disciples and pilgrims who are seeking a city whose builder and maker is God. And as such it is always provisional, incomplete, an antepast or appetiser rather than the real banquet. Thus we can still sing, but perhaps with a slightly different emphasis:

> O thou who at thy Eucharist didst pray
> That all thy Church might be for ever one,
> Grant us at every eucharist to say,
> With longing heart and soul, 'Thy will be done.'
> Oh, may we all one bread, one body be,
> One through this sacrament of unity.
>
> So, Lord, at length when sacraments shall cease,
> May we be one with all thy Church above,
> One with thy saints in one unbroken peace,
> One with thy saints in one unbounded love:
> More blessed still, in peace and love to be
> One with the Trinity in Unity.[19]

11

Worship, ethics and unity

Worship is the definitive and central activity of the people of God. It is something we do rather than observe, or listen to, or talk about. It is the strange practice which is characteristic of Christians. In worship the Church manifests itself most clearly, and in worship Christians are nourished for the broader 'divine service' or 'liturgy after the liturgy' in the life of the world. In worship we are involved in the life of heaven; we experience in a fragmentary way the life that is to come, and we glimpse God's purposes for everyone and for the whole of creation. Worship expresses and creates community, *koinonia*, and in worship we find an ethic, a lifestyle, embodied and sustained. In authentic Christian worship we discover a deeper experience of unity, the unity, harmony and reconciliation that God has in store for God's people. In worship the search for the fuller institutional actualization of unity is actively fostered, and worshippers are invited and encouraged to involve themselves in struggles for peace and justice and liberation.[1]

Worship is a kind of template of the Christian life. The worship of communities of expectant faith anticipates God's future and challenges the present. Those who sing God's song in a strange land are thereby disturbing the existing order and proclaiming an alternative. As they reappropriate the tradition in celebrating together the love and the justice of God, they discover that there are opportunities of renewal, transformation and liberation offered to them.

Worship and the service of God

Orthodox Christians in particular have reminded us all that when we speak of worship we do not mean simply or exclusively set times of worship, the 'cult', a particular and rather odd compartment of life.

The wholeness of the Christian life should be rooted in the times set apart; any sharp disjunction between worship and the Christian life is a distortion of each. 'Christ did not establish a society for the observance of worship, a "cultic society"', wrote the Orthodox theologian Alexander Schmemann, 'but rather the Church as the way of salvation, as the new life of re-created [hu]mankind'.[2] Only too often we have made of the worship which should sanctify and illumine the whole of life, which should be the leaven of the lump and the sign of God's love for the world, a temporary escape from reality and a way of avoiding the ethical task. But in fact worship ought to be a resource for the enrichment and humanization of the life of the world.

Worship should shape and enrich the practice and the ethics of the community of faith, for it is 'condensed action that is intended to focus and concentrate meaning so that what is done in this nexus of sacred time and place ripples out onto all prior and subsequent doings, the doings that take place in the "profane" or outside world, resonating in these ordinary affairs with interpretive possibilities'.[3] Christian worship, in other words, is the heart of Christian practice and ethics, which expresses the significance of the whole, and sustains and illumines the Christian life. In worship and in action which flows from worship we learn how to be Christians; and in the doing we explore the nature and the claim of faith.

None of this is done in isolation. In worship we experience what it is to be 'Church'; together we encounter God in worship, and this is inseparable from our meeting and responding to our neighbours with their needs. In worship we find that together we are opened to God and to the world that God has made and redeemed in Christ. In worship the unity of the Church is displayed in such a way that we know that it is costly unity, the unity that has been won for us by Christ. The Church, as the Russian Orthodox theologian, Vitaly Borovoi, proclaimed at the Vancouver Assembly of the World Council of Churches, 'is called to be a sign, a pledge, and a manifestation of … life in unity'.[4] This unity, he went on, is most fully shown in the worshipping Church, particularly when that Church gathers to celebrate the Eucharist. Unfortunately, that magnificent declaration was almost immediately followed by a statement that only Orthodox Christians would be welcome to receive communion at the Orthodox liturgy the following morning!

The Methodist Stanley Hauerwas in a key passage wrote:

> The task of the church [is] to pioneer those institutions and practices that the wider society has not learned as forms of justice. (At times it is also possible that the church can learn from society more just ways of forming life.) The church, therefore, must

act as a paradigmatic community in the hope of providing some indication of what the world can be but is not... The church does not have, but rather is a social ethic. That is, she is a social ethic inasmuch as she functions as a criteriological institution – that is, an institution that has learned to embody the form of truth that is charity as revealed in the person and work of Christ.[5]

But *how* is the Church a social ethic, how does it 'pioneer new institutions and practices', how does it function as 'a paradigmatic community'? The Orthodox theologian Vigen Guroian responds to this question in terms with which Hauerwas would have no difficulty, 'For Orthodoxy the answer is that this social ethic originates in baptism and is continued in all of the Church's liturgical and sacramental acts.'[6] Christian ethics which is not rooted in and nourished by worship is in constant danger of dilution into something very different. 'Christian ethics', writes Guroian, 'is possible because a new people has come into existence by baptism and chrismation, is reconstituted and nourished in eucharistic celebration, is diversified and deepened in agapeic union by the sacraments of baptism and orders, and is reconciled and healed through penance and anointing'.[7]

From the Reformed side a not dissimilar view emerges. For Karl Barth, the theologian should be seen primarily as one who holds an office in the Church rather than as an academic; Christian theology must be done in the context of the Church, as a critical service to the Church and its witness in the world to the truth of God. The same is true of Christian ethics: Barth and his disciples deny that you can have a free-floating Christian ethics, as it were. Christian ethics is 'koinonia ethics', in Paul Lehmann's phrase. It is necessarily Church ethics, tied to the life of the community of faith, serving that community and articulating the insights that that community has received and witnesses to as 'public truth'. Thus 'Church ethics' is closely related to worship. When Barth published his Gifford Lectures as *The Knowledge of God and the Service of God*[8] some English-speaking readers were surprised to discover in a book they assumed was about the relation between theology and ethics substantial discussions of the service of God in worship (*Gottesdienst*) alongside long treatments of the political worship or service of God, the state as the servant of God, and so on. Barth was suggesting, in this book as elsewhere, that worship, including necessarily the preaching of the Word, was a central dimension of the broader service of God in responding to the needs of the world and confronting the principalities and powers that hold sway there.[9]

A caveat has to be entered here. There are dangers, particularly of a Church trying to be the Church in an enclosed way, washing its hands of 'the world' and its concerns, unwilling to be challenged and enriched by what happens beyond its bounds. A Church that in its life and worship is turned in on itself (*incurvatus in se*) and not open to the world and to the coming Reign of God is in a thoroughly problematic position. A Church that forgets its mission or assimilates into the power structures of society is neither making nor exemplifying a lively Christian ethic. Empirically the social ethic that Churches in some contexts present is more a reflection and reinforcement of the align-ments, divisions, hostilities and suspicions of the societies in which they exist. And a ghetto existence, isolated from others by a belief system and lifestyle which make no claim to broader relevance, like the Amish people in Pennsylvania, is not really an option for Christian Churches striving to be faithful in pointing to God's Reign. Hauerwas is right in affirming that '[T]he first social ethical task of the church is to be the church – the servant community... The church does not have a social ethic; the church is a social ethic.'[10] But his preface to this quotation is more questionable: 'I am in fact challenging the very idea that Christian social ethics is primarily an attempt to make the world more peaceable or just.' Because the life and worship of the Church are orientated on the Reign of God, they inevitably have a bearing on the life of the world.

The ambiguity of worship

Such a relationship between worship, the central, sustaining activity of the household of faith, and ethics has not gone unchallenged. For Miranda, the OT prophets are seen as uniformly opposed to the cult because 'to know Jahweh is to do justice and compassion and right to the needy'; but worship has become understood as an *alternative* to the service of the neighbour, which is the only path to the true God. The cult, in other words, leads remorselessly to idolatry and sinful practice.[11] Sobrino, in similar vein, argues that we gain access to Jesus *only* through the praxis of discipleship which is always in tension with 'cultic worship'.[12] There is, he says, no 'direct access to God in cultic worship. It can come only indirectly through service to human beings, specifically to those who can represent and embody the total otherness of God in historical terms, namely the poor and oppressed'.[13] Interest in worship, Sobrino argues, converts Christianity into 'a religion', using that term in a pejorative way reminiscent of Karl Barth. Worship for such liberation theologians is not just superfluous – it is a distraction from discipleship, a temptation and a disguise for the doing of injustice.

But there are other theologians. Some sympathetic critics of liberation theology have been surprised and even offended that so many liberation theologians are actively and apparently uncritically involved in 'ordinary' Christian worship. In so doing, they are accused of failure to assimilate Marx's criticisms of religion, and encouraging behaviour which is archaic, alienating and fundamentally superstitious. Thus liberation theology, because of its continuing and rather traditional affirmation of the importance of the practice of worship, has failed the very people to whom it is committed.[14] This line of argument cannot be lightly dismissed, particularly by Protestants. There is much to suggest that what is labelled 'Christian worship' can indeed obstruct faithful Christian practice and offer a false way to God which by-passes the neighbour and all the ethical issues of justice, peace and the integrity of creation.

Theologians such as Miranda, Sobrino and Kee who are suspicious of the actual effects of worship are clearly influenced by the assumption that worship and ritual are essentially reinforcements of the existing order of things, and thus inherently conservative and opposed to transformation. The prevailing orthodoxy in social science was for a long time that worship and ritual were in fact no more than ways of confirming the social order and enabling individuals to accept oppression and injustice. More recently there have been effective challenges to this view, most notably perhaps from Victor Turner.[15] Building on the work of Turner and others, the American theologian Tom F. Driver has emphasized the capacity of ritual to liberate and transform. Using the concept of liminality, Driver sees worship as taking place in liminal space, 'at the edge of, or in the cracks between' the mapped regions of what we like to call 'the real world'.[16] An alternative world is established there which by its existence challenges 'the real world'. Ritual, it is true, is concerned with order and with community as well as with transformation. But the greatest of these is transformation:

> Social order is not an end in itself but is necessary to make possible the benefits of communal love. But even love is not an end in itself unless, allied to justice, it is devoted to freeing individuals and groups from the forces that oppress them. Static love is never enough, and genuine love reaches out to invoke powers and techniques of liberative transformation.[17]

Worship therefore is capable of challenging the temporal order by presenting a higher order that is to come. Christian worship is essentially transformative. The worship of an expectant and faithful Church is liberating. Accordingly it is proper to look in the worship of the Church for insights and resources for the moral life, and to expect that if the Church is a social ethic this should be most clearly manifest in its worship, service and sacrifice.

And yet the empirical reality continues to be ambiguous. Totalitarian regimes in this century have tended to prohibit evangelistic and educational activity on the part of the Church, and to strive to control preaching, but to regard the worship that takes place within a recognized church building as relatively inoffensive. There have even been suggestions that the Nazis, so far from being worried by the movement for liturgical renewal, secretly encouraged it on the grounds that it made church people less concerned with the political, economic and social processes around them.[18] Nevertheless, both the Nazi and the Communist dictatorships were at great pains to develop alternative secular rituals and forms of 'worship' – baptism, marriage, confirmation, funerals, and so on – to wean the people away from the Church: evidence of the continuing power and influence over behaviour and belief of worship.[19] Accordingly it is proper for us to explore in a theologically responsible way that is chastened by empirical reality the ethical content and force of two central dimensions of Christian worship – the Lord's Supper, and baptism – in the light of the ecumenical convergence most strikingly crystallized in the Faith and Order Commission of the World Council of Churches' *Baptism, Eucharist and Ministry* (henceforth abbreviated to BEM), and of an awareness of the powerful political and economic forces at work in the world today.

Baptism

The sacrament of baptism is a celebration of grace, a recognition of God's choice, and also a recentring of life, a reorientation, a new beginning. It is a turning to God from idols,[20] so that now we must 'live lives worthy of the God who calls you into his kingdom and glory'.[21] Repentance, conversion and baptism thus give a new identity, a new orientation, a new goal. It is not simply a rite; it is a life lived to God, which finds its fulfilment only at the end, as Jesus' baptism found its fulfilment on the cross. Baptism is entry into a community of forgiven sinners, a fellowship of reconciliation, not a company of moral heroes.

Baptism, Eucharist and Ministry on baptism gives considerable attention to the ethical content of baptism, particularly in para. 7:

Baptism initiates the reality of the new life given in the midst of the present world. It gives participation in the community of the Holy Spirit. It is a sign of the Kingdom of God and of the life of the world to come. Through the gifts of faith, hope and love, baptism has a dynamic which embraces the whole of life, extends to all nations, and anticipates the day when every tongue will confess that Jesus Christ is Lord to the glory of God the Father.

'Baptism', writes Vigen Guroian, 'is where reflection upon Christian ethics ought to begin'.[22] For in baptism we embark upon the life and discipline of discipleship, and are called to be people of a certain character, showing love, generosity and graciousness in our dealings and struggling against the selfishness, pride, violence and arrogance which are endemic in a sinful world. Incorporation into Christ has a powerful ethical component, and in baptism we are assured of support and forgiveness in our ethical struggles. Guroian quotes the words used in the Armenian Church during the anointing in the baptismal rite:

Sweet ointment in the name of Jesus Christ is poured upon thee as a seal of incorruptible heavenly gifts.
The eyes:
This seal in the name of Jesus Christ enlighten thine eyes, that thou mayest never sleep unto death.
The ears:
This holy anointing be unto thee for the hearing of divine commandments.
The nostrils:
This seal in the name of Jesus Christ be to thee a sweet smell from life unto life.
The mouth:
This seal in the name of Jesus Christ be to thee a guard for thy mouth and a strong door for thy lips.
The hands:
This seal in the name of Jesus Christ be to thee a cause for good works and for all virtuous deeds and conduct.
The heart:
This seal establish in thee a pure heart and renew within thee an upright spirit.
The back:
This seal in the name of Jesus Christ be to thee a shield of strength thereby to quench all the fiery darts of the Evil One.
The feet:
This divine seal direct thy goings unto life everlasting that thou mayest not be shaken.[23]

Although baptism is administered to individuals, it is incorporation into Christ and entry into a community. The ethics and the way of life that baptism signifies is therefore from start to finish a communal matter. We are never alone, but are constantly in solidarity with countless others, who encourage, guide and warn. As part of the body we are responsible to and for one another. And in baptism we experience and enter a fuller unity, a more comprehensive and reconciled community, a more total *koinonia*, than the divided Churches have yet actualized. The main denominations and confessions today recognize each other's baptism, but often do not accept baptized Christians from other Churches as full members, or admit them to the Lord's Table. This is a painful ecumenical anomaly, but it may also be a step towards the realization of a fuller unity.

Enda McDonagh, the Irish theologian, reminds us that baptism as incorporation into the dying and rising of Christ is baptism into the *one* Church, which is the body of Christ. This is not a purely legal point – that different denominations accept the validity of baptismal initiation into membership – but goes far deeper. In our divisions, or rather, despite our divisions, we all share in Christ. The celebration of a baptism involves, he argues, not only the congregation, denomination or confession in which it takes place, but all the other Christian communities. Only so is it capable of signifying credibly the coming unity of all humankind. McDonagh goes on:

> In the more confined world of Northern Ireland, with its overspill in Scotland, England and the Republic of Ireland, this understanding of Baptism presents a particular challenge. When asked what the Churches could do to help overcome the divisions in Northern Ireland, I sometimes, as a shock tactic, reply: 'They should stop baptising'. After the inevitable shock effect I go on to explain how the theological and ecclesiological significance of baptism may be undermined by its social and political significance. Baptism of a new member into the local Church of Ireland or Presbyterian Church or Catholic Church has the same profound theological and ecclesiological significance. It is baptism into the one Christ, the one great Church. All the Churches are called to recognise this... However, at this level of history and politics, of peoples' attitudes and divisions, the unity in Christ, the surrender to Christ, is obscured, if not rendered entirely futile. Baptism into a particular Church, Protestant or Catholic, expresses integration into a particular historical community of Christians with its own cultural and political traditions which set it apart from and indeed against another community of Christians... To preserve the sacraments from such futility should one not stop the practice of Baptism?[24]

McDonagh's suggestion arises out of a passion that the authentic meaning and significance of baptism should shine forth, and an awareness that distortion often enters in. In the baptismal liturgy of my own Church, the parents are enjoined to 'unfold to her the treasure she has received today'. We should all be concerned with the constant unfolding of the ethical treasure that is given to us in baptism, in Eucharist and in the proclamation of the gospel.

Eucharist

Like the new-born infants you are, you should be craving for unadul-
terated spiritual milk so that by it you may *grow* towards salvation;
for surely you have *tasted that the Lord is good*.[25] The Eucharist may
be understood as nourishment for moral growth and formation. Like
all worship, this central liturgy has an important function of edifying,
of building up the community and its members. Individualistic
worship, like speaking in tongues without an interpreter, does not edify
and should be discouraged. As should the modern extremes of individualistic worship.

The Lord's Supper thus has an important formative role, both in
relation to the community and the individual. As at Jesus' table there
was an open invitation and deeply entrenched suspicions, divisions and
hostilities were overcome, so at the eucharistic table Jew and Gentile,
rich and poor, weak and strong come together and experience a new
and challenging depth of community. When the poor are despised, the
sacrament is invalid;[26] in the eucharistic sharing the divisions of the
world are challenged and a better way is shown. The Eucharist involves
a commitment (*sacramentum*) to sharing with the needy neighbour, for
Jesus said, 'The bread that I shall give is my own flesh; given for the
life of the world'.[27] It is not bread for believers, but for the life of the
world (*kosmos*). The reverent use and sharing of the sacramental
elements likewise involves a commitment to this as the proper use of
the natural environment, and is a necessary component of a eucharistic
lifestyle. In and through the Eucharist we are called to be holy people
in a world that is being made holy.

The Eucharist is also food for a journey and an anticipation
(*antepast*) of the coming heavenly banquet. We find in the Eucharist
an authentic but partial expression of the conviviality of the realm of
God, the taste of the future, which encourages us to seek the Realm
of God in hope. There is thus in the Eucharist a proper kind of play-
acting involved. We are trying out the roles that will be fully ours in
the Realm of God, as young children play 'let's pretend' games to get
the feel of being mothers or fathers, or train-drivers, or soldiers.

Other examples could be multiplied from various contexts. In
worship we receive a new identity, we are formed morally. By encountering God we learn how to be disciples. We learn to love by being
loved; we learn to forgive by being forgiven; we learn generosity by
being treated generously. 'At heart', writes Vigen Guroian, 'Christian
ethics should be an invitation to the great banquet.'[28] Only when two

or three are gathered together in Christ's name and when people come from east and west and north and south to sit at table in the Kingdom of God, is Christian ethics possible. At that table the stranger is always welcome: 'Then the king will say to those at his right hand, "Come, O blessed of my Father, inherit the kingdom prepared for you from the foundation of the world; for I was hungry and you gave me food, I was thirsty and you gave me drink, I was a stranger and you welcomed me."'[29] And eating and drinking at the anticipation of that banquet on earth provides more than food and drink: 'The kingdom of God does not mean food and drink but righteousness and peace and joy in the Holy Spirit.'[30]

BEM is notable for the strength of its concern with the ethical dimension. In the Eucharist section the key paragraphs are 19–24:

> It is in the eucharist that the community of God's people is fully manifested... The eucharist embraces all aspects of life... The eucharistic celebration demands reconciliation and sharing among all those regarded as brothers and sisters in the one family of God and is a constant challenge in the search for appropriate relationships in social, economic and political life... All kinds of injustice, racism, separation and lack of freedom are radically challenged when we share in the body and blood of Christ... As participants in the eucharist, therefore, we prove inconsistent if we are not actively participating in this ongoing restoration of the world's situation and the human condition. The eucharist shows us that our behaviour is inconsistent in face of the reconciling presence of God in human history: we are placed under continual judgement by the persistence of unjust relationships of all kinds in our society, the manifold divisions on account of human pride, material interest and power politics and, above all, the obstinacy of unjustifiable confessional oppositions within the body of Christ... The eucharist opens up the vision of the divine rule which has been promised as the final renewal of creation, and is a foretaste of it. Signs of this renewal are present wherever the grace of God is manifest and human beings work for justice, love and peace... Reconciled in the eucharist, the members of the body of Christ are called to be servants of reconciliation among men and women and witnesses of the joy of resurrection.

The challenge of these words in today's world is more acute perhaps than we sometimes recognize. How, in a deeply divided world, can we celebrate the Lord's Supper so that it transforms the situation by challenging and transcending divisions and hostility? Camilo Torres, the Colombian priest who died as a guerrilla, believed that in a society as profoundly unjust and divided as Colombia it was impossible for the Eucharist to be properly celebrated. Hence he said, 'I took off my cassock to be more fully a priest', and gave up celebrating Mass.[31] Was he in this reflecting Paul's words to the Corinthian Christians whose celebrations humiliated the poor and confirmed division: 'The result is that when you meet as a congregation, it is not the Lord's Supper that you eat'?[32] The Spanish theologian, José M. Castillo, has declared, 'Where there is no justice, there is no eucharist'.[33] 'Participation in the eucharist...as it is celebrated today', declared Gustavo Gutierrez, 'appears to many to be an action which, for want of the support of an authentic community, becomes an exercise in make-believe'.[34] Even more sharply, Ulrich Duchrow asks whether a Church which 'is divided among active thieves, passive profiteers, and deprived victims', is indeed the body of Christ, capable of celebrating the Eucharist.[35] And nearer to my own home, we should ask what is the relation between eucharistic division in Northern Ireland and the deadly social and political divisions there – and whether the brave words of BEM have in fact made any contribution whatever to the peace process that is now, thank God, under way, if sometimes falteringly.

Nevertheless, we need to recognize that the Eucharist is not the messianic banquet, but a foretaste. We are not yet in the Kingdom for the coming of which we pray. The Eucharist is nourishment for those *seeking* the Kingdom and its justice, and not the feast at the end of the journey. Passive acceptance of injustice, hostility and division may well make our Eucharists questionable. We need today to recover ways in which the Eucharist may be a healing, effective, transforming sign of community and of hope, as well as of commitment to the overcoming of division.

It is significant that the same Gutierrez who pointed to the danger of the Eucharist becoming an exercise in make-believe, also says: 'The first task of the Church is to celebrate with joy the gift of the salvific action of God in humanity, accomplished through the death and resurrection of Christ. This is the Eucharistic memorial and thanksgiving'.[36] Such celebration inevitably takes place in a defective Church and a deformed world, full of sin and suffering, and injustice and oppression. But rightly used, the Supper can be a mighty instrument for the transformation and renewal both of the Church and of the world. For here we have an authentic anticipation of God's future, an appetiser for the coming Kingdom which nourishes expectation and hope. As antepast the Supper is an *arrabon*, a real, if partial, experience of what God has in store for us, which is also the guarantee that it will come. At the table, believers prefigure the future, play out their roles in the Kingdom, present an image, a model of the Kingdom, and themselves enjoy something here and now of the conviviality of the messianic banquet.

Archbishop Trevor Huddleston once said that he felt sometimes that the Church's concern with the Real Presence of Christ in the Eucharist distracted her from the Real Presence of Christ in the neighbour. The Eucharist should, of course, open our eyes to the presence of Christ in the world. Another Anglo-Catholic, Frank Weston, the Bishop of Zanzibar, made a similar point in the 1920s:

> You cannot worship Jesus in the tabernacle if you do not pity Jesus in the slum... And it is folly, it is madness, to suppose that you can worship Jesus in the sacrament and Jesus on the throne of glory when you are sweating him in the souls and bodies of his children... Go out and look for Jesus in the ragged, in the naked, and in the oppressed and sweated, in those who have lost hope, in those who are struggling to make good. Look for Jesus. And when you see him, gird yourself with his towel, and try to wash his feet.[37]

In the Eucharist we learn to discern Jesus where he is, and find the resources to serve him.

*   *   *

All Christians should be concerned with the constant unfolding of the ethical treasure that is given to us in baptism, in Eucharist and in the proclamation of the gospel. For, as Stanley Hauerwas says, baptism and Eucharist 'are the essential rituals of our politics'. They are not simply motives or causes for social witness, 'these liturgies are our effective social work. For if the church *is* rather than *has* a social ethic, these actions are our most important social witness. It is in baptism and the eucharist that we see most clearly the marks of God's kingdom in the world. They set our standard, as we try to bring every aspect of our lives under their sway.'[38]

An ethic that strives to be Christian must, I believe, be rooted in the being and the activity of the Church which has at its heart in the unity of Word and Sacrament a proclamation of the Christian mystery which is our truest and deepest contribution to the life of the world. In authentic Christian worship believers are nourished to seek God's Reign and God's righteousness, and learn to discern the Lord's presence in the hungry, thirsty, naked, sick and imprisoned neighbour. Thus Christian witness and service emerge from the heart of the life of the Church; and if they do not, the very integrity of the congregation's faith is impugned. Unless believers are striving to be disciples, witnessing to the truth, loving their neighbours and seeking God's Reign and God's justice the significance of the Church as a sign and foretaste of the Reign of God is put into question.

IV

Issues

12

Politics and reconciliation[1]

A Christian understanding of reconciliation is primarily in the indicative mood. It rests on something that has happened, something that has been achieved, accomplished, done. The situation has been changed; something objective has happened, which has made everything different. And this reconciliation is more than a change of mind or a call for alteration of behaviour, although it is of course good if behaviour and thought respond to the realities of the situation. Furthermore, this reconciliation that has been achieved does not belong in a 'religious' world, nor is it something affecting only that artificial intellectual construct the isolated individual. 'God was in Christ reconciling the *world* [i.e. the cosmos] to himself', we read, and it is only in this broad cosmic context that 'he has reconciled us to himself through Christ' (2 Cor. 5.18–19). The passage, of course, goes on to speak of 'the ministry of reconciliation' and 'the message of reconciliation' which have been entrusted to us. The objective change, in other words, calls for a response: we cannot be detached and impassive in face of it. We have to do something about it. We have to spread the message and minister the reconciliation in which we participate. Reconciliation has been achieved; it is already there, even if not recognized; we are called to point to, to declare what has been done, and adapt ourselves to this gracious reality. Similar points are made powerfully in Ephesians 2 in a passage which deals unambiguously with the relations between communities: on the cross Christ has in fact broken down 'the barrier of enmity' and annulled the law, the two paradigmatic signs of division, suspicion and hostility. He has thus reconciled Jew and Gentile in one new humanity, so making peace. Accordingly there is good news of peace and reconciliation to proclaim: a gospel rather than a law, a declaration that something decisive for good has happened rather than a call to action or an ethical demand. The indicative is prior to the imperative. We are dealing with facts rather than values.

I want to make these points as strongly as possible right at the beginning because of the pervasive assumption in the modern world that the Church is primarily concerned with values, with ethics, with good behaviour, with the 'moral fabric of society', and that the gospel is a narrative way of communicating ideals and moral education to the masses, not an account of things that have happened, events rather than fairy stories with edifying lessons attached. And I also want to affirm that the gospel belongs in the public realm where it engages with issues of communities and nations as well as the individual heart, and the matters that are commonly labelled 'religion'. Remember that in Matthew 25 it is the *nations* that are called to account.

Such assumptions do not, of course, dispose of imperatives and calls to action; they simply place them in their proper light, as responses to a gracious context, the recognition of the deeper realities of life, allying oneself with God's just and loving purposes, rather than desperate attempts to transform a hostile reality into love and fellowship. This gracious context generates confidence, generosity, pertinacity and hope and provides an alternative to a narrow realism which is circumscribed by the hostilities and suspicions of the moment. *Christian* ethics is a response to the God of justice and love who has in Christ reconciled the cosmos to himself and has already overcome the hostilities and suspicions of today.

There remains the widespread assumption that reconciliation and forgiveness belong in some religious sphere and are relevant in face-to-face relationship, but do not belong in politics. Traditionally, this position has sometimes been grounded in theories of the two kingdoms: reconciliation, grace and forgiveness belong in the spiritual sphere, while the temporal sphere operates on quite other principles. In modern days similar conclusions flow from the assumption that theological language is simply the in-house converse of the Church and can have no validity in the public realm. It is not too hard to show that this leads to a massive impoverishment of public political discourse, as well as a drastic narrowing and domestication of theological language. It is easy to pooh-pooh the two kingdoms theory by citing extreme expressions of it, which appear to set politics free from any theological constraint, such as Luther's declaration that 'the hand that wields this sword and slays with it is then no more man's hand but God's, who hangs, tortures, beheads, slays and fights',[2] or his savage call: 'Quick, head off, away with it, in order that the earth does not become full with the ungodly'.[3] And such quotations could be paralleled with examples of a no less alarmingly distorted individualistic understanding of the Christian faith.

But for all that, it is still necessary to affirm that there are two different spheres, that the Church is not the state, and must not try to act as such, and that the state must not attempt to operate as a Church. Even theological documents as politically challenging as the Barmen Declaration (1934) are careful to draw limits and define functions. The central attack on the Nazi regime here is that it refused to recognize its boundaries, it usurped the task of the Church, and it made exaggerated claims for itself. For Barth the alternative was not politicization, the Church striving to take over the task of the state, but rather that the Church should do its own task more faithfully.[4]

But it is clear that there are reciprocal responsibilities between the Church and the political realm. For Barth, the Church is responsible for what happens within politics because this is closely related to the gospel of the Kingdom. And the gospel provides some knowledge of the context, the significance and the purpose of political activity and offers a language – particularly the discourse of reconciliation, forgiveness and justice – without which politics becomes distorted and malign.

So the Church and theology in their responsibility to God for the political sphere have to offer an account of reality, a language which is adequate to the intractable problems of politics, and a call to respond creatively to the reconciliation which has been achieved in Christ.

Within this frame I wish to discuss three aspects of the relation of reconciliation and politics – politics as safeguarding space for reconciliation; reconciliation as a *telos* or goal for political activity; and politics as an agent of reconciliation.

Politics as safeguarding space for reconciliation

Here we are considering politics in traditional terms as a 'dyke against sin', a function which may appear initially somewhat negative but which is in fact very important if positive processes are to develop properly. We have to recognize that there are in existence powerful inner and outer forces which divide, disrupt and nourish hostility and suspicion – forces, that is, which are opposed to reconciliation and erode any kind of authentic community. Particularly in ways of thought influenced by Augustine a major function of politics has been seen as restraining, limiting, excluding these destructive, sinful forces.

They must be confined and disciplined if reconciliation and community are to be experienced as contemporary public realities in a still sinful world. This dyke against sin is not like the old Berlin Wall, keeping people apart and making fellowship impossible. It is not even like the so-called Peace Wall in Belfast which has the function of stopping people attacking and threatening one another, and thus provides a fragile and partial security – although that in some circumstances is a good which should not be underestimated.

The image of politics as a dyke against sin has to do not with creating and enforcing frontiers which keep people apart, recreating, that is, the dividing walls of hostility which Christ has destroyed. It is not boundary maintenance as much as the creation of space within which reconciliation may take place and community emerge.

Boundaries, of course, need to be defended, and the space within provided with a degree of order. This is the police function of politics: politics should provide the sort of environment in which people can function normally, without fear or uncertainty. Politicians in this model have a vocation as creators of community, not leaders of the pack, or referees regulating a ritualized political game which has become, in Alasdair MacIntyre's phrase, 'civil war carried on by other means'.[5] The politician sees the role as acting on behalf of the community in the broadest sense rather than taking sides in group conflicts. The task is to bring people together rather than keep them apart, in a context where they dare to speak the truth and relate to one another with confidence. The referee model of politics is not to be despised – channelled, limited and ritualized conflict is better than anarchy. Fouls must be recognized and dealt with if conflict is not to become intolerably destructive. *Ius in bello* is better than no *ius* at all! But there are, of course, massive problems when police and security forces are perceived, rightly or wrongly, as taking sides.

The space that is protected by dykes and policed by politics provides an alternative arena for working through conflicts and seeking their resolution through talk, and bargaining, and sharing. This space is neutral ground; it is not the territory of either party or group in which others are interlopers. It is space for non-political methods to be used. Here in this context, what the sociologists call intermediate institutions which cut across class and interest groups flourish and help people to understand and relate to one another. In schools, and trade unions, clubs and churches, civil society is given substance, misapprehensions are gradually broken down and friendships are created. Such institutions, of course, may be recruited into tribal politics, in whole or part, and become cadres in conflict, or organs of one or other ghetto in the city. But their true function is to be agents of reconciliation and community building in the space that politics provides. This is why integrated education is so important. When the children of two opposed communities are educated apart from one another, misunderstandings and suspicions inevitably arise and the community-building function of education is compromised.

This is also space for the Church to *be* the Church, to work for the healing of relationships, to announce that reconciliation has been achieved, and to show that it works. But the Church as a visible institution, a network of congregations belonging to various denominations, is frequently hijacked by warring parties, so that the divided Church proclaiming a gospel of reconciliation reflects and reinforces the divisions of the warring parties and thereby denies the reconciliation it preaches. When I returned to Scotland in the late 1970s I found a Baptismal Certificate in common use in the Church of Scotland. At its top there was a symbol which could be seen in two ways. It was simultaneously a dove descending and a thistle, and both were unambiguously tartan! What a vivid reminder of the dangers of confusing membership in the Body of Christ with membership in an ethnic community! Similarly, for example, Enda McDonagh has pointed out how the understanding of baptism is commonly distorted in Northern Ireland:

> Baptism in a particular Church, Protestant or Catholic, expresses integration into a particular historical community of Christians with its own cultural and political traditions which set it apart from and against another community of Christians. Affiliation to the Unionist or Nationalist community is the other side of the baptism event in Northern Ireland, which is in opposition to and sometimes in deadly conflict with integration into the Body of Christ.[6]

This is the danger, McDonagh suggests, of rendering baptism futile. The easy solution in a way would be to stop baptizing. But that would be to lose 'the challenge and empowerment' which baptism offers Christians in these hard days in Northern Ireland. Thus he suggests that both branches of the Christian Church should be fully represented in every baptism as a sign of the true Church and a symbol of reconciliation.

Only if the Church takes with profound seriousness the damage done by its own divisions and the urgent need to show that in the Church – at every level – reconciliation is a recognized and recognizable reality can the Church faithfully point to reconciliation in the space that politics provides.

Reconciliation as the goal of politics

Two schools in contemporary thought are particularly vehement in suggesting that politics has no goal, no *telos* beyond itself; they see politics as a self-contained game which has no need to justify itself in relation to some external standard. Politics, according to many propon-ents of political realism, is about the rational pursuit of the national interest. There is no *telos* beyond this national interest, and since there are many nations there are many interests in tension with one another. Politics thus becomes the business of balancing and channelling conflicting interests. Out of this process, if the protagonists are reasonably restrained and sensible, a rather tenuous kind of order emerges in which a good proportion of interests find at least partial satisfaction and the scales provide a tolerable degree of stability as a kind of by-product of the pursuit of national interest. This stability is on the whole an accidental benefit rather than a conscious goal of policy.

The second type of theory which rejects the notion that political activity should be orientated towards a goal or *telos* explicitly rejects the possibility or desirability of goals such as the 'common good' or 'social justice'. Modern societies, the argument runs, are large and complex, and individuals and groups have very diverse understandings of the good. The state should recognize this and acknowledge that no arbitrator is possible between these divergent notions of the good. Thus the state, according to Bruce Ackerman and others, must be morally neutral and see its role as simply enabling individuals and groups to pursue their interests with the minimum of interference, in the expec-tation that through the benign impersonal operations of an 'invisible hand' some general benefit may emerge. Northern Ireland might be seen as a standing refutation of this process.

But in this imbroglio of differing and often conflicting goods no such thing as a common good can be found, and indeed the attempt to establish a common good for a complex modern society inevitably leads to totalitarian tyranny, or so the argument runs. In what Friedrich Hayek calls 'teleocratic societies', freedom is eroded and dictatorship is the only way to sustain a common good. Society, to this way of thinking, should be like a hotel – a set of facilities available to guests to enable them to pursue their diverse purposes with as little inter-ference and as few rules as possible. It is not at all like a family or a sports team, closely integrated and held together by a common destiny and a network of shared commonalities.

The majority Christian tradition has, of course, strongly stressed community and the common good. The Aristotelian/Thomist tradition sees the human being as a social and political animal whose individual good cannot be separated from the common good, and whose destiny transcends the political and the worldly. Here politics can only be understood in the light of the *telos*, which is to do with reconciliation and the restoration of community.

Politics, then, is directed to something beyond itself. If it is not understood within such a transcendent frame it becomes warped and destructive. To give a specific instance: if just war thinking is detached from two fundamental theological convictions – that violence is sinful and evil, and that the aim is reconciliation and the restoration of fellowship – it quickly is transformed from being a way of limiting damage into being a justification, even sometimes a glorification, of violence and destruction.

Presenting reconciliation as the *telos* of politics is by no means to reject or question what I said earlier about reconciliation as something that has happened, something that has been achieved. Indeed it is integral to Christian belief that the fellowship which has been established by Christ is also the end, the goal. But when we speak of reconciliation, as Christians we see it as a gift, a promise and a hope on the basis of the reconciliation which has already been achieved. The future indicative is grounded in the past indicative. Thus we should understand reconciliation as a central dimension of the Christian hope. We hope for the fullness of the *telos* which God will give us as a gift. People in situations of long-drawn-out conflict are frequently condemned to despair, deprived of hope. They begin to assume that hostility and conflict are perennial aspects of their situation, that there is no escape. Without hope we are imprisoned in the present. Christian hope is the seeking of a city, not one that we design but one whose architect and builder is God. The seeking of the city is the proper function of politics, although attempts to construct the heavenly city are projects doomed to frustration. What we can and must strive for is the kind of partial anticipations of that city which give people its flavour and help to sustain hope and the constant seeking of the city. And that is also the Christian vocation of the politician.

Politics as an agent of reconciliation

There is much conflict in life, and conflict can sometimes be productive. But when adversarialism is accepted as a fundamental principle it becomes profoundly destructive. In medicine, for example, it has been argued that when the model of care and healing is replaced by an emphasis on struggle between the physician and the ailment or tumour, a struggle in which 'defeat' must never be acknowledged, and secondly, when patient and doctor regularly see themselves as potential antagonists in court, the situation and the relationships are fundamentally adulterated.

So it is in politics, if conflict is accorded finality. Then the politician becomes simply the leader of the pack, pursuing with the minimum of restraint the interests of the group represented. Adversarial politics exacerbates the existing tensions and divisions in society, and politics becomes defensive – or offensive, depending on one's point of view – rather than creative, looking forward to a broader sense of community, and attempting to move towards that community. Augustine argued that 'political authority exists to resolve at least some of the tensions in human society ... [It] serves to remedy the conflict, tension and disorder of society'.[7] Only if this can be recovered as a central dimension of the vocation of politics can we reaffirm a broader and more Christian understanding of community, and overcome the heresy that politics is a war to be won through total victory and unconditional surrender. Politicians are not generals, or leaders of the pack, or shop stewards; they have a broader vocation as pastors, ministers, creators of community, mediators, healers – somewhat like the shepherd-kings of the Bible.

This does not mean plastering over the cracks, disguising real conflicts of interest, suggesting that sordid settlements imposed by the powerful are in fact *shalom*. There has been and continues to be too much of this. The fruits are there for all to see in the former Yugoslavia today – and closer to home as well! Conflicts need to be recognized and worked through with integrity. Martin Luther King and other leaders in the American Civil Rights Movement or Gandhi in India show both how difficult and how costly it is to struggle to right wrongs, heal antagonisms and overcome deep-seated conflicts of interest, and simultaneously create a broader and more authentic sense of community.

The *Kairos Document* from South Africa raises a series of very important caveats about glib or hasty or simplistic appeals for reconciliation, in effect for seeking instant reconciliation which is simply crying, 'Peace, peace where there is no peace'. Its criticisms of what it calls 'church theology' are fair; and it makes a number of important points about reconciliation. The passage is so important that it deserves to be cited at length:

'Church Theology' takes 'reconciliations' as the key to problem resolution. It talks about the need for reconciliation between white and black, or between all South Africans. 'Church Theology' often describes the Christian stance in the following way: 'We must be fair. We must listen to both sides of the story. If the two sides can only meet to talk and negotiate they will sort out their differences and misunderstandings, and the conflict will be resolved'. On the face of it this may sound very Christian. But is it?

The fallacy here is that 'reconciliation' has been made into an absolute principle that must be applied in all cases of conflict or dissension. But not all cases of conflict are the same. We can imagine a private quarrel between two people or two groups whose differences are based upon misunderstandings. In such cases it would be appropriate to talk and negotiate to sort out the misunderstandings and to reconcile the two sides. But there are other conflicts where one side is a fully armed and violent oppressor while the other side is defenceless and oppressed. There are conflicts that can only be described as the struggle between justice and injustice, good and evil, God and the devil. To speak of reconciling these two is not only a mistaken application of the Christian idea of reconciliation, it is a total betrayal of all that Christian faith has ever meant...

In our situation in South Africa today it would be totally unchristian to plead for reconciliation and peace before the present injustices have been removed. Any such plea plays into the hands of the oppressor by trying to persuade those of us who are oppressed to accept our oppression and to become reconciled to the intolerable crimes that are committed against us. That is not Christian reconciliation, it is sin. It is asking us to become accomplices in our own oppression, to become servants of the devil. No reconciliation is possible in South Africa *without justice*. What this means in practice is that no reconciliation, no forgiveness and no negotiations are possible *without repentance*...

There is nothing that we want more than true reconciliation and genuine peace – the peace that God wants and not the peace the world wants (Jn 14:27). The peace that God wants is based upon truth, repentance, justice and love. The peace that the world offers us is a unity that compromises the truth, covers over injustice and oppression and is totally motivated by selfishness.[8]

This passage, I think, has important things to say to us, even if we feel we read it in a very different context where the rights and wrongs are much less clear and where serious Christians are much more divided about the way forward. First, we must attend to the assertion that most deep conflicts have their roots in situations of injustice which must be remedied and put right if reconciliation is to be actualized. We must also recognize that concepts of justice become weapons in social conflict, with their meaning warped to serve the interests of groups. It seems to me that as Christians we should be suspicious of any understanding of justice with which we can be entirely comfortable. F. Hayek's account of justice, for example, at no point is calculated to disturb the wealthy and the powerful. A Christian understanding of justice seem to me to be profoundly disturbing, because it calls for more than fairness, for a move to generosity. This is particularly relevant in situations where the entail of history cannot be undone, where it is impossible for past injuries to be cured or full restitution made. In such situations healing depends on the generosity of the victims. Secondly, there is the need for repentance if forgiveness and reconciliation are to be realized. It is very hard for collectivities to repent, and there are few instances of this happening. But without repentance the way forward is closed. 'A politics of forgiveness…might be the ultimate realism, the recognition of the inevitable imperfection of society.'[9] And repentance and forgiveness are only real way to reconciliation. Thirdly, premature or wrongly timed attempts at reconciliation are worse than useless as James Cone emphasizes.[10] Real deep-seated conflicts have to be analysed, worked through and there must be genuine repentance. Evils and obstacles must be named, unmasked, and repented of. This all takes time. And only after these matters have been worked through is reconciliation on the agenda. Haddon Willmer puts the point well:

> Forgiveness in politics cannot be an easy-going acceptance of what is, a whitewashing tolerance. It has to be a practicable policy in which what is wrong is reckoned with, but forgivingly rather than punitively. Forgiveness is not reconciliation on any terms but takes form in the agreement to work together a political system which expresses the will to forgive, is sustained by forgiveness and encourages and enables men to enter into it. 'Forgiveness' in politics must be a quality of events, institutions, processes and participants.[11]

And The *Kairos Document* reminds us that Christian politicians must endeavour seriously to read the signs of the times, to analyse their situation objectively in order to glimpse what God is doing and saying through it. They must rise above group interests which distort and confuse.

Finally, a word about the politics of hope and the necessity of hope for any politics worth the name – a theme reiterated in The *Kairos Document* and also, I believe, one of the most urgent responsibilities of Christianity in the public realm today. Is it possible that in societies which have lost their grip on social hope the Christian faith, in all its obvious frailty and weakness, may stand as more than an empty husk of unfulfilled expectations and a bastion of group interests? Can Christian faith give shape to hope and sustain hope even here – the kind of hope that strengthens and comforts the weak and vulnerable, that disturbs the comfortable, and rouses the complacent? For this is the kind of hope which makes reconciliation and community possible. And without it we are doomed to continuing internecine strife and suspicion.

13

The media and theology: some reflections[1]

The modern mass media raise few, if any, *entirely* new issues for theology. But they make inescapable some questions that theology has attempted for a long time to dodge. The media highlight and emphasize old problems and possibilities in theology. They challenge comfortable and complacent orthodoxies. In a real sense, then, the media are capable of arousing theology from its 'dogmatic slumbers', and hold forth fascinating possibilities of theological renewal and the recovery of long-neglected emphases and insights. It is a dangerous over-simplification to see the media as nothing but a threat to faith and to theological integrity, the trivialization of all that is sublime, serious or holy. And it is naïve to regard the media as simply a new and immensely powerful channel for the communication of the unchanging gospel. If theologians pay any serious attention to the media today, they tend either to see the media as the new Moloch, the modern idol to which faith, truth and human values are being sacrificed; or, alternatively, they treat the media as a powerful and theologically neutral instrument which can be used to get across the message more compellingly than ever before, an opportunity to communicate Christian truth to millions around the world simultaneously. But only too rarely is it recognized that the media are not simply a tool of theology, but an invitation to new things, an opportunity for the deepening and renewal of theology – a challenge rather than a threat.

Medium and message

The older tradition of academic theology insisted that the primary task, the really important and significant operation, was the establishment of the message. Thereafter, attention might be given to technical issues of how to communicate that message effectively. Here the message is

147

understood as something which is eternal, unchanging. Once it is established it is the same for all cultures and ages. The medium, on the other hand, is variable in accordance with contextual factors of time, place, and culture. The establishment of the message is not only an exercise distinct from its communication, but it is the scientific, the academically respectable operation. The communication of the message is secondary – craftsmanship rather than science. The communicator is a technician, transferring a message determined elsewhere. Accordingly, communication, usually in the guise of homiletics, came to have no more than a tenuous toehold in those sectors of the academic theological world which were concerned with professional formation. It had nothing like the significant place that clinical studies have in medicine. It was a kind of postscript to the serious tasks of exegesis and dogmatics, which wrestled with the exploration and elucidation of the message, which was then handed over to the preacher. This was why many of us were unhappy with the notion that communication was the central concept of the discipline of practical theology. It made the subject a kind of 'applied theology', conveying, communicating and implementing truths independently arrived at elsewhere, but not itself involved in any serious way in wrestling with truth. Such an understanding makes practical theology's claim to being an academic subject very tenuous indeed,[2] and also narrowed extraordinarily the understanding of theology as such by making theology-as-theory's links with practice and with communication equally tenuous.

This split between theory and communication, and indeed any kind of practice, encouraged strange distortions in the way theology was understood and practised. The assumption that theology was a scientific, academic study which deals with unchanging and ahistorical truths, reinforced a tendency to see its task as the establishment of the original meaning of a text *simpliciter*. Much less attention was given to the possibility that the meaning of the text for today might be different, or to allowing the text to speak afresh for itself. The concern was almost entirely with the original horizon of meaning, and hardly at all with the often very different modern horizon. Exegetes or dogmaticians who gave substantial attention to the modern meaning of the text – Rudolph Bultmann is a good example – tended to see the heart of the message as timeless truths, which had to be translated from one terminology into another – from Paul to Heidegger, for example. In such a process communication easily becomes accommodation to modernity. The assumption is that the kernel of the message, the timeless and universal meaning, may be detached from the husk, the original medium of communication, and then presented in modern form with only the inessentials, the time-bound frame, set aside. Such an approach leads easily to the assumption that the one truth, the universal message, can be packaged and transmitted in various ways, but at the heart we have an objective, universal, truth. This is something that can be exchanged, possessed, sold or even 'banked' – to use Paulo Freire's term for inauthentic education: 'The teacher issues communiqués and makes deposits which the students patiently receive, memorize and repeat ... knowledge is a gift, bestowed by those who consider themselves knowledgeable upon those whom they consider to know nothing.'[3] The 'bankers' are the members of an intellectual elite who possess the truth, who control the message, and who convey it to the masses in measured doses, sometimes sugar-coated or otherwise disguised in order to make it palatable. The elite shares its message, at least in part, with the masses. But it also conceals from the people the truths that are regarded as too hard for them, or as likely to prove dangerous in their hands. The elite in fact retains power for itself through its power over the message. And this gives them immense possibilities for manipulation and ideological control.

Truthful communication

Then we have the sophists, attacked by Socrates as cynical abusers of truth, the Gnostic heretics who despised the masses, the medieval prelates who believed the Scriptures were too dangerous to be put into the hands of the people, the Grand Inquisitor of Dostoevsky, always fearful of allowing freedom to the people, or indeed to Jesus.[4] Here too the place of narrative and of image is usually played down. Rather than being means whereby things hidden from the wise and understanding are revealed unto babes according to God's gracious will,[5] the story and the image become codes to be cracked and then translated into a new academic jargon which is the domestic language of the elite and excludes others.

These tendencies have been struggled against, with more or less vigour and conviction, in the Church down the ages, from the conflicts with the Gnostics in the early centuries to the educational methods of Paulo Freire today. Among modern thinkers who have argued that truth and communication must not be separated, and indeed are inter-dependent, pride of place may be given to the extraordinarily original nineteenth-century Danish thinker, Søren Kierkegaard. Kierkegaard found key, and very similar, clues to the proper relationship of truth and communication in the lives of Socrates and Jesus. Socrates attacked the sophists, and Jesus attacked the Pharisees, in both cases objecting to a radically distorted understanding of the relation of truth, the message, and communication, the medium. The sophists, according to Socrates, regarded themselves as free to manipulate the message so as to 'make friends and influence people'. Truth was subordinated to their own objectives and goals. It was something they could manipulate and possess, apportion, sell or use to get their own way. The teacher, the communicator, conveyed information to the recipient. Socrates and Jesus, on the other hand, believed in dialogue, in probing and searching together for the truth. For Socrates, any attempt at manipulation, or foreclosing the discussion, or determining its conclusion in advance, destroys authentic dialogue. Truth cannot be imposed by power; it must be freely sought and freely appropriated. Socrates taught and practised a self-involving, probing and practically orientated kind of dialogue which always involved respect for the participants as people. This is a radically open style of dialogue, in this respect different from the traditional Christian catechetical method, where the answers as well as the questions are laid down authoritatively and thus become a form of thought control. But it is surely good to teach people to ask questions, and to realize that their lives and their practice are implicated in the questions and in the answers. The old catechisms were not simply a form of thought control; they encouraged people to question, and gave them basic resources and a model for serious dialectical enquiry.

Authentic dialogue is impossible if it is assumed that one side *has* both truth and power in its hands, is the giver, the authority, the possessor of the truth, and the other side is simply the passive recipient of the communication, of the truth. The powerful prefer this model, and find true dialogue to be profoundly disturbing, precisely because it encourages people to question established certainties. Socrates was condemned for encouraging the young in particular to probe the 'truths' on which power and authority were believed to rest. He was denounced as a traitor and an infidel although he effectively demonstrated his own patriotism and respect for the gods of the city; but his encouragement of questioning was seen as deeply disturbing to the established order of things. Similarly Jesus was condemned to death as a threat to the political establishment, as one who claimed to be the King of the Jews, and as a blasphemer who questioned the place of the temple and the law in the order of things. Both men encouraged people to probe, to question, to enter into open dialogue. And this in itself was seen as a direct threat to the existing powers.

Power, Kierkegaard suggests, always seeks to control communication and regards open, dialogical communication as a threat. And the market, likewise, seeks to package and sell the truth, commodifying communication. This, in relation to Christian truth, leads to various serious distortions. The electronic evangelists, for example, proclaim themselves to be Evangelicals, that is, people who believe in the priority of grace and justification by faith, but their pervasive message is that one can in some sense earn one's salvation by writing in, by asking for prayers, and above all by contributing 'to keep the gospel ministry on the air'. Here there is a subtle but pervasive reversal of the heart of the message encouraged by the pressures integral to the medium. Or consider the following advice issued some years ago via radio and TV speakers by the Protestant Council of New York:

> Subject matter should project love, joy, courage, faith, hope, trust in God, goodwill. Generally avoid criticism, condemnation, controversy. In a very real sense we are 'selling' religion, the good news of the Gospel. Therefore admonitions and training of Christians on cross-bearing, forsaking all else, sacrifices, and service usually cause the average listener to turn the dial. Consoling the bereaved and calling sinners to repentance, by direct indictment of the listeners, is out of place (with designated exceptions) .... As Apostles, can we not extend an invitation, in effect: 'Come and enjoy our privileges, meet good friends, see what God can do for you?'[6]

The medium here is allowed to determine the message in a one-sided way. Or consider how the modern pedagogical orthodoxy can be used to make the message conform to a whole series of fairly arbitrary assumptions about children and their capacity to appropriate complex, disturbing and challenging truths. Ronald Goldman, for example, long a guru of religious education in Britain, argued that young children should not be told the story of the crucifixion of Jesus because they would find it disturbing:

> Young children should not be exposed, for obvious reasons, to the painful, horrific and often morbid details of the Crucifixion, although they cannot be protected from knowledge of these events ... The emphasis in schools should be emotional rather than intellectual, and it is the Resurrection with its hope, joy and new life which should be the emotional focus.[7]

By way of contrast, Kierkegaard suggests in a passage which is clearly autobiographical that the message which is inherently disturbing and challenging must find an appropriate medium which communicates its authentic challenge. A child, he writes, is shown by a loving parent or a caring teacher a series of pictures – remember this comes long before the age of TV and the movies! Here is a knight on a charger; there is Napoleon, leading his troops to victory. Then comes a picture of a huntsman, dressed in green, his bow in his hand staring ahead as he takes aim. That is William Tell. The stories are told to the child as the pictures are shown: the Swiss patriot-hero is taking aim with consummate skill, determined not to harm his beloved son, concentrating on hitting the apple, devoted to the liberation of his people and the welfare of his child.

In among the pictures which delight and instruct the child there is one that is different – the image of a man on a cross. This one will puzzle and disturb the child as much as the others delight him. It does not belong with the other images. The child will be confused by this one, ugly picture among all the lovely ones, by the picture of a criminal suffering torture among all the pictures of heroes in their moment of triumph. He will ask questions: Why does he hang painfully upon the tree? Why is he being executed like the worst of criminals? Who is he? What has he done? Why do people do this to him? And as he listens to the story which gradually unfolds in response to his questions he will find within himself a turmoil of conflicting emotions and a stream of constant questions about why this happened and the strange meaning of it all.[8]

This tale of Kierkegaard's, about the central Christian image among other images and the dialogue which ensues, raises the issue of the sense in which Christianity can 'belong' in a powerful medium such as broadcasting, which delights and instructs, and broadens horizons, and challenges – and can easily distort or trivialize. Can religious truth and Christian dialogue survive in a medium which amuses and advertises? Kierkegaard's answer, I am sure, would be that Christianity does indeed belong in that medium, rubbing shoulders with the other images and stories, and amusements and instruction to be found there, like the picture of the crucifixion alongside the pictures of Napoleon and William Tell, and heroes rescuing damsels in distress, to say nothing of the more trivial and violent modern hero figures such as Rambo or Superman. Its place is there, but it belongs there in a disjointed and disturbing way. It does not sit easily alongside much that is displayed in the box of delights. It is inherently different from a great many of the other things that are to be found there. It belongs because it claims to be true, to be public truth, open to inspection and examination and discussion, not simply the arbitrary choice of a declining group in our culture. It belongs because it is interesting and important. It belongs because it interacts, to confirm and question and be challenged by much else that is on offer. But if it itself becomes frothy and amusing, the selling of religion that disturbs no one, challenges nothing, and overlays truth with an impenetrable layer of candyfloss, we would be better without it. If it wallows in the razzmatazz and nostalgia of old-time religion, without any contemporary cutting edge, we should get rid of it as quickly as possible. If it gives way to the seductions of power and wealth, so that it can no longer speak the truth to power, or proclaim good news to the poor, or show that God has chosen the weak to shame the strong, it should be consigned to the dustbin as quickly as possible as totally lacking integrity.

Subjectivity is truth

Kierkegaard also insisted that the truth is something that is self-involving. When he reiterated his slogan, 'subjectivity is truth', part of his meaning was that truth is not something objective, 'over there', to which one can appropriately relate in a detached way. The truth grabs one, challenges one, demands a response if it is to be known; the truth is elicited by love, and the truth is itself to be loved. The truth is not something to which one may relate in a dispassionate way; indeed for Kierkegaard as for Christian orthodoxy, the truth is not a 'something' but personal, a Someone; and that Someone is Jesus Christ, who calls to discipleship, to searching for and following the truth. The truth that cannot be possessed possesses the disciple. But Kierkegaard goes further: there is not, he says, a natural and universal tendency to recognize and follow truth. Human beings are in *error*, turned away from truth, content to live in lies rather than living in the truth. They need to be brought up short, shocked perhaps, caught unawares, surprised or startled if they are to turn towards the truth and be reconciled to that from which they have been alienated. This all suggests some features which should mark Christian communication, in the mass media or in more traditional forms of communication. Its function is not to repeat the conventional wisdom of the age, adding only a religious sugar-coating; it is essentially against the stream, at odds with the *Zeitgeist*. It should arouse passion, not simply a cold intellectual interest. It is challenging, disturbing, unexpected. It calls for decision and for action. It may be consoling, but it is not amusing. It makes a claim and it calls for a response. We should expect many people to turn away from it, to switch channels to something less demanding, confusing, disturbing. So here's a problem for the viewer statistics! And here also is a reminder of how easily Christian communication becomes diluted and attenuated if the market forces of the modern mass media are allowed to determine content and presentation.

Communication and community

Kierkegaard also taught that communication draws people into community, into communion – and only in communion is the fullest and most authentic communication possible, when people speak the truth in love.[9] Both Socrates and Jesus insisted that they could only have as their disciples those whom they loved; only so is the most profound and honest communication possible. Communication of truth creates and sustains community – and destroys the bogus fellowship that rests upon lies. Yet the community does not *possess* the truth, it cannot use or shape or transform the truth as it wills. It stands under the truth, it is sustained by the truth, it passes on the truth. And this truth is an explosive challenge to closed and rigid forms of social structure – and to narrow, complacent ways of being Church.

Socrates, who sought truth with a total passion, and Jesus, whose disciples declared him to be the truth embodied, each represented, simply by being who they were, an inescapably seditious challenge to the existing social order. For they reveal in their various ways that these orders, which claim to be based upon truth and ceaselessly promote this claim, in fact are founded upon lies, have inherently unstable foundations and will inevitably collapse. Václav Havel pointed to a similar situation in the now mercifully defunct dictatorships of Eastern Europe and reflected also, he argued, in the consumerist societies of the West. The East holds up a mirror to the West. Both systems depend on ideologies, opposed in form but very similar in content, which have the function of providing people 'with the illusion that the system is in harmony with the human order and with the order of the universe'.[10] These ideologies, sedulously fostered by the media, legitimate power by suggesting that 'the centre of power is identical with the centre of truth'.[11] Ideology thus serves to internalize a false reality, to convince people that the lie is the truth, to encourage them to live happily in the lie.

But Havel affirms, and his own personal experience is here very much to the point, that even in a totalitarian dictatorship, even when the media have become an instrument for presenting lies as truth, it is possible for individuals or groups to live in the truth. This means dissent, for living in the truth is inevitably a direct challenge to the whole vast interlocking structure of lies. Hence Havel's call is to all of us, but particularly to those involved in communication:

> It seems to me that all of us, East and West, face one fundamental task from which all else should follow. That task is one of resisting vigilantly, thoughtfully and attentively, but at the same time with total dedication, at every step and everywhere, the irrational momentum of anonymous, impersonal and inhuman power – the power of ideologies, systems, *apparat*, bureaucracy, artificial languages and political slogans. We must resist their complex and wholly alienating pressure, whether it takes the form of consumption, advertising, repression, technology, the cliché – all of which are blood brothers of fanaticism and the wellspring of totalitarian thought.[12]

Even the total political control of the media cannot destroy truth if there are some dissenters, some who are striving to live in the truth. Even when lies are propagated as truth and power systematically supports falsehood, sooner or later there is someone who, like the little boy in the Hans Christian Andersen's story, tells the simple truth: 'The Emperor has no clothes on!' and such simple truths are inherently seditious.

Indirect communication

Kierkegaard also stressed the need for what he called 'indirect communication' of Christian truth. Religious and moral truths cannot be packaged and transferred or sold without distortion of a fundamental sort. These are matters which affect the deepest levels of a person's being. They must be appropriated, welcomed, responded to, and allowed to shape the personality and behaviour. They cannot be imposed by power or transferred as commodities in a market transaction. They must be subjectively appropriated. But truth is often uncongenial; men and women prefer to turn away from truth, and shut their eyes and block their ears. Accordingly Kierkegaard compares the Christian communicator to the Socratic gadfly, stinging people awake, rousing them from their dreams and their dogmatic slumbers so that they may encounter reality, truth. The gadfly's task is to disturb accepted certainties and challenge the received wisdom, allowing people space to engage for themselves with the truth which must pervade their inwardness before it makes acclaim to the public domain. Each person must appropriate the truth individually; the communicator's task, according to Kierkegaard (and here again he follows Socrates) is *maiuetic* – the midwife role, assisting to bring to birth, to bring into the open, the truth that the midwife has not created or shaped, and does not control. This all suggests important lessons for the Christian communicator today. The task is to help people to become open to the truth, and then the communicator must step back and allow a direct relationship to the truth to be established. The gadfly role suggests that the truth is often best expressed through the unexpected, the shocking and the disturbing. Authentic Christian communication perhaps takes place at least as much through drama, news, documentary programmes as through the formal 'God-slot'. The test is the ability of a programme to plumb the depths and reach the heights, to get at people's hearts and wills rather than shimmering over the surface.

Kierkegaard is, of course, presenting an understanding of *Christian* communication which is, I believe, both a call to the recovery of Christian authenticity in communication and also has very important general lessons for effective and non-oppressive communication in general. The ultimate model is God's self-communication, which down the ages has taken place 'in many and various ways', but is summed up fully in the person of the Son who communicates perfectly the reality of God, and to whom people are able freely to relate.[13] Since the truth ultimately is personal and we are called to relate to truth in a personal way, it follows that narrative and image are particularly apt forms of communication. The modern media can play a liberating role here, restoring the centrality of narrative and image in communication and safeguarding against some kinds of theological reductionism, particularly the assumption that the Word, the message, the truth, can be adequately captured in words.

The modern media challenge the wordy didacticism of most theology, and through a renewed emphasis on story and on image help in the restoration of the Reformation insights that while the truth cannot be captured in words, the words that point to it must be in a language 'understanded of the people', and not in some esoteric academic jargon, the modern equivalent of church Latin.

A great deal has been written on the dangers of the modern mass media. The media are not unreasonably presented as for many people fulfilling the traditional functions of religion in a modern consumerist society as well as giving a twist to the practice of religion in its more traditional and organized forms. As an alternative Church which presents a kind of world-view which is experienced as coherent and total and which is normally under the effective control of power and wealth, it is not surprising that Christians often find the media threatening and dangerous, a competitor rather than an ally, an idol rather than a place where the truth may be encountered. But there is another side to the matter which I have tried to suggest in this chapter. If Christian communicators do not lose their nerve or compromise with the false values and untruths so often promoted in our society, they may find that the media can trigger and strongly assist important styles of theological renewal, deepening the understanding of the Gospel and the Church, and presenting opportunities of Christian communication in the modern age which are in fact given by God.

14

Welfare and human nature: public theology in welfare policy debates[1]

In the present debates about welfare, theological issues inevitably arise, usually relating to understandings of human nature and of community. How can public theology relate constructively to consultations about welfare, and what kind of theology is the most apt, relevant and incisive contributor? Key Christian ethical and theological ideas have been major factors in shaping welfare policy in the past both in Britain and the US, and various types of public theology have been brought into play. In today's more secular and plural atmosphere, despite determined efforts to base policy on purely secular considerations and premises, specifically and identifiably Christian notions of human nature, character, behaviour, duty and community remain influential in the ongoing debate – or are they perhaps no more than ornaments in a discussion which proceeds on entirely secular assumptions? In the past a 'public theology' underlying public policy was commonly assumed, and discussions about welfare, poverty and deprivation could seldom proceed without frequent explicit theological reference. And today, despite secularization and the growth of pluralism, public theology is surprisingly vigorous in public debate, either explicitly or just below the surface.

It is clear that different approaches to welfare provision depend on varying understandings of character, behaviour, and human nature. And accounts of human nature in turn reflect underlying assumptions about relationships and reality, the way things are and the way things ought to be. In dealing with such issues, theologians have always had to relate their thinking to the secular ideologies of welfare of the day.

Traditionally, thinkers of the left have emphasized social conditioning: the poor are the victims of social forces, with very limited ability to respond creatively or responsibly to their situation. Change the society by way of innovative and imaginative social engineering, they taught, and you will transform character, behaviour, and indeed human nature itself. Left-wingers tended to be optimistic about the possibilities of transformation and confident in their ability to usher in a utopia and a new human nature once they had control of the levers of power; their understanding of social reform was rather mechanical. People were 'pawns' who could be moved around for their own good and the welfare of society; ultimately they could be remade by judicious policymaking so that they became 'knights'. The shapers of policy assumed that they were themselves knights, disinterested and altruistic, capable of determining with substantial objectivity what was good for others. Even 'knaves' could usually be transformed into knights by calculated changes in their social circumstances.[2] At the extreme, this way of thinking is both utopian and authoritarian.

Right-wing thinkers were more aware of boundaries, limitations and what they believed to be the recalcitrance of an unmalleable human nature, the same always and everywhere, capable of subverting the most idealistic of projects of reform. In theological terms, right-wing thinkers were Augustinian, constantly aware of sin and of the fallenness of things. The art of politics for them consisted of diverting the flow of the sin, aggression and selfishness of people into channels where it could be converted into an energy that holds society together and produces the goods that all need. People were for the most part seen by right-wing thinkers as knaves who did not naturally and spontaneously act altruistically, generously or justly, but wise policy could put selfishness and even sin to work for the good of all. As David Hume put it:

> Political writers have established it as a maxim, that, in contriving any system of government, and fixing the several checks and controls of the constitution, every man ought to be supposed a *knave* and to have no other end, in all his actions, than private interest. By this interest we must govern him, and, by means of it, make him, notwithstanding his insatiable avarice and ambition, co-operate to public good.[3]

Welfare policy, for such thinkers, must go with the grain of human nature; otherwise it is doomed to frustration and becomes destructive. Selfishness rather than altruism, self-interest rather than generosity, must be the basis for welfare provision. Welfare recipients are not passive pawns, but knaves who will play the system, given half a chance. The framers of welfare policy must be able to show that welfare provision is in some clear sense in the interest of all. At its extreme, this line of thinking becomes cynical in its realism.

These two poles are understood in modern social theory in almost entirely secular terms, although occasionally there is an awareness that theological notions still lurk in the discussion like ghosts in the machine. For its part, theology is sometimes overawed in face of social science and ends up reflecting the latest sociological orthodoxy, or claiming that it can proceed entirely independently of social theory, presenting as it were a 'pure theology' which owes nothing to social science or ideology. That public theology can still be recognized as relevant and constructive is evidenced by the very different, but immensely influential, challenges to the simplistic optimism of liberal anthropology that came from Reinhold Niebuhr and Karl Barth in the middle decades of the twentieth century – reminders that theology may still today offer a crucial word which is recognized as true by many who do not share Christian faith. Perhaps something like that might be public theology's distinctive contribution to the contemporary debate about welfare in the volatile, fragmented and confusing public forum of today.

I will explore two examples of the kinds of public theology that were influential in relation to welfare issues at two past moments – the nineteenth-century debate about 'pauperism', and the discussion of post-war reconstruction, and in particular the kind of welfare state that was desired, during and immediately after the Second World War. I then turn to the rather odd phenomenon that in today's very much more secular atmosphere, public theology still seems a frequent, perhaps indispensable, element in the debate about the future of welfare. These three moments suggest very different understandings of the scope and nature of public theology, largely because of the varying place of religion, the Church and theology in the social scenario over time.

A theology of pauperism[4]

A typical nineteenth-century theology of welfare might well be represented by the towering figure of Thomas Chalmers, theologian, leader of the Free Church of Scotland and distinguished intellectual. Chalmers was as significant in his day in political economy as in theology; he was one of the leaders in what Boyd Hilton calls 'the baptism of political economy',[5] and he even received the accolade of being denounced by Marx as 'the arch-Parson Thomas Chalmers', a pupil of 'Parson Malthus'.[6] Chalmers taught Political Economy as a branch of Natural Theology.[7] For him, public theology as natural theology was so closely associated with classical political economy as to be almost indistinguishable. The clear implication of this was, of course, that the market was a kind of divine ordering, and therefore to that extent beyond human critique or control. 'The whole science of Political Economy', he wrote, 'is full of those exquisite adaptations to the wants and the comforts of human life, which bespeak the skill of a master-hand, in the adjustment of its laws, and the working of its profoundly constructed mechanism.'[8] The workings of the market point to a beneficent God who gives good gifts to his children through market transactions, which harness human self-interest to the achievement of the common good. Thus the selfishness of human beings results in 'cheapening and multiplying to the uttermost all the articles of human enjoyment, and establishing a thousand reciprocities of mutual interest in the world'; accordingly it displays 'the benevolence and comprehensive wisdom of God'.[9]

The market, as part of the providential ordering of a just and loving God, is beyond critique, and should be left undisturbed to pursue its benign course. Interference with the market causes social havoc, and transforms the economy into a malign, destructive force. For the mechanism of trade demonstrates 'the hand of a righteous Deity' in all its free working.

In addition to this sacralizing of economic processes, Chalmers was also one of the leading figures in commending a way to combat what people at the time called 'pauperism'. The term is significant. It suggests that the problem is *poor people*, who develop in an industrial society communities and cultures and patterns of behaviour which actually perpetuate and exacerbate poverty. Essentially, Chalmers taught, pauperism is caused, not by society or economic structures, or by injustice, but by interference with economic processes. By 'trying to mend the better mechanism which nature had instituted', evils such as the multiplication of pauperism are engendered.[10] The Poor Law taking the place of private and ecclesiastical charity, Chalmers believed, simply makes the situation worse, as do common patterns of behaviour and attitudes among poor people. The solution to pauperism is also largely in the hands of the poor themselves; charity and government intervention often do more harm than good. Official policies of relief which ran counter to 'economic laws' usually make the situation worse. In Malthusian tones, Chalmers declared:

> There is no possible help for them [the poor] if they will not help themselves. It is to a rise and reformation in the habits of our peasantry that we look for deliverance, and not to the impotent crudities of a speculative legislation... This will at length save

the country from the miseries of a redundant population – and this we apprehend, to be the great, the only specific for its worst moral and its worst political disorders.[11]

'The remedy against the extension of pauperism', he declares elsewhere, 'does not lie in the liberalities of the rich; it lies in the hearts and habits of the poor. Plant in their bosoms a principle of independence. Give a high tone of delicacy to their characters. Teach them to recoil from pauperism as a degradation.'[12] The state and the broader community are not responsible for 'pauperism', nor is its solution in their hands: 'Neither government nor the higher classes of the state, have any share in those economical distresses to which every trading and manufacturing nation is exposed', for 'the high road to the secure and permanent prosperity of labourers, is through the medium of their own sobriety, and intelligence, and virtue'.[13]

Paupers have no claim in justice; only on the compassion of their neighbours, most desirably expressed in Chalmers's view through a revitalized parish system. The local community, best represented by the parishes of an established Church in which the rich and the poor are held together in mutual responsibility, was the most appropriate agency for *disciplining* and caring for paupers, for the local community knew the individuals and families concerned, as well as local conditions, and could adapt their treatment appropriately. The Church, in Chalmers's thought, while it had close relations to the state, was essentially a body independent of the state. In spiritual and moral matters it had its own proper sphere, in which the state should not interfere.

Chalmers resisted with vehemence the suggestion that the Scottish Poor Law should be reformed to make it more liberal and to give the state a greater role. The Poor Law reformers, led by Professor William Alison, showed that less was done for the poor in Scotland than in other European countries. But their proposal that there should be a massive increase in government funding for the relief of poverty was denounced by the church journal, *The Witness*, as 'a mere physical remedy for a moral disease'.[14] This typifies the whole approach: poverty is a spiritual and moral ailment of the poor, to be cured by spiritual and moral change on their part. The poor were divided into the deserving and the undeserving, or those that can be helped and the unhelpable.[15] It was as if the poor had a different, and inferior, human nature from that of the more prosperous members of society. But the leaders in Church and state were on the whole assumed to be capable of rising above their own selfish interests to embrace a wise and chastened concern for the welfare of all.

Chalmers's social thought was profoundly conservative; he saw the social as well as the economic system as part of the divine ordering of things, and thus as beyond question.[16] At the laying of the foundation stone of New College, Edinburgh, he declared:

> We leave to others the passions and politics of this world, and nothing will ever be taught, I trust, in any of our [theological] halls, which shall have the remotest tendency to disturb the existing order of things, or to confound the ranks and distinctions which now obtain in society.[17]

Pauperism and economic distress were caused by well-intentioned tinkerings with God-given systems, and the solution depended upon the character of the poor and a true, that is Christian, account of human nature, together with the moral paternalism of an established Church which was concerned with nurturing the poor in virtue and responding wisely and guardedly to the misery of the poorest.

We have in Chalmers an example of a kind of public theology which was immensely influential in policymaking. It rested on an apparently Calvinist/Augustinian account of human nature, but it embraced and endorsed almost without qualification the dominant contemporary economic and social theories. Its central problem was that which Barth identified a century later: a freefloating natural theology has an inbuilt tendency to sanctify existing orders and to assimilate to secular theories and philosophies. Chalmers's account of human nature in fact owed more to Adam Smith than to the gospel, and it suggested behaviour towards the poor that was often callous and even cynical rather than generous. Perhaps Donald Macleod is right in suggesting that it is not theology at all, because '[Chalmers] is merely lending the weight of his authority as a churchman to a purely secular economic theory'.[18]

In Chalmers, then, we find a natural theology which claims to be detached from revelation and Scripture and grounded on reason, a kind of prelude to revealed theology. As such it is explicitly detached from biblical narrative and from explicitly Christian insights. It is not surprising perhaps that such a natural theology is peculiarly liable to take on the colour of its context, even when this involves a rather sharp contrast with dominant biblical attitudes to the poor, for example.

Chalmers's social theology attempted, with some success, to set the terms of debate in the public forum. In this respect his project was similar to the recent endeavour of some prominent US Catholic thinkers who see contemporary public discourse as at the mercy both of special interests and of ideological distortion. Accordingly they

offer the natural law approach of Catholic social teaching as a structural resource for public debate and for adjudicating between the
various interest groups' claims, just as Chalmers offered 'natural
theology'. American society, Weigel, Neuhaus, McCann and others
believe, is at a 'Catholic moment' in which coherent ethical discourse
based on Catholic understandings of natural law might give the
Church a leading role in public moral discourse, and the public forum
an objective language for debate.[19]

W. D. Lindsey, in a fascinating article, sees McCann's proposal as 'a
strategy of management that will "orchestrate" dissonant voices so that
their unique tonalities will be muted and their specific textures
suppressed'.[20] The structure of the argument, Lindsey argues, is disinterested and claims a kind of objectivity; but in fact it is intended to
discipline dissident voices, all positions which unashamedly claim to
represent special interests, and all other approaches which claim to be
privileged. Both a 'preferential option for the poor' and a Niebuhrian
understanding of the task as the balancing out of competing claims to
reach a proximate and temporary settlement are excluded. McCann's
position, claims Lindsey, is 'first and foremost *managerial* – a strategy
for disciplining and silencing difficult Others'. The Church and theology
appear as legislator and law enforcer, the body which makes the rules
and the referee or umpire which enforces them. It does not have
interests of its own, or so it pretends, nor does it promote the special
interests of any group. Its task is not that of attending to, incorporating,
privileging or responding to the voice of the disempowered, the
voiceless, the Other. Rather, it regulates the game magisterially, with
authority, from above not from the margins, arbitrating from on high
on the ebb and flow of the disputes in the public square. Under the
appearance of objectivity it is in fact more malleable than it purports
to be, and since it is not rooted in the distinctive particularities of the
Christian message there is a constant danger that it ends up reflecting
dominant ideas of the time. The example of Chalmers and others in the
nineteenth century might make us cautious about embracing too enthu-
siastically today such a public theology from above which is essentially
a natural theology as an adequate account of Christian responsibility
for the welfare of the poor and the marginalized.[21]

Recent social encyclicals base their arguments far more on biblical
material than was the case in the past. While this does not necessarily
involve a move away from natural law as a mode of reasoning or the
suggestion that Catholic social teaching can be commended entirely
independently of specifically Christian arguments, it is a welcome

recognition that Christian social teaching cannot be adequately treated independently of the gospel. While documents such as the English Roman Catholic bishops' report on *The Common Good*, produced in the run-up to the 1997 election are very useful and significant contributions to debate, it is extremely doubtful whether they can or should provide a framework for political deliberation in a secular, pluralist age.

Depression, warfare and welfare

When the welfare settlement in Britain of the 1940s was established it had strong convictions at its roots, convictions which had been shaped and nourished by the experiences of the Depression and of the Second World War, and which were in some cases explicitly Christian.[22] Cumulatively it was a vision of society which led some people to a willingness to make sacrifices of their interests for a greater social good; it acted for a time as a kind of restraint to collective selfishness, or at least the open glorification of selfishness.

A major factor in the shaping of proposals for a welfare state during the Second World War was revulsion at the attitudes, procedures and institutions which emerged from the dominant nineteenth-century social theories, strongly and effectively endorsed by public theologies of the style of Thomas Chalmers. In reaction, many influential theorists and public figures now spoke of the poor as entirely *victims* of social processes who deserved compensation from society as a right without any regard to their behaviour, responsibility or contribution. Discussions of behaviour and character, which had been so central in the nineteenth century, were now taboo.[23] Such an account of human beings as victims, or 'pawns', is perhaps understandable as a reaction to a demeaning and inadequate system, but it does not itself accord much dignity to the human being, and seems equally unbalanced in the new direction.

The British welfare state as it emerged in the late 1940s was not simply a reaction against the individualistic excesses of the nineteenth century. Out of the experiences of the Depression and the Second World War there emerged a new solidarity in shared suffering and shared joys, together with a determination that the sacrifices of the hard years of unemployment and hunger marches and of the war should not be wasted, but that a better Britain in which William Beveridge's five 'giants' – Want, Disease, Ignorance, Squalor and Idleness – were defeated should emerge. During the war, middle-class people who had been insulated from the worst horrors of the Depression came face to face with children evacuated from the slums of the cities, malnourished, unhealthy and unschooled. They saw what poverty and slum conditions did to children. The two nations met one another and felt in a new way responsibility for and to one another. As a result, hardly anyone questioned the need for cheap or free school meals and the provision of milk and orange juice and cod liver oil for all children. The common goal of winning the war united all classes in a new quality of fellowship, which a huge majority of the population wished to see continue after the war.

Out of the war emerged a new and positive vision of the state and its role in society, radically different from the view common in the 1920s and 30s that the state was on the side of the owners and the managers and against the workers. The state was now seen as the genial guardian of the common good, helping to forge community and capable of looking after the weak and the vulnerable on behalf of the whole society. Few people questioned that welfare was best provided by the state, which had shown that it could deliver welfare on a just and acceptable basis in time of warfare. In peacetime it could do the same. The state, political leaders, civil servants and professionals were on the whole trusted to behave altruistically.

Frank Field, the Christian socialist and for some time Minister for Welfare Reform in the UK government, believes that the welfare state as it was established in the 1940s was based largely on an unduly optimistic understanding of human nature and destiny. This, Field argues, was expressed particularly clearly in the work of Richard Titmuss. Titmuss taught that an effective and just welfare system both depends on, and in its turn encourages, a high degree of altruism. His classic study of blood donation policies, *The Gift Relationship* (1973), provided some empirical support to this notion, and a kind of general rationale of the pattern of welfare provision that emerged after the Second World War. Titmuss showed that the British system whereby volunteers freely provide their blood to help strangers through a nationwide service was more effective than a more mercenary provision of blood where donors demand payment, and the market nature of the transaction makes the system more expensive and the dangers of lethal infection greater. Altruism, it seemed, had been demonstrated to be more efficient and cheaper than a system which depends on self-interest and emphasizes market transactions. Altruism rather than self-interest, Titmuss argued, binds people together in fellowship, giving practical expression to their responsibility for and to one another. The Titmussian welfare state was a noble project for the moralization of society. In this respect alone it was like Chalmers's social vision – only far less judgemental.

But Titmuss's approach was also top-down. The other side of this project for the promotion of altruism among the people was that Titmuss and his school – indeed Fabian social reformers in general – had a striking confidence in the altruism and ability to rise above their self-interest of intellectuals, bureaucrats, politicians, social workers, and others from the ranks of the powerful. The Platonic idea that Guardians, intellectuals, when properly educated have a unique ability to take an objective view and decide what was good for others had been recently revived by Karl Mannheim in his *Ideology and Utopia* (1936). It was easy for left-wing intellectuals to see their role as doing good to others and defining what is good for them. This is, of course, classically paternalist and top-down. It does not recognize that intellectuals and professionals have their own interests, and unavoidably these interests often, and usually unconsciously, give a skew to their judgements. It is no easier for intellectuals than it is for other people to be altruistic, and their claim to be surveying reality from a mountaintop of objectivity is usually largely spurious. Furthermore, because of their position in society, their view is necessarily partial and distorted. For these reasons, well-intentioned schemes of welfare devised by intelligent and caring people and imposed in a paternalistic way often went seriously wrong. Power is often abused, and welfare schemes turn out often to do more for those already prosperous than for the poor.[24] Paternalism and a failure to take fully into account the pervasiveness of sin are deep-seated in British Fabianism and in Christian socialism. For Frank Field and others it is clear that Titmuss-style paternalism and rather simplistic emphasis on altruism and human goodness don't work. Indeed, they make things worse.[25]

British theological advocates and defenders of the welfare state were not hard to find, but it is not so easy to show that public theology *shaped* the welfare state to any significant degree. William Temple, Archbishop of York and then of Canterbury, declared that the Beveridge Report on social security was the first attempt ever to embody the whole ethic of the Sermon on the Mount in an act of parliament! As a thinker he was influenced, like most other social reformers at the time, by the philosophical idealism of T. H. Green, Edward Caird, and the 'Balliol men'. Theologically he argued that the incarnation provided a kind of template for reality. For most of his life his social theology was typically liberal, progressivist, optimistic and moralistic. He was deeply shaken by the rise of Nazism and the outbreak of the Second World War, which seemed to confirm the validity of the attack on theological liberalism associated with the

names of Karl Barth and Reinhold Niebuhr. Temple's public theology
moved from a typically liberal optimism to a more Niebuhrian
position. His influence on the post-war reshaping of education was
notable, but his little book, *Christianity and Social Order* (1942),
had the general effect of enlisting Christian support for the development of the welfare state as an expression of a Christian social order,
rather than making a specific contribution towards its shaping.

In Scotland the Commission on God's Will in the Present Crisis, led
by Principal John Baillie, was quite explicit in calling for sweeping
changes in the way British society was organized in an egalitarian
direction. It in effect mobilized a major denomination behind the idea
of a welfare state as it was to be established after 1945. Neither
Temple nor Baillie in fact did much more than endorse on theological
grounds the emerging left-of-centre welfare consensus.

The more original, creative and influential theologian was in fact a
lay economic historian, R. H. Tawney. He affirmed that Christians
could not responsibly abstract themselves from the debate about
welfare, for they had important and distinctive contributions to offer.
He himself attacked the mammon worship which he believed
dominated capitalist society, and commended Christian values, usually
in secular garb. He saw the issue as fundamentally a religious one, and
'the proper bodies to propagate it are the Christian churches'.[26]

For Tawney, Christianity presented a true understanding of human
nature, taking into account both the heights and the depths of which
humans were capable, and resolutely affirming human equality as the
only basis for true fellowship. Human beings have the right to equal
consideration. Equality does not mean a dreary sameness; for Tawney
the flowering of individuality and freedom is possible only if inequal-
ities are significantly diminished. Society should cultivate this common
humanity by putting stress on institutions and procedures which meet
common needs, and are the source of common enjoyments and enlightenment. But it is, I think, fair to say that Tawney was more revered than
listened to, especially after the initial post-war euphoria was over. But
his ideas, along with those of John Macmurray, another Christian
thinker who was for a time almost forgotten, have recently had a
renaissance.

In general I believe that David Nicholls is right in suggesting that a
close relationship existed between Christian theology and the development of the welfare state in Britain. But the theology that was
operative was largely based on a benign liberal notion of a benevolent
and paternal God; sin, selfishness and the shadow side of human

nature were rarely in evidence.[27] Theology in Britain in the 1940s no longer set the terms of the debate, but it was still an influential player. On the whole it operated by endorsing policies developed on a secular basis rather than itself shaping policy.

Welfare and human nature since the 1990s

Lady Thatcher inaugurated the modern renaissance of conviction politics in Britain. The 'Sermon on the Mound' which she delivered in Edinburgh in 1988, for instance, claimed to root both the general orientation and the particular policies of her government squarely on the central affirmations of the Christian faith. After a generation when most people in Britain assumed that politics was either a pragmatic matter of 'fine-tuning heaven', or a sordid business of horse-trading, when politicians such as Harold Wilson dismissed any reference to theory or principle as so much 'theology', it was refreshing to find a Prime Minister who affirmed adamantly that fundamental principles mattered, and that religious convictions had a relevance beyond the private and domestic spheres.

Insistently Margaret Thatcher affirmed that she acted on principle, not on expediency, and that this gave her and her government an effective lodestar and a coherent strategy. In a speech she described the orientation of her government:

> It was not a set of policies cobbled together from minute to minute, begged, borrowed or stolen from other people. It was successful because it was based on clear, firmly-held principles which were themselves based on a right understanding of politics, economics and above all human nature.[28]

Lady Thatcher was, of course, recovering an understanding of the necessity of conviction politics, of the place of religion in public debate, and of the importance of a true account of human nature.

There is a vigorous debate today in Britain and the US and in other Western countries as well about the future of welfare, which often makes explicit reference to theories of human nature. This has been sparked off partly by a sense that previous massive welfare projects such as the British welfare state or the American war on poverty have not succeeded, and might in some cases have made the situation worse, as has been argued by theorists such as Charles Murray and Lawrence Mead, and partly by an increasingly widespread conviction that at the root of present problems with welfare lie misunderstandings of human nature, motivation, behaviour and character.

The earliest and strongest critiques of established forms of welfare provision came from the right wing. For example, David Marsland, a British neo-conservative academic, sees the welfare state as corrupting the nation, and wishes to replace it with Victorian self-help. He regards the welfare state as 'a lethal threat to our freedom' which has 'made the British people a nation of greedy wastrels and an ungovernable mob, bereft of values and scornful of rules'. Welfare, he says, damages the economy, creates an underclass, fails to help the needy, and destroys the dynamism necessary for a healthy and prosperous society. We don't need the welfare state, we can't afford it, it doesn't work, and it 'inflicts damaging levels of moral and psychological harm on its supposed beneficiaries'. It is, in fact, he concludes, 'an enemy of society'.[29]

More moderate forms of such arguments are now being used by left-of-centre figures, and sometimes there is explicit reference to the need for religious notions to illuminate the situation and inform policy, even in a radically secularized society. For example, Frank Field has urgently affirmed the need for an adequate and *truthful* account of human nature to undergird policy. And this leads to a new concern in the framing of welfare policy with issues of character and behaviour – matters which in Britain were virtually taboo for several decades. Field believes that the British welfare state as it was established in the 1940s was based, not on R. H. Tawney's Christian understanding of human nature and destiny, but on the unduly optimistic views of Richard Titmuss. Tawney's ability to hold a 'utopian' vision of a fraternal society free from exploitation and injustice, together with a hard-headed realism about political and economic realities, made him concerned not only with goals but with the strategy and tactics of realizing the vision. He was convinced that the Christian vision generated social values which stand in sharp opposition to the operative values of possessive individualism. And his ability to hold together reality and utopia makes him, according to Frank Field, a surer guide than Titmuss in reforming welfare provision.

For Frank Field the simple point so long ignored, that human nature underpins all political activities, must become a central determining force in the political debate on welfare's reconstruction.[30] An effective welfare system, he argues, must be founded on 'a realistic view of human nature' which is unambiguously Christian, for,

> We are less than perfect creatures and it is partly because of this most fundamental aspect of each of us that a distinction has continually to be drawn between where we are now and our destiny, on the one hand, and what might ideally be hoped for

now in the bosom of the family and what can operate in the wider public arena, on the other.[31]

He suggests that a Christian account of human nature, particularly as propounded in the 1940s and 50s by R. H. Tawney, provides a far more adequate foundation for welfare provision than a one-sided stress on altruism because it takes into account the depths as well as the heights of which humans are capable, is hopeful without being naïve, and realistic without becoming cynical. 'Self-interest', Field argues, 'is the most powerful motivating force in each of us.'[32] Self-interest, not altruism, is humankind's main driving force.[33] 'Part of the necessary moral order', he writes, 'is not to do with decrying or thwarting self-interest, but with attempting to satisfy it in a way which is consistent with the public good. The most deadly charge which can be made against Britain's welfare state is that it increasingly ignores this cardinal principle.'[34] In welfare, as in other issues of public policy, the task is 'setting a legal framework where natural decent instincts guided by self-interest are allowed to operate in a manner which enhances the common good'.[35]

Particularly through means-testing, the older form of welfare provision was profoundly corrupting; a reformed welfare system, Field suggests, is capable of contributing effectively towards the remoralization of society. There are feckless, dishonest and idle welfare claimants as in all social groups. But much dishonesty and 'scrounging' is a rational response to the welfare framework which has been imposed from on high by politicians. A properly designed and realistic welfare system is 'one of the great teaching forces open to advanced societies' and a way of affirming right conduct and discouraging wrong conduct.[36]

There are some significant changes of emphasis in the way Field reads Tawney. It is true that Tawney sees human beings as capable of great evil and also as capable of generosity and altruism, as sinners called to salvation, in short. But Tawney is more explicitly egalitarian in his account of human nature, and he roots his egalitarianism in his Christian faith:

In order to believe in human equality it is necessary to believe in God... What is wrong with the modern world is that having ceased to believe in the greatness of God, and therefore the infinite smallness (or greatness – the same thing!) of *man*, it has to invent distinctions between *men*. It does not say, 'I have said, "Ye are gods!"' Nor does it say, 'all flesh is grass'. It can neither rise to the heights nor descend to the depths... What it does say is that *some* men are gods, and that some flesh is grass, and that the former should live off the latter (combined with pâté de foie gras and champagne), and this is false.[37]

Tawney saw welfare as a way of creating greater equality, and emphasized the inevitability of confronting the structures of power which
sustain inequality. He saw inequality and poverty as essentially structural matters, and resisted the tendency which has once again come
into fashion to blame the poor for poverty, and the unemployed for
their lack of work.

It is not necessary for present purposes to pursue the debate stimulated by Frank Field further. I simply want to note that here what I
have elsewhere called a 'theological fragment' has been injected into
public debate in a context where the discourse of politics has become
radically secularized. This fragment – an account of human nature –
is presented as true, its validity being in a sense empirically verifiable.
It cannot claim truth as part of a generally accepted truthful system,
because Christian belief is so widely rejected or misunderstood today.
The truthfulness of the fragment is related to the fact that when it
becomes the presupposition of policy or of behaviour it 'works', while
both naïvely sunny and cynical views of human nature seem to make
problems worse rather than better.[38]

This process of offering fragments of insight may indeed be the most
appropriate contribution of Christian theology to public debate today.
But it has its problems. In the first place, 'theological fragments'
abstracted from their place within the Christian narrative, and unsup-
ported by that narrative, can easily become vulnerable to ideological
distortion and misuse. Indeed, to present the Christian contribution in
terms of timeless general truths, such as an account of human nature,
is inherently problematic. The alternative is not to offer some vast
system of theology or theologically informed moral philosophy, but
rather a series of illuminating fragments which sustain the life of the
community of faith which nurtures and exemplifies them, and claim
also to be in some sense 'public truth'.[39]

Such fragments may be a peculiarly important contribution when
public debate appears to be impoverished, when real issues are being
avoided, old ideologies showing themselves to be exhausted, and
people as a result getting hurt. Frank Field and his colleagues believed
they had identified just such a moment in relation to issues of welfare
and poverty in British public debate. And during the 1997 General
Election the British Churches felt so strongly that the campaign was
avoiding a whole range of vital issues that they produced in time for
the election two major documents – the Roman Catholic Bishops' *The
Common Good* and the Council of Churches of Britain and Ireland's
Unemployment and the Future of Work. Such endeavours to serve and

enrich public discourse can be an important form of confession, especially when people recognize a fragment as true, and trace it back to its provenance, the quarry from which it came.

I have looked, albeit rather cursorily, at three different ways of deploying Christian understandings of human nature in relation to issues of welfare. In the nineteenth century we saw in the thought and work of Thomas Chalmers an account of human nature which claimed to be rooted in a comprehensive system of natural theology. The separation of natural from revealed theology and the paucity of scriptural references made it easy for this way of thinking to capitulate to the dominant economic ideology of the time. In Britain, at any rate, the prevailing theological thrust in the 1940s in relation to welfare was simply to endorse the plans for post-war reconstruction developed by William Beveridge and others. It is not easy to argue that theology had any significant role in shaping the proposals for the welfare state, or examining them critically. In both these situations the Christian faith and the Christian Church in Britain had a very much more prominent and influential position than they have today. Theology was expected to have a say, and was listened to with respect.

That has all changed today. Theology has to earn its right to be heard in the public realm, but in some ways it is easier today for theology to speak for the marginalized, the poor and the voiceless than it was in the past. Theology should seek opportunities of helping when policy debates get into the kind of impasse that hurts people and communities. It is just this role that Frank Field hopes a Christian account of human nature can serve. But the setting for such a theory of human nature matters. The example of Thomas Chalmers might warn us about the dangers of locating it within a natural theology, or indeed within a repristinated public philosophy based on natural law and claiming to express universal and rational insights, rather than in the setting of the Christian narrative. But if an account of human nature is indeed an attempt to offer as a 'theological fragment' distinctive and truthful insights of Christian faith, and particularly a preferential option for the poor, it may be both a constructive contribution to public debate and a way of confessing the faith in the public realm.

Notes

Chapter 1. Theology in fragments

1 Samuel Wells, *Improvisation: The Drama of Christian Ethics* (Grand Rapids: Brazos Press, 2004).

2 Plato, *Apology* 30.6.

3 Luke 23.14.

4 John 3.21 NRSV.

5 Alexander Dru (ed.), *The Journals of Kierkegaard* (London: Oxford University Press, 1938), p. 583.

6 Walter Lowrie, *Kierkegaard* (London: Oxford University Press, 1938), pp. 507–8; S. Kierkegaard, *Papers and Journals: A Selection* (trans. A. Hannay; Harmondsworth: Penguin, 1996), pp. 491–2.

7 Cited in Lowrie, *Kierkegaard*, p. 507.

8 C. Wright Mills, *The Sociological Imagination* (Oxford: Oxford University Press, 1959), pp. 195–226.

9 M. F. A. Voltaire, *Letter to d'Alembert*, 23 June 1760.

10 See Marcella Althaus-Reid's comments in this connection in Andrew Morton and William Storrar (eds.), *A Public Theology for the 21st Century* (London: T & T Clark, 2004), p. 369.

11 See Elaine Graham's comments in Morton and Storrar, *Public Theology*, p. 402.

12 F. Dostoevsky, *The Brothers Karamazov* (London: Heinemann, 1912), pp. 52–3.

13 Thomas Hobbes, *Leviathan*, Part 3, ch. 32.

14 *Book of Common Order of the Church of Scotland* (Edinburgh: St Andrew Press, 1994), p. 89.

15 1 John 4.7–8 (NRSV); my emphasis.

16 1 John 4.16 (NRSV).

17 Numbers 12.6–8.

18 1 Cor. 13.12.

19 Morton and Storrar, *Public Theology*, pp. 218–19.

20 Cited in Stephen K. White, *Political Theory and Postmodernism* (Cambridge: Cambridge University Press, 1991), pp. 4–5.

21 Václav Havel, *Living in Truth* (London: Faber & Faber, 1987), p. 54.

22 Havel, *Living in Truth*, p. 39.

23 Havel, *Living in Truth*, p. 50.

[24] See Zygmunt Bauman, *Life in Fragments: Essays in Post-modern Morality* (Oxford: Blackwell, 1995), pp. 44–55.

[25] Alasdair MacIntyre, *After Virtue: A Study in Moral Theory* (London: Duckworth, 1981), pp. 104–5.

[26] MacIntyre, *After Virtue*, p. 236.

[27] Larry L. Rasmussen, *Moral Fragments and Moral Community: A Proposal for Church in Society* (Minneapolis: Fortress, 1993), p. 11.

[28] Jeffrey Stout, *Ethics after Babel: The Languages of Morals and their Discontents* (Boston: Beacon Press, 1988), p. 74.

[29] See Jeffrey Stout, *Democracy and Tradition* (Princeton: Princeton University Press, 2004), p. 225.

[30] See Charles R. Pinches, *Theology and Action: After Theory in Christian Ethics* (Grand Rapids: Eerdmans, 2002) for a shrewd critique of the idea of bricolage, esp. pp. 5–7.

[31] MacIntyre, *After Virtue*, pp. 244–5.

[32] S. Hauerwas, *The Peaceable Kingdom: A Primer in Christian Ethics* (London: SCM Press, 1983), p. 99. The phrase is repeated frequently in Hauerwas's writings.

[33] S. Hauerwas, *Christian Existence Today* (Durham, NC: Labyrinth Press, 1988), p. 73.

[34] Stout, *Democracy and Tradition*, p. 110.

[35] *Lumen Gentium* 1.1.

[36] *The Uppsala Report 1968* (Geneva: WCC, 1968), p. 17.

[37] This paragraph is much indebted to G. Gassmann's article, 'The Church as Sacrament, Sign and Instrument', in Gennadios Limouris (ed.), *Church, Kingdom, World: The Church as Mystery and Prophetic Sign* (Geneva: World Council of Churches, 1986), pp. 1–17.

[38] Notice that Z. Bauman characterizes 'the postmodern perspective' as 'above all the tearing off of the mask of illusions; the recognition of certain pretences as false and certain objectives as neither attainable or, for that matter, desirable'. *Postmodern Ethics* (Oxford: Blackwell, 1993), p. 3.

[39] John 6.51.

[40] This section is a development of my 'Afterword – Working in the Quarry: A Response to the Colloquium', in Morton and Storrar, *Public Theology*, pp. 436–8.

[41] F. A. Hayek, *The Intellectuals and Socialism* (London: Institute of Economic Affairs, 1998), p. 26.

Chapter 2. The mystery of the human person in community

[1] The first version of this essay was prepared for the Faith and Order Commission of the World Council of Churches's Study Group on Theological Anthropology.

[2] Augustine, *Confessions* 10.1.

[3] See the illuminating discussion in A. A. McFadyen, *The Call to Personhood* (Cambridge: Cambridge University Press, 1990), ch. 1.

[4] Genesis 1.26–27, NRSV.

[5] For still useful studies, see David S. Cairns, *The Image of God in Man* (London: Collins, 1973), and G. C. Berkouwer, *Man: The Image of God* (Grand Rapids: Eerdmans, 1962).

[6] Jonathan Sacks, *The Dignity of Difference* (London: Continuum, 2002), p. 92.

[7] Joe Corrie, 'The Image o' God', in Meg Bateman *et al.* (eds.), *Scottish Religious Poetry: An Anthology* (Edinburgh: St Andrew Press, 2000), p. 230.

[8] For a fuller treatment of this see my *On Human Worth: A Christian Vindication of Equality* (London: SCM Press, 2001), esp. ch. 3. Chesterton's adage is very similar to an old rabbinic saying, cited by Jonathan Sacks in his *The Dignity of Difference*, p. 60.

[9] See Robert Veatch, *The Foundations of Justice: Why the Retarded and the Rest of Us have Claims to Equality* (New York: Oxford University Press, 1986).

[10] Sacks, *The Dignity of Difference*, p. 17.

[11] Sacks, *The Dignity of Difference*, p. 166.

[12] Genesis 2.18.

[13] This insight has been particularly influential among the communitarians, and was classically expressed in the thought of the Christian philosopher John Macmurray.

[14] *The Church Hymnary* (trans. T. Carlyle; London: Oxford University Press, 3rd edn, 1973), no. 406.

[15] 2 Cor. 4.4; Col. 1.15.

[16] E. Jüngel, *Karl Barth: A Theological Legacy* (Philadelphia: Westminster, 1985), p. 128; my emphasis.

[17] Blaise Pascal, *Pensées* (London: Dent, 1908), no. 526, p. 143.

[18] Philippians 2.5–11.

[19] John D. Zizioulas, *Being as Communion: Studies in Personhood and the Church* (London: Darton, Longman & Todd, 1985).

[20] Zizioulas, *Being as Communion*, p. 15.

[21] I try to do this in relation to Stanley Hauerwas's ecclesiology in 'The Church and the Concentration Camp: Some Reflections on Moral Community', in Mark Theissen Nation and Samuel Wells (eds.), *Faithfulness and Fortitude: In Conversation with the Theological Ethics of Stanley Hauerwas* (Edinburgh: T & T Clark, 2000), pp. 189–207, which is a preliminary version of Chapter 7 of this book.

[22] See Wolfhart Pannenberg, *Anthropology in Theological Perspective* (Philadelphia: Westminster, 1985), ch. 3.

[23] Reinhold Niebuhr, *The Nature and Destiny of Man*. I: *Human Nature* (London: Nisbet, 1941), p. vii.

[24] J. Habermas, 'The New Obscurity and the Exhaustion of Utopian Energies', in *idem* (ed.), *Observations on the Spiritual Situation of the Age* (Cambridge: MIT Press, 1984).

[25] J. Moltmann, *Man: Christian Anthropology in the Conflicts of the Present* (London: SPCK, 1971), pp. 116–17.

Chapter 3. Good and gay?

[1] A version of this chapter will appear in Terry Brown (ed.), *Other Voices, Other Worlds* (London: Darton, Longman and Todd, 2006).

[2] Walter Scott, *Old Mortality* (London: John Nimmo, 1893), p. 283.

Chapter 4. Divinity in use and practice

[1] First published in D. Forrester (ed.), *Theology and Practice* (London: Epworth Press, © Epworth 1990. Used with permission of the Methodist Publishing House), pp. 3–10.

[2] W. Hazlitt (trans.), *The Table Talk of Martin Luther* (London: Bell, 1895), p. 179.

[3] Luther, *Werke* Weimarer Ausgabe, TR1, no. 153.

[4] The text of Mrs Thatcher's speech, together with a critical analysis, is to be found in J. Raban, *God, Man and Mrs Thatcher* (London: Chatto & Windus, 1989).

[5] R. Garaudy, *The Alternative Future* (Harmondsworth: Penguin, 1976), p. 89.

[6] Luther, *Weimarer Ausgabe*, V, 84, 39.

[7] W. Pannenberg, *Theology and the Philosophy of Science* (London: Darton, Longman & Todd, 1976), p. 435.

[8] Pannenberg, *Theology and the Philosophy of Science*, p. 438–9.

Chapter 5. The pastoral significance of Mary: a Protestant perspective

[1] First published in *The Clergy Review*, August 1981, vol. LXVI no. 8:276–281.

[2] H. Küng, *The Council and Reunion* (London: Sheed & Ward, 1962), p. 187.

[3] Quoted in R. Ruether, *Mary – the Feminine Face of the Church* (London: SCM Press, 1979), p. 53. A good instance of what I am objecting to is to be found in Paul VI's 1974 *Marialis Cultus*: 'Mary, the New Woman, stands at the side of Christ, the New Man'.

[4] E. Schillebeeckx, *Mary, Mother of the Redemption* (London: Sheed & Ward, 1964), pp. 180–1.

[5] J. H. Newman, *Essay on the Development of Christian Doctrine* (London: Pickering, 1878), p. 424.

[6] Julian of Norwich, *Revelations of Divine Love*, trans. C. Walters (Harmondsworth: Penguin Books, 1966), pp. 165–73.

[7] *The Prayers and Meditations of St Anselm* (Harmondsworth: Penguin Books, 1973), p. 153, cf. pp. 154–6.

[8] So Karl Barth, *Church Dogmatics*, 1/2 (ed. G. W. Bromily and T. F. Torrance; Edinburgh: T & T Clark, 1956), p. 138.

[9] See Raymond E. Brown *et al.* (eds.), *Mary in the New Testament* (Philadelphia: Fortress, 1978), pp. 286–7.

[10] Brown *et al.*, *Mary in the New Testament*, p. 142.

[11] George Caird, *Pelican Commentary on Luke* (Harmondsworth: Penguin Books, 1963), pp. 55–6.

[12] Ernesto Cardenal, *The Gospel in Solentiname* (Maryknoll, NY: Orbis, 1977), pp. 30–1.

Chapter 6. Biblical interpretation and cultural relativism

[1] First published in Michael Wadsworth (ed.), *Ways of Reading the Bible* (Brighton: Harvester Press, 1981), pp. 118–29.

[2] N. N. Glatzer (ed.), *The Passover Haggadah* (New York: Schocken Books, 1969), pp. 21–3.

[3] S. Kierkegaard, *Efterladte Papirer*, vol XI, p. 389, cited in W. Lowrie, *Kierkegaard* (London: Oxford University Press, 1938), p. 539.

[4] D. E. Nineham, *The Use and Abuse of the Bible* (London: SCM Press, 1976), pp. 5 and 27.

[5] Nineham, *Use and Abuse of the Bible*, p. 229.

[6] Nineham, *Use and Abuse of the Bible*, p. 230.

[7] E. Winslow, cited in K. L. Parry (ed.), *Companion to Congregational Praise* (London: Independent Press, 1953), p. 128.

Chapter 7. The Church and the concentration camp: some reflections on moral community

[1] I am indebted to various friends and colleagues for helpful comments on drafts of this essay, especially to Peter Hayman, Michael Northcott, and my wife, Margaret. It was originally published in Mark Theissen Nation and Samuel Wells (eds.), *Faithfulness and Fortitude: In Conversation with the Theological Ethics of Stanley Hauerwas* (Edinburgh: T & T Clark, 2000), pp. 189–207. Used with the permission of T & T Clark International.

[2] H. J. Goldhagen, *Hitler's Willing Executioners: Ordinary Germans and the Holocaust* (New York: Vintage, 1997), p. 170. Goldhagen gives a succinct and horrifying account of the development and scale of the camps, pp. 167–78.

[3] Martin Gilbert, *The Holocaust: The Jewish Tragedy* (London: Fontana, 1987), pp. 32–3.

[4] Gilbert, *The Holocaust*, p. 40.

[5] Gilbert, *The Holocaust*, pp. 57–8.

[6] Goldhagen, *Hitler's Willing Executioners*, pp. 172–3.

[7] Zygmunt Bauman, *Life in Fragments: Essays in Postmodern Morality* (Oxford: Blackwell, 1995), p. 201. See also his *Modernity and the Holocaust* (Ithaca, NY: Cornell University Press, 1991).

[8] Tzvetan Todorov, *Facing the Extreme: Moral Life in the Concentration Camps* (London: Weidenfeld and Nicolson, 1999).

[9] Todorov, *Facing the Extreme*, p. 35.

[10] Todorov, *Facing the Extreme*, pp. 72–3.

[11] Todorov, *Facing the Extreme*, p. 83.

[12] Todorov, *Facing the Extreme*, p. 84.

[13] Todorov, *Facing the Extreme*, pp. 148–9.

[14] Todorov, *Facing the Extreme*, pp. 57–8.

[15] Todorov, *Facing the Extreme*, p. 86.

[16] Todorov, *Facing the Extreme*, p. 123.

[17] Todorov, *Facing the Extreme*, pp. 96–7.

[18] Stephen Eric Bonner, 'Making Sense of Hell: Three Meditations on the Holocaust', *Political Studies* 47 (1999), p. 328.

[19] Samuel Wells, 'The Disarming Virtue of Stanley Hauerwas', *Scottish Journal of Theology* 52.1 (1999), pp. 82–8.

[20] Stanley Hauerwas, *The Peaceable Kingdom: A Primer in Christian Ethics* (London: SCM Press, 1983), p. 99.

[21] Hauerwas, *The Peaceable Kingdom*, p. 99.

[22] S. Hauerwas, *Christian Existence Today* (Durham, NC: Labyrinth Press, 1988), p. 101.

[23] S. Hauerwas, *Vision and Virtue* (Notre Dame: University of Notre Dame Press, 1981), p. 240.

[24] Hauerwas, *Vision and Virtue*, p. 216.

Chapter 8. Lex orandi, lex credendi

[1] First published in D. Forrester (ed.), *Theology and Practice* (London: Epworth Press, 1990), pp. 71–80. © Epworth 1990. Used with permission.

[2] J. P. Miranda, *Marx and the Bible* (London: SCM Press, 1977).

[3] M. Polanyi, *Personal Knowledge* (London: Routledge, 1962), p. 199.

[4] Those who wish to do so can turn to P. de Clerck, '"Lex Orandi Lex Credendi": Sens original et avatars historiques d'un adage équivoque', *Questions liturgiques et paroissiales* 59 (1978), pp. 193–212 and G. Wainwright, *Doxology: The Praise of God in Worship, Doctrine and Life* (London: Epworth Press, 1980), pp. 218–83, esp. n. 523.

[5] K. Barth, 'The Gift of Freedom', in *The Humanity of God* (London: Collins, 1961), p. 88.

[6] M. Wiles, *The Making of Christian Doctrine* (Cambridge: Cambridge University Press, 1967), ch. 4.

[7] Larry Hurtado, *At the Origins of Christian Worship* (Carlisle: Paternoster, 1999).

[8] B. Wicker, *First the Political Kingdom* (London: Sheed & Ward, 1967), pp. 84–85.

[9] Wainwright, *Doxology*, pp. 237–8.

[10] S. Sykes, *The Identity of Christianity* (London: SPCK, 1984), p. 277.

Chapter 9. The liberation of worship

[1] The Dr Robert Lee Lecture delivered in Greyfriars Kirk, Edinburgh, in 1980. Part of this chapter has been published in Duncan B. Forrester, *Truthful Action* (Edinburgh: T & T Clark, 2000) and is used here by permission of T & T Clark.

[2] J. H. Cone, cited in G. Wainwright, *Doxology: The Praise of God in Worship, Doctrine and Life* (London: Epworth, 1980), p. 419.

[3] J. de Santa Ana, (ed.), *Towards a Church of the Poor* (Geneva: World Council of Churches, 1979), pp. 11–12.

[4] J. Moltmann, *The Crucified God* (London: SCM Press, 2nd edn, 1973), p. 53.

[5] Psalm 126, Grail Version.

[6] S. Galilea, 'Les messes de protestation', *Parole et Mission* 14 (1971), p. 334.

[7] John Miller, *Problems of the Ministry and Mission of the Church in New Housing Areas and Other Working Class Parishes* (Glasgow [privately circulated], 1976), p. 2.

[8] E. Muir, 'The Incarnate One', in *Collected Poems* (London: Faber & Faber, 1963), p. 228.

[9] Isaiah 1.11–17. Jerusalem Bible.

[10] Cited in E. Schillebeeckx, *Jesus: An Experiment in Christology* (London: SCM Press, 1979), p. 674.

Chapter 10. The end of sacraments?: sacramental action and discipleship

[1] This is a revised version of the Presidential Address I gave to the Church Service Society in May 2001.

[2] Søren Kierkegaard, *The Last Years: Journals 1853–1855* (London: Collins, 1965), p. 177.

[3] Kierkegaard, *The Last Years*, p. 177.

[4] Kierkegaard, *The Last Years*, p. 177.

[5] Karl Barth, *Church Dogmatics* (ed. T. F. Torrance and G. W. Bromily; Edinburgh: T & T Clark, 1956–75, II/4, pp. 484, 504.

[6] Barth, CD, IV/4, p. 46.

[7] Barth, CD, IV/4, p. 46.

[8] Cf. Reinhold Niebuhr's suggestion that prophetic faith is opposed to 'idolatrous sacramentalism'. Dennis McCann, *Christian Realism and Liberation Theology* (Maryknoll, NY: Orbis, 1981), p. 44.

[9] Barth, CD, IV/4, p. ix.
[10] Barth, CD, IV/4, p. ix; CD II/2, p. 640.
[11] Barth, CD, IV/1, p. 326; IV/4, p. 112.
[12] A. C. Cochrane, *Eating and Drinking with Jesus: An Ethical and Biblical Inquiry* (Philadelphia: Westminster, 1974), p. 128.
[13] W. D. Maxwell, *The Liturgical Portions of the Genevan Service Book* (Edinburgh: Oliver & Boyd, 1931), p. 126.
[14] On this see Leigh Eric Schmidt, *Holy Fairs: Scottish Communions and American Revivals in the Early Modern Period* (Princeton: Princeton University Press, 1989).
[15] Cochrane, *Eating and Drinking*, p. 77.
[16] 1 Cor 11.20.
[17] John 6.33 and 51.
[18] John 13.15.
[19] William Henry Turton, in *The Church Hymnary Third Edition* (Oxford: Oxford University Press, 1973), no. 492.

Chapter 11. Worship, ethics and unity

[1] See Thomas F. Best and Dagmar Heller (eds.), *So We Believe, So We Pray: Towards Koinonia in Worship* (Geneva: WCC Publications, 1995), pp. xi–xii. This chapter originally appeared as Chapter 4 in my book *The True Church and Morality: Reflections on Ecclesiology and Ethics* (Geneva: World Council of Churches, 1997). It appears here with permission.
[2] Alexander Schmemann, *Introduction to Liturgical Theology* (Crestwood, New York: St Vladimir's Seminary Press, 1986), p. 29.
[3] Wayne A. Meeks, *The Origins of Christian Morality* (New Haven: Yale University Press, 1993), p. 92.
[4] Vitaly Borovoi, 'Life in Unity', unpublished address, WCC Sixth Assembly, Vancouver, August 1983.
[5] Stanley Hauerwas, *Truthfulness and Tragedy* (Notre Dame: Notre Dame University Press, 1977), pp. 142–3.
[6] Vigen Guroian, *Incarnate Love: Essays in Orthodox Ethics* (Notre Dame: Notre Dame University Press, 1989), p. 69.
[7] Guroian, *Incarnate Love*, p. 54.
[8] London: Hodder & Stoughton, 1938.
[9] On this see particularly Bernd Wannenwetsch, 'The Political Worship of the Church: A Critical and Empowering Practice', *Modern Theology* 12.3 (1996), pp. 269–99, and *Political Worship: Ethics for Christians* (Oxford: Oxford University Press, 2004).
[10] Stanley Hauerwas, *The Peaceable Kingdom* (London: SCM Press, 1984), p. 99.
[11] José P. Miranda, *Marx and the Bible* (London: SCM Press, 1977), p. 53.
[12] Jon Sobrino, *Christology at the Crossroads* (London: SCM Press, 1978), p. 275. 'I would help the Salvadoreans to replace their popular "superstitious" religiosity with a more sophisticated kind', he wrote of his initial intentions on going from Europe as a missionary to El Salvador. 'Awakening from the Sleep of Inhumanity', *The Christian Century* 3 (April 1991), pp. 364–70.
[13] Sobrino, *Christology at the Crossroads*, p. 277.
[14] Alasdair Kee, *Marx and the Failure of Liberation Theology* (London: SCM Press, 1990).

[15] Victor Turner, *The Ritual Process: Structure and Anti-structure* (Harmondsworth: Penguin Books, 1969).

[16] Tom F. Driver, *The Magic of Ritual* (New York: HarperCollins, 1991), p. 80.

[17] Driver, *The Magic of Ritual*, p. 132.

[18] For the relevant citations, see Dermot A. Lane, *Foundations for a Social Theology* (Dublin: Gill and Macmillan, 1984), pp. 143–4, 182.

[19] On this see especially Christel Lane, *The Rites of Rulers: Ritual in Industrial Society – The Soviet Case* (Cambridge: Cambridge University Press, 1981).

[20] 1 Thess. 1.9

[21] 1 Thess. 2.2

[22] Vigen Guroian, *Incarnate Love: Essays in Orthodox Ethics* (Notre Dame: University of Notre Dame Press, 1987), p. 56.

[23] Cited in Guroian, *Incarnate Love*, pp. 63–4.

[24] Enda McDonagh, *Between Chaos and New Creation* (Dublin: Gill and Macmillan, 1986), pp. 84–5.

[25] 1 Peter 2.2–3.

[26] 1 Cor. 11.20.

[27] John 6.51.

[28] Guroian, *Incarnate Love*, p. 70.

[29] Matt. 25.34–35.

[30] Romans 14.17.

[31] J. Gerassi (ed.), *Camilo Torres: Revolutionary Priest* (Harmondsworth: Penguin Books, 1979), p. 9.

[32] 1 Corinthians 11.20.

[33] Cited in G. Wainwright, *Doxology: The Praise of God in Worship, Doctrine and Life* (London: Epworth, 1980), p. 402 n. 987, p. 568.

[34] G. A. Gutiérrez, *Theology of Liberation* (London: SCM Press, 1974), p. 137.

[35] U. Duchrow, *Global Economy* (Geneva: WCC, 1987), p. 137.

[36] Gutiérrez, *Theology of Liberation*, p. 262.

[37] Cited in Kenneth Leech, *The Eye of the Storm: Spiritual Resources for the Pursuit of Justice* (London: Darton, Longman & Todd, 1992), p. 149.

[38] Hauerwas, *The Peaceable Kingdom*, p. 108.

Chapter 12. Politics and reconciliation

[1] First published in M. Hurley (ed.), *Reconciliation in Religion and Society* (Antrim: Institute of Irish Studies, 1994), pp. 111–22. I am indebted to Professor Ted Weber of Emory University and various participants in the Reconciliation in Religion and Society Conference, held by the Irish School of Ecumenics and the University of Ulster, in May 1993, for comments on the draft of this chapter.

[2] M. Luther, 'Whether Soldiers too can be Saved', in *The Works of Martin Luther* (Philadelphia: A. J. Holman, 1915–32), p. 36.

[3] Cited in D. Garland, *Punishment and Modern Society* (Oxford: Clarendon, 1991), pp. 226–7.

[4] See E. Jüngel, *Christ Justice and Peace: Toward a Theology of the State in Dialogue with the Barmen Declaration* (Edinburgh: T & T Clark, 1992). This includes a translation of the Barmen Declaration by Douglas S. Bax.

[5] MacIntyre, *After Virtue*, p. 236.

[6] E. McDonagh, *Between Chaos and New Creation* (Dublin: Gill and Macmillan,

1986), p. 85.
7   P. D. Bathory, *Political Theory as Public Confession: The Social and Political Thought of St. Augustine of Hippo* (New Brunswick: Transaction Books, 1981), p. 160.
8   C. Villa-Vicencio (ed.), *Between Christ and Caesar: Classical and Contemporary Texts on Church and State* (Cape Town: David Philip, 1986), pp. 256–7.
9   P. Hinchcliff, *Holiness and Politics* (London: Darton, Longman & Todd, 1980), p. 190.
10 J. Cone, *God of the Oppressed* (New York: Seabury, 1975), pp. 243–4.
11 H. Willmer, 'Forgiveness and Politics', *Crucible* (July–September 1979), pp. 103–4.

Chapter 13. The media and theology: some reflections

1   First published in C. Arthur (ed.), *Religion and the Media: An Introductory Reader* (Cardiff: University of Wales Press, 1993), pp. 67–79. Reprinted with permission.
2   My own university gave the subject intellectual 'respectability' in the 1930s by linking it to a 'recognized discipline', Christian ethics!
3   P. Freire, *Pedagogy of the Oppressed* (Harmondsworth: Penguin Books, 1972), pp. 45–6.
4   F. Dostoevsky, *The Brothers Karamazov* (London: Heinemann, 1912), p. 253.
5   Matt. 11:25–26; Luke 4:10–21.
6   Cited in W. H. Whyte, *Organization Man* (Harmondsworth: Penguin Books, 1960), p. 48.
7   R. Goldman, *Readiness for Religion* (London: Routledge and Kegan Paul, 1965), p. 99.
8   S. Kierkegaard, *Training in Christianity* (trans. W. Lowrie; Princeton: Princeton University Press, 1942), pp. 174–9.
9   Ephesians 4.15.
10 V. Havel, *Living in Truth* (London: Faber & Faber, 1987), p. 43.
11 Havel, *Living in Truth*, p. 39.
12 Havel, *Living in Truth*, p. 153.
13 Hebrews 1.1–4.

Chapter 14. Welfare and human nature: public theology in welfare policy debates

1   Reprinted with permission of Sage Publications Ltd from *Studies in Christian Ethics* 13.2 (2000), pp. 1–14.
2   I borrow the categories of knights, knaves and pawns from Julian Le Grand's article, 'Knights, Knaves or Pawns? Human Behaviour and Social Policy', *Journal of Social Policy* 26.2 (1997), pp. 149–170. The article's conclusion, that what are needed are 'robust policies which are not dependent on any simple view of human behaviour' might be seen as making the discussion largely otiose; but perhaps he is seeking an account of human beings which takes the measure of the greatness as well as the misery of the human condition.
3   David Hume, *Essays Moral, Political and Literary* (London: Longmans, Green, 1898), I, pp. 117–18.
4   The nineteenth-century distinction between poverty and pauperism is important here. Poverty is simply the absence of the resources to sustain a proper subsistence for oneself and one's dependants. Pauperism is a distinctive feature of industrial societies, a massive and destructive social, moral and spiritual problem. See Gertrude Himmelfarb, *The Idea of Poverty: England in the Early Industrial Age* (London: Faber & Faber, 1984), ch. 6.

5   Boyd Hilton, *The Age of Atonement: The Influence of Evangelicalism on Social and Economic Thought, 1785–1865* (Oxford: Clarendon, 1988), p. 56.

6   Karl Marx, *Capital*, I (Moscow: Progress Publishers, 1965), p. 617.

7   The best modern study of Chalmers is S. J. Brown, *Thomas Chalmers and the Godly Commonwealth in Scotland* (Oxford: Oxford University Press, 1982). And an incisive discussion of Chalmers's social policy is Donald Macleod, 'Thomas Chalmers and Pauperism', in S. J. Brown and Michael Fry (eds.), *Scotland in the Age of the Disruption* (Edinburgh: Edinburgh University Press, 1993), pp. 63–76.

8   Thomas Chalmers, *On the Power, Wisdom and Goodness of God as Manifested in the Adaptation of External Nature to the Moral and Intellectual Constitution of Man*, II (London: William Pickering, 1834), p. 36.

9   Chalmers, *On the Power, Wisdom and Goodness of God*, p. 36.

10 Chalmers, *On the Power, Wisdom and Goodness of God*, p. 30.

12 Thomas Chalmers, *On Political Economy*, pp. 25–6, cited in Donald C. Smith, *Passive Obedience and Prophetic Protest: Social Criticism in the Scottish Church 1880–1945* (New York: Peter Lang, 1987), p. 113. It is instructive to see how such attitudes worked out in the Irish Famine of the 1840s. Charles Trevelyan, the permanent head of the Treasury and thus the British official most directly responsible for dealing with the famine, declared, 'The great evil with which we have to contend is not the physical evil of the famine, but the moral evil of the selfish, perverse and turbulent character of the people'. At every point he resisted outdoor relief; even while recognizing the existence of a famine in which thousands would die. At the height of the hunger he warned: 'if the Irish once find out there are any circumstances in which they can get free government grants…we shall have a system of mendicancy such as the world never saw'. Cecil Woodham-Smith, *The Great Hunger* (New York: Old Town Books, 1989), pp. 156, 171.

12 Cited in Smith, *Passive Obedience*, p. 117.

13 Cited in Smith, *Passive Obedience*, p. 88.

14 Cited in Smith, *Passive Obedience*, p. 116.

15 The undeserving were described in the late nineteenth century by Helen Bosanquet, one of the leading lights of the Charity Organisation Society (COS), in terms that would have been approved by Chalmers: 'The Residuum displayed all the defects of character which rendered it industrially incompetent: absence of foresight and self-control; recklessness; aimless drifting; self-indulgence; an insuperable aversion to steady work; low intellect; degradation of the natural affections to animal instincts; a disposition unfavourable to the acquisition of skill and many other vices of similar kinds.' Cited by Alan Deacon in Andrew R. Morton (ed.), *The Future of Welfare* (Edinburgh: Centre for Theology and Public Issues, 1979), p. 121. For a recent defence of the COS, see A. W. Vincent, 'The Poor Law Reports of 1909 and the Social Theory of the Charity Organisation Society', in David Gladstone (ed.), *Before Beveridge: Welfare Before the Welfare State* (London: Institute of Economic Affairs, 1999), pp. 64–85.

16 A. M. C. Waterman, *Revolution, Economics and Religion: Christian Political Economy, 1798–1833* (Cambridge: Cambridge University Press, 1991), ch. 6.

17 Cited in Hugh Watt, *New College, Edinburgh: A Centenary History* (Edinburgh: Oliver & Boyd, 1946), pp. 3–4.

18 Macleod, 'Thomas Chalmers and Pauperism', p. 70.

19 See especially Dennis McCann, *New Experiments in Democracy* (London: Sheed & Ward, 1987) and (with Charles R. Strain), *Polity and Praxis: A Program for American Practical Theology* (Minneapolis: Winston, 1985). For critique see W. D.

Lindsey, 'Public Theology as Civil Discourse: What Are We Talking About?' *Horizons* 19.1 (1992), pp. 44–69.

[20] Lindsey, 'Public Theology as Civil Discourse', p. 51.

[21] For a similar British initiative, see Paul Vallely, (ed.), *The New Politics: Catholic Social Teaching for the Twenty-first Century* (London: SCM Press, 1999).

[22] I have explored the Christian roots of the welfare state in my *Christianity and the Future of Welfare* (London: Epworth, 1985).

[23] Alan Deacon in Morton (ed.), *The Future of Welfare*, p. 121.

[24] This point has been classically made by Julian Le Grand, in his *The Strategy of Equality: Redistribution and the Social Services* (London: Allen & Unwin, 1982), and in his subsequent writing.

[25] On this see Jose Harris, 'Political Thought and the Welfare State 1870–1940: An Intellectual Framework for British Social Policy', in David Gladstone, (ed.), *Before Beveridge: Welfare Before the Welfare State* (London: Institute of Economic Affairs, 1999), pp. 43–63.

[26] R. H. Tawney, *Equality* (Brighton: Harvester, new edn, 1982), p. 227.

[27] David Nicholls, *Deity and Domination: Images of God and the State in the Nineteenth and Twentieth Centuries* (London: Routledge, 1989), chs 2 and 3.

[28] *The Scotsman*, 23 November 1996. Italics mine.

[29] D. Marsland, *Welfare or Welfare State? Contradictions and Dilemmas in Social Policy* (London: Macmillan, 1966). Behind Marsland's position lies, of course, the more temperate and measured thought of Charles Murray and Lawrence Mead; an attentive reader will not fail to notice echoes of Chalmers and his like in the nineteenth century.

[30] Frank Field *et al.*, *Stakeholder Welfare* (London: Institute of Economic Affairs, 1996), p. i.

[31] Field *et al.*, *Stakeholder Welfare*, p. 109.

[32] Frank Field, in Morton (ed.), *The Future of Welfare*, p. 143.

[33] Field *et al.*, *Stakeholder Welfare*, p.19.

[34] Ibid., p. 20.

[35] Ibid., p. 144.

[36] Field *et al.*, *Stakeholder Welfare*, p. 111.

[37] J. M. Winter and. D. M. Joslin, *R.H. Tawney's Commonplace Book* (Cambridge: Cambridge University Press, 1972), pp. 53–4.

[38] This may be the sort of understanding of human nature that Julian Le Grand is seeking to undergird 'robust policies'. See endnote 1.

[39] Duncan B. Forrester, *Christian Justice and Public Policy* (Cambridge: Cambridge University Press, 1997), p. 202.

Bibliography

Barth, Karl, *The Knowledge of God and the Service of God* (London: Hodder & Stoughton, 1938).

——, *Church Dogmatics 1/2* (ed. G. W. Bromily and T. F. Torrance; Edinburgh: T & T Clark, 1956).

——, 'The Gift of Freedom', in *The Humanity of God* (London: Collins, 1961).

——, *The Christian Life* (Church Dogmatics, IV/4, Lecture Fragments; Edinburgh: T & T Clark, 1981).

Bathory, P. D., *Political Theory as Public Confession: The Social and Political Thought of St. Augustine of Hippo* (New Brunswick: Transaction Books, 1981).

Bauman, Zygmunt, *Modernity and the Holocaust* (Ithaca, NY: Cornell University Press, 1991).

——, *Postmodern Ethics* (Oxford: Blackwell, 1993).

——, *Life in Fragments: Essays in Post-modern Morality* (Oxford: Blackwell, 1995).

Berkouwer, G. C., *Man: The Image of God* (Grand Rapids: Eerdmans, 1962).

Best, Thomas F. and Dagmar Heller (eds.), *So We Believe, So We Pray: Towards Koinonia in Worship* (Geneva: WCC Publications, 1995).

Bonner, Stephen Eric, 'Making Sense of Hell: Three Meditations on the Holocaust', *Political Studies* 47 (1999), pp. 314–28.

Brown, Raymond E., *et al.*, (eds.), *Mary in the New Testament* (Philadelphia: Fortress, 1978).

Brown, S. J., *Thomas Chalmers and the Godly Commonwealth in Scotland* (Oxford: Oxford University Press, 1982).

Caird, George, *Pelican Commentary on Luke* (Harmondsworth: Penguin Books, 1963).

187

Cairns, David S., *The Image of God in Man* (London: Collins, 1973).

Cardenal, Ernesto, *The Gospel in Solentiname* (Maryknoll, NY: Orbis, 1977).

Chalmers, Thomas, *On the Power, Wisdom and Goodness of God as Manifested in the Adaptation of External Nature to the Moral and Intellectual Constitution of Man* (London: William Pickering, 1834).

Clerck, P. de, '"Lex Orandi Lex Credendi": Sens original et avatars historiques d'un adage équivoque', *Questions liturgiques et paroissiales* (1978), pp. 193–212.

Cochrane, A. C., *Eating and Drinking with Jesus: An Ethical and Biblical Inquiry* (Philadelphia: Westminster, 1974).

Cone, J., *God of the Oppressed* (New York: Seabury, 1975).

Dostoevsky, F., *The Brothers Karamazov* (London: Heinemann, 1912).

Driver, Tom F., *The Magic of Ritual* (New York: HarperCollins, 1991).

Dru, Alexander (ed.), *The Journals of Kierkegaard* (London: Oxford University Press, 1938).

Duchrow, U., *Global Economy* (Geneva: WCC, 1987).

Field, Frank, *et al.*, *Stakeholder Welfare* (London: IEA, 1996).

Forrester, Duncan B., *Christianity and the Future of Welfare* (London: Epworth, 1985).

——, *Christian Justice and Public Policy* (Cambridge: Cambridge University Press, 1997).

——, *The True Church and Morality: Reflections on Ecclesiology and Ethics* (Geneva: World Council of Churches, 1997).

——, *On Human Worth: A Christian Vindication of Equality* (London: SCM Press, 2001).

Forrester, Duncan B. (ed.), *Theology and Practice* (London: Epworth Press, 1990).

Forrester, Duncan B., J. I. H. McDonald and Gian Tellini, *Encounter with God: An Introduction to Christian Worship and Practice* (Edinburgh: T & T Clark, 2nd edn, 1996),

Freire, P., *Pedagogy of the Oppressed* (Harmondsworth: Penguin Books, 1972).

Galilea, S., 'Les messes de protestation', *Parole et Mission* 14 (1971), p. 334.

Garaudy, R., *The Alternative Future* (Harmondsworth: Penguin, 1976).

Garland, D., *Punishment and Modern Society* (Oxford: Clarendon, 1991).

Gerassi, J. (ed.), *Camilo Torres: Revolutionary Priest* (Harmondsworth: Penguin Books, 1979).

Gilbert, Martin, *The Holocaust: The Jewish Tragedy* (London: Fontana, 1987).

Gladstone, David (ed.), *Before Beveridge: Welfare Before the Welfare State* (London: Institute of Economic Afairs, 1999).

Glatzer, N. N. (ed.), *The Passover Haggadah* (New York: Schocken Books, 1969).

Goldhagen, H. J., *Hitler's Willing Executioners: Ordinary Germans and the Holocaust* (New York: Vintage, 1997).

Goldman, R., *Readiness for Religion* (London: Routledge and Kegan Paul, 1965).

Guroian, Vigen, *Incarnate Love: Essays in Orthodox Ethics* (Notre Dame: Notre Dame University Press, 1987).

Gutiérriez, G. A., *Theology of Liberation* (London: SMC Press, 1974).

Habermas, J. *idem* (ed.) 'The New Obscurity and the Exhaustion of Utopian Energies', in *Observations on the Spiritual Situation of the Age* (Cambridge: MIT Press, 1984).

Hauerwas, Stanley, *Truthfulness and Tragedy* (Notre Dame: Notre Dame University Press, 1977).

——, *Vision and Virtue* (Notre Dame: University of Notre Dame Press, 1981).

——, *The Peaceable Kingdom: A Primer in Christian Ethics* (London: SCM Press, 1983).

——, *Christian Existence Today* (Durham, NC: Labyrinth Press, 1988).

Havel, Václav, *Living in Truth* (London: Faber & Faber, 1987).

Hayek, F. A., *The Intellectuals and Socialism* (London: Institute of Economic Affairs, 1998).

Hilton, Boyd, *The Age of Atonement: The Influence of Evangelicalism on Social and Economic Thought, 1785–1865* (Oxford: Clarendon, 1988).

Himmelfarb, Gertrude, *The Idea of Poverty: England in the Early Industrial Age* (London: Faber & Faber, 1984).

Hinchcliff, P., *Holiness and Politics* (London: Darton, Longman & Todd, 1980).

Hume, David, *Essays Moral, Political and Literary* (London: Longmans, Green, 1898).

Hurley, M. (ed.), *Reconciliation in Religion and Society* (Antrim: Institute of Irish Studies, 1994).

Hurtado, Larry, *At the Origins of Christian Worship* (Carlisle: Paternoster, 1999).

Julian of Norwich, *Revelations of Divine Love* (Harmondsworth: Penguin, 1966).

Jüngel, E., *Karl Barth: A Theological Legacy* (Philadelphia: Westminster, 1985).

——, *Christ, Justice and Peace: Toward a Theology of the State in Dialogue with the Barmen Declaration* (Edinburgh: T & T Clark, 1992).

Kee, Alasdair, *Marx and the Failure of Liberation Theology* (London: SCM Press, 1990).

Kierkegaard, Søren, *Philosophical Fragments* (trans. David F. Swenson; Princeton: Princeton University Press, 1936 [1844]).

——, *Training in Christianity* (trans. W. Lowrie; Princeton: Princeton University Press, 1942).

——, *The Last Years: Journals 1853–1855* (London: Collins, 1965).

——, *Papers and Journals: A Selection* (trans. Alastair Hannay; Harmondsworth: Penguin, 1996).

Küng, Hans, *The Council and Reunion* (London: Sheed & Ward, 1962).

Lane, Christel, *The Rites of Rulers: Ritual in Industrial Society – The Soviet Case* (Cambridge: Cambridge University Press, 1981).

Lane, Dermot A., *Foundations for a Social Theology* (Dublin: Gill and Macmillan, 1984).

Le Grand, Julian, *The Strategy of Equality: Redistribution and the Social Services* (London: Allen & Unwin, 1982).

——, 'Knights, Knaves or Pawns? Human Behaviour and Social Policy', *Journal of Social Policy* 26.2 (1997), pp. 149–70.

Leech, Kenneth, *The Eye of the Storm: Spiritual Resources for the Pursuit of Justice* (London: Darton, Longman & Todd, 1992).

Limouris, Gennadios (ed.), *Church, Kingdom, World: The Church as Mystery and Prophetic Sign* (Geneva: World Council of Churches, 1986).

Lindsey, W. D., 'Public Theology as Civil Discourse: What are we Talking About?' *Horizons* 19.1 (1992), pp. 44–69.

Lindsey, W. D., (with Charles R. Strain), *Polity and Praxis: A Program for American Practical Theology* (Minneapolis: Winston, 1985).

——, 'Public Theology as Civil Discourse: What Are We Talking About?' *Horizons* 19.1 (1992), pp. 44–69.

Lowrie, Walter, *Kierkegaard* (London: Oxford University Press, 1938).

Luther, Martin, *The Works of Martin Luther* (6 vols.; Philadelphia: A. J. Holman Co., 1915–32).

MacIntyre, Alasdair, *After Virtue: A Study in Moral Theory* (London: Duckworth, 1981).

Macleod, Donald, 'Thomas Chalmers and Pauperism', in S. J. Brown and Michael Fry (eds.), *Scotland in the Age of the Disruption*

(Edinburgh: Edinburgh University Press, 1993).

Mannheim, Karl, *Ideology and Utopia: An Introduction to the Sociology of Knowledge* (London: Kegan Paul, Trench, Trubner and Co., 1936).

Marsland, D., *Welfare or Welfare State? Contradictions and Dilemmas in Social Policy* (London: Macmillan, 1966).

Marx, Karl, *Capital* (Moscow: Progressive Publishers, 1965).

Maxwell, W. D., *The Liturgical Portions of the Genevan Service Book* (Edinburgh: Oliver & Boyd, 1931).

McCann, Dennis, *Christian Realism and Liberation Theology* (Maryknoll, NY: Orbis, 1981).

——, *New Experiments in Democracy* (London: Sheed & Ward, 1987).

McCann, Dennis, and Charles R. Strain, *Polity and Praxis: A Program for American Practical Theology* (Minneapolis: Winston, 1985).

McDonagh, Enda, *Between Chaos and New Creation* (Dublin: Gill and Macmillan, 1986).

McFadyen, A. A., *The Call to Personhood* (Cambridge: Cambridge University Press, 1990).

Meeks, Wayne A., *The Origins of Christian Morality* (New Haven: Yale University Press, 1993).

Miller, John, *Problems of the Ministry and Mission of the Church in New Housing Areas and Other Working Class Parishes* (Glasgow [privately circulated], 1976).

Mills, C. Wright, *The Sociological Imagination* (Oxford: Oxford University Press, 1959).

Miranda, J. P., *Marx and the Bible* (London: SCM Press, 1977).

Moltmann, J., *Man: Christian Anthropology in the Conflicts of the Present* (London: SPCK, 1971).

——, *The Crucified God* (London: SCM Press, 2nd edn, 1973).

Morton, Andrew and William Storrar (eds.), *A Public Theology for the 21st Century* (London: T & T Clark, 2004).

Morton, Andrew R. (ed.), *The Future of Welfare* (Edinburgh: Centre for Theology and Public Issues, 1979).

Muir, E., 'The Incarnate One', in *Collected Poems, 1912–1958* (London: Faber & Faber, 1963).

Nation, Mark Theissen and Samuel Wells (eds.), *Faithfulness and Fortitude: In Conversation with the Theological Ethics of Stanley Hauerwas* (Edinburgh: T & T Clark, 2000).

Newman, J. H., *Essay on the Development of Christian Doctrine* (London: Pickering, 1878).

Nicholls, David, *Deity and Domination: Images of God and the State in the Nineteenth and Twentieth Centuries* (London: Routledge, 1989).

Niebuhr, Reinhold, *The Nature and Destiny of Man*. I: *Human Nature* (London: Nisbet, 1941).

——, *The Nature and Destiny of Man*. II: *Human Destiny* (London: Nisbet, 1943).

Nineham, D. E., *The Use and Abuse of the Bible* (London: SCM Press, 1976).

Pannenberg, Wolfhart, *Theology and the Philosophy of Science* (London: Darton, Longman & Todd, 1976).

——, *Anthropology in Theological Perspective* (Philadelphia: Westminster, 1985).

Pascal, Blaise, *Pensées* (London: Dent, 1908).

Pinches, Charles R., *Theology and Action: After Theory in Christian Ethics* (Grand Rapids: Eerdmans, 2002).

Polanyi, M., *Personal Knowledge* (London: Routledge, 1962).

Raban, J., *God, Man and Mrs Thatcher* (London: Chatto & Windus, 1989).

Rasmussen, Larry L., *Moral Fragments and Moral Community: A Proposal for Church in Society* (Minneapolis: Fortress, 1993).

Ruether, R., *Mary – the Feminine Face of the Church* (London: SCM Press, 1979).

Sacks, Jonathan, *The Dignity of Difference* (London: Continuum, 2002).

Santa Ana, Julio de (ed.), *Towards a Church of the Poor* (Geneva: World Council of Churches, 1979).

Schillebeeckx, E., *Mary, Mother of the Redemption* (London: Sheed & Ward, 1964).

——, *Jesus: An Experiment in Christology* (London: SCM Press, 1979).

Schmemann, Alexander, *Introduction to Liturgical Theology* (Crestwood, NY: St Vladimir's Seminary Press, 1986).

Schmidt, Leigh Eric, *Holy Fairs: Scottish Communions and American Revivals in the Early Modern Period* (Princeton: Princeton University Press, 1989).

Scott, Walter, *Old Mortality* (London: John Nimmo, 1893).

Smith, Donald C., *Passive Obedience and Prophetic Protest: Social Criticism in the Scottish Church 1880–1945* (New York: Peter Lang, 1987).

Sobrino, Jon, *Christology at the Crossroads* (London: SCM Press, 1978).

Stout, Jeffrey, *Ethics after Babel: The Languages of Morals and their Discontents* (Boston: Beacon Press, 1988).

——, *Democracy and Tradition* (Princeton: Princeton University Press, 2004).

Sykes, S., *The Identity of Christianity* (London: SPCK, 1984).

Tawney, R. H., *Equality*, (Brighton: Harvester, new edn, 1982).

Temple, W., *Christianity and Social Order* (Harmondsworth: Penguin Books, 1942).

Titmuss, Richard, *The Gift Relationship* (Harmondsworth: Penguin Books, 1973).

Todorov, Tzvetan, *Facing the Extreme: Moral Life in the Concentration Camps* (London: Weidenfeld & Nicolson, 1999).

Turner, Victor, *The Ritual Process: Structure and Anti-structure* (Harmondsworth: Penguin Books, 1969).

Vallely, Paul (ed.), *The New Politics: Catholic Social Teaching for the Twenty-first Century* (London: SCM Press, 1999).

Veatch, Robert, *The Foundations of Justice: Why the Retarded and the Rest of Us have Claims to Equality* (New York: Oxford University Press, 1986).

Villa-Vicencio, C., (ed.), *Between Christ and Caesar: Classical and Contemporary Texts on Church and State* (Cape Town: David Philip, 1986).

Wainwright, G., *Doxology: The Praise of God in Worship, Doctrine and Life* (London: Epworth, 1980).

Wannenwetsch, Bernd, 'The Political Worship of the Church: A Critical and Empowering Practice', *Modern Theology* 12.3 (1996), pp. 269–99.

——, *Political Worship: Ethics for Christians* (Oxford: Oxford University Press, 2004).

Waterman, A. M. C., *Revolution, Economics and Religion: Christian Political Economy, 1798–1833* (Cambridge: Cambridge University Press, 1991).

Watt, Hugh, *New College, Edinburgh: A Centenary History* (Edinburgh: Oliver & Boyd, 1946).

Wells, Samuel, 'The Disarming Virtue of Stanley Hauerwas', *Scottish Journal of Theology* 52.1 (1999), pp. 82–88.

——, *Improvisation: The Drama of Christian Ethics* (Grand Rapids: Brazos Press, 2004).

White, Stephen K., *Political Theory and Postmodernism* (Cambridge: Cambridge University Press, 1991).

Whyte, W. H., *Organization Man* (Harmondsworth: Penguin Books, 1960).

Wicker, B., *First the Political Kingdom* (London: Sheed & Ward, 1967).

Wiles, M., *The Making of Christian Doctrine* (Cambridge: Cambridge University Press, 1967).

Willmer, H., 'Forgiveness and Politics', *Crucible* (July–September 1979) pp. 100–105.

Winter, J. M. and D. M. Joslin, *R.H.Tawney's Commonplace Book* (Cambridge: Cambridge University Press, 1972).

Woodham-Smith, Cecil, *The Great Hunger* (New York: Old Town Books, 1989).

Zizioulas, John D., *Being as Communion: Studies in Personhood and the Church* (London: Darton, Longman & Todd, 1985).

Index

Ackerman, Bruce 142
Alison, William 162
Allan, Tom 114
Althaus-Reid, Marcella 175n
altruism 166–7, 171
Amish people 125
anamnesis (remembering) 88–9, 116–17, 118
Anselm of Canterbury 61, 97, 178n
Antelme, Robert 86
anti-semitism 79
Apollo 51
Aquinas, Thomas 99
Aristotle 51, 89
Athanasius 98
Augustine of Hippo 25, 39, 139, 144, 176n
Auschwitz concentration camp 79, 87

Baalshem (Jewish teacher) 111
Baillie, John 168
baptism 6, 112, 113, 114, 127–9, 133, 141
Baptism, Eucharist and Ministry 127–8, 131, 132
Barmen Declaration 17, 139
Barth, Karl 178n, 180n, 181nn
  and Christology 29–30
  and Mary 58
  and natural theology 163
  and politics 139
  and religion 125
  and sacraments 112–15, 121

and Scripture 72
and theological liberalism 160, 168
and theology 13, 17, 124
and worship 97, 102
Barth, Markus 112
Basil of Caesarea 98
Bathory, P.D. 183n
Bauman, Zygmunt 85, 176nn, 179n
Bax, Douglas S. 182n
Bell, Daniel 50
Berdyaev, Nikolai 37
Berkouwer, G.C. 176n
Bernard of Clairvaux 99
Best, Thomas F. 181n
Beveridge Report 167, 173
Beveridge, William 165, 173
biblical criticism 70, 71
biblical interpretation
  across cultures 72, 73, 74–5
  across time 71–2, 74
  contexts
    academy 69, 70, 71–2
    church 69, 70, 72, 74
    India 74–5
    overlapping 71–2
    political 76–7
    social 76
  principles 38–9
Blake, William 33–4
Bloch, Ernst 33
Bonner, Stephen Eric 89, 179n
Book of Common Order 175n
Borovoi, Vitaly 123, 181n

195

Bosanquet, Helen   184n
Brown, Raymond E.   178nn
Brown, S.J.   184n
Bruce, F.F.   76
Bruce, Robert   114
Buber, Martin   111
Bultmann, Rudolph   148

Caird, Edward   167
Caird, George   64, 178n
Cairns, David S.   176n
Calvin, John   114
canon of Scripture   73
Cardenal, Ernesto   64, 76, 178n
caring vs solidarity   86–7
Castillo, Jose M.   132
catechisms   150
celibacy   42, 44–5
Chalmers, Thomas   160, 161–3,
   164, 165, 166, 173, 184nn, 185n
Chambon-sur-Lignon   82
Charity Organisation Society   184n
Chesterton, G.K.   27, 177n
Christ
   as communicator   150, 154
   death of   151–2
   and family   62–3
   incarnation   55–9, 110
   as Logos   52
   and Mary   58, 59–60, 61, 62
   as mother   61
   presence in church   109
   as reconciler   137–8
   as true human being   29–31
Christendom, end of   113–14
Christology   29–31, 97–8
church
   as alternative society   13–15
   as communion   31
   mission   15–16, 110, 125
   as pilgrim   109
   and the poor   109
   and presence of Christ   109
   as reconciler   141
   Scripture in   69, 71–2, 73, 74
   secular context   of 89–91
   as social ethic   124, 125
   and the state   138–9, 162
   and theology   144–5

and unity   15–16, 123, 129, 133
Churchill, Winston   83
Cochrane, A. C.   115, 118, 181nn
Collingwood, R. G.   72
Commission on God's Will in the
   Present Crisis   168
common good   142–3, 165, 166
Common Good, The   165, 172
communication
   and Christ   150, 154
   Christian   151–4
   and community   154–5
   indirect 155–6
   and Socrates   150, 154
   truthful   149–53
community building   12–13
concentration camps
   Auschwitz   79, 87
   Dachau   78, 79, 83–6, 89–91
   life in   86–9, 90
   Soviet gulag   88
Cone, James H.   104, 146, 180n, 183n
conflict   144–5
contentment, culture   of 33
conviction politics   50, 169
Corrie, Joe   26, 176n
creation
   Genesis story   26, 28
   Hindu myth   27
criminal justice reform   4–5
cultural relativism   71, 73
cultural totality   71, 73, 74
Cyprian   98

Dachau church   80–3, 86, 89, 90, 91
Dachau concentration camp   78, 79,
   83–6, 89–91
de Clerck, P.   180n
de Santa Ana, J.   180n
Deacon, Alan   184n, 185n
detachment   3, 19
dialogue   56–7, 66, 150–1
Dionysus   51–2
dissent   155
Dostoevsky, F. 5,   149, 175n, 183n
Douglas, Willie   65–6, 67
Driver, Tom F.   126, 182nn
Duchrow, Ulrich   132, 182n
Duncan, John ('Rabbi' Duncan)   115

education, integrated   141
electronic evangelists   151
emotion vs reason   51–2
equality   25–8, 75, 168, 171–2
eschatology   32–3
eucharist *see* Lord's Supper

family, ideal Christian   62–3
Fanon, Frantz   82
Ferdinand of Austria, Archduke   79
Field, Frank   17, 166, 167, 170–2,
   173, 185nn
folk religion (religiosity)   58, 181n
forgiveness   5, 9, 17, 138, 146
Forrester, D. F.   176n, 177nn, 185n
fragmentation
   social and moral,   10–11, 12
   theological, *see under* theology
Francis of Assisi   42
Freire, Paulo   149, 183n

Galbraith, J. W.   33
Galilea, S.   180n
Gandhi, M. K.   4, 61, 144
Garaudy, Roger   50, 178n
Garland, D.   182n
Gassmann, G.   176n
Gerassi, J.   182n
Gilbert, Martin   84, 179nn
Ginzburg, Eugenia   86
God
   and gender specific language   60–1
   image of   25–9, 33–4
   knowledge of   7
   as liberator   106–7, 110
   love of   6–7, 39–40, 45
   as mother   61
   and sexism   61
Goldhagen, H. J.   84, 85, 179nn
Goldman, Ronald   151, 183n
Gradowski, Zalmen   88
Graham, Billy   114
Graham, Elaine   175n
Gray, John   8
Green, T. H.   167
Grossman, Vasily   88
Guroian, Vigen   124, 128, 130,
   181nn, 182nn
Gustafson, James   14

Gutierrez, G.   132, 182nn

Habermas, J.   33, 177n
Harris, Jose   185n
Hauerwas, Stanley   176nn, 177n,
   179nn, 181nn,   182n
   and church   13, 83, 89–91,
      123–4, 125
   and sacraments   133
   and theology   14
Havel, Vaclav   9–10, 12, 154–5,
   175nn, 183nn
Hawking, Stephen   3
Hayek, Friedrich A.   20–1, 142, 145,
   176n
Hegel, G. W. F.   2
Heller, Dagmar   181n
Hilton, Boyd   160, 184n
Himmelfarb, Gertrude   183n
Hinchcliff, P.   183n
history   67
Hitler, Adolf   80, 88
Hobbes, Thomas   6, 8, 175n
Holocaust,   78, 89, *see also*
   Auschwitz; Dachau
Holy Spirit   98, 100, 104
homiletics   53, 148
homophobia   35
homosexuality   35, 37, 43
   and celibacy   42, 44–5
   and homosexual behaviour   44,
      45, 46
   and homosexual orientation   44
   and homosexual unions   45–6
   and scripture   38–9
hope   32–3, 143, 146
Huddleston, Trevor   118, 132
human beings, individual worth
   26–8
human nature
   optimistic views   158–9, 165,
      166, 167, 168–9
   pessimistic views   159, 163
   realistic views   168, 169, 170–1,
      172, 173
humans in community   29–34
Hume, David   52, 159, 183n
Hurtado, Larry   180n
hymnody   100–1

ideology   9–10, 11, 16, 50, 154
image of God   25–9, 33–4
indicative and imperative   137–8
involvement   3, 150
Irish Famine 1840s   184n

Joslin, D. M.   185n
Jüngel, E.   177n, 182n
Julian of Norwich   61, 178n
just war thinking   143
justice   108, 110, 132, 145–6

Kairos Document   144–5, 146
Kant, Immanuel   4
Kee, Alasdair   126, 181n
Kierkegaard, Søren   175nn, 178n,
   180nn, 183n
   and Christian message   151–2,
      153
   and communication   149–50,
      151, 154, 155–6
   and Jesus   1–2, 150
   and sacraments   113
   and Scripture   70, 76
   and Socrates   1–2, 150
   and theology   2–3
   and truth   6, 9, 149–50, 153, 156
King, Martin Luther   144
knowledge   7
Knox, John   114, 116
Kolbe, Maximilian   88
Küng, Hans   57, 60, 178n

Lane, Christel   182n
Lane, Dermot A.   182n
Last Supper   116–17
Le Grand, Julian   183n, 185n
Leech, Kenneth   182n
Lehmann, Paul   124
Levi, Primo   87
Lewis, C. S.   39, 41
lex orandi lex credendi   96–7
liberal democracy   11–12
liberation theology   18, 126
lies   154–5
liminality   126
Lindsey, W. D.   164, 184n, 185nn
liturgical movement   101
Lord's Prayer   98

Lord's Supper
   and *anamnesis*   116–17, 118
   as anticipation of heavenly banquet
      121, 130–1, 132
   as challenge to service   119–20
   as context of Christian story   67
   as crown of ethics   115
   and fencing of the Table   115–16
   and justice   132
   and Karl Barth   112, 113–15
   and liberation   106–7
   and presence of Christ in the world
      133
   and protest   108
   as real feast   117–18
   theology and ethics of   98–9
   and transformation   132
   and unity   119
love
   divine   6–7, 39–40, 45
   human   40–1, 45, 46
Lowenberg (Jewish prisoner, Dachau)
   84
Lowrie, Walter   175nn, 178n
Lowy (Jewish prisoner, Dachau)   85
Lumen Gentium   176n
Luther, Martin   29, 39, 49, 52, 138,
   177n, 178n, 182n
Lyotard, Jean-François   9

McCann, Dennis   164, 180n, 184n
McDonagh, Enda   129, 141, 182n,
   182nn
MacDonald, George   35
McFadyen, A. A.   176n
MacIntyre, Alasdair   10–11, 12–13,
   14, 140, 176nn, 182n
Macleod, Donald   163, 184nn
MacLeod, George   114
Macmurray, John   168, 177n
Magnificat   63–4, 76
Mala Christians, Muthialapad (India)
   103–4, 109
Malthus, Thomas   160
Mannheim, Karl   167
Marialis Cultus 1974   178n
market forces   161
Marsland, David   170, 185n
Marx, Karl   126, 160, 184n

Mary, Mariology
  in Catholic doctrine   58, 99
  and Christology   58, 59–60, 61,
    62
  as mother of God   57
  political significance   63–4
  and the poor   63–4
mass media
  as challenge to theology   147, 157
  dangers of   156
Maxwell, W. D.   181n
Mead, Lawrence   169, 185n
means-testing   171
medium vs message   147–9, 151–2
Meeks, Wayne A.   181n
Milbank, John   89
Miller, John   109, 180n
Mills, C. Wright   3, 175n
Miranda, Jose P.   95, 125, 126,
  179n, 181n
missiology   54
modernity   74, 148
Moltmann, Jürgen   33, 177n, 180n
moral bricolage   12
moral Esperanto   12
Morton, Andrew   175n
Muir, Edwin   110, 180n
Murray, Charles   169, 185n
mystery   25
myth   67

natural law   37, 164
natural theology   160, 163–4, 173
Neuhas, Richard John   164
Newman, J. H.   60, 178n
Nicholls, David   168, 185n
Niebuhr, Reinhold   17, 32, 53, 108,
  160, 168, 177n,   180n
Nineham, Dennis   71–4, 178nn
Northcott, Michael   8

objectivity   19

Pannenberg, Wolfhart   53, 177n,
  178nn
Pascal, Blaise   30, 113, 177n
Passover   66, 67, 106, 116–17
Pasternak, Boris   5
paternalism   167

Paul, Apostle   7, 29, 119, 131–2
Paul VI, Pope   178n
pauperism   160–5
perichoresis   28, 39
phronesis (practical wisdom)   51
Pilate   50
Pinches, Charles R.   176n
Pinochet, General   82
Plato   51, 67–9, 175n
Polanyi, Michael   96, 97, 179n
political theology   54
politics
  adversarial   144
  and community building   140–1
  of conviction   50, 169
  as dyke against sin   139–40
  and reconciliation   139–41,
    142–6
poor, the
  and the church   109
  deserving and undeserving   162,
    172
  and Mary   63–4
  poverty vs pauperism   183n
  preferential option for   173
  relief of   162
Popper, Karl   73
postmodernism   8, 9–10, 16, 176n
practical theology   49, 50, 53–5, 148
practical vs theoretical sciences   51,
  52–3
practice / praxis, nature of   52, 54
preaching   96
priesthood of believers   110
providence   33
public theology   8, 19, 158
  and natural theology   160
  and political economy   161
  and US Catholic thought   163–4
  and welfare policy   160

Raban, J.   178n
radical orthodoxy   14
Rasmussen, Larry L.   12, 176n
Rawls, John   9
reconciliation   5
  in Christ   137–8
  and forgiveness   138
  and politics   139–41, 142–6

premature 146
redemption, cosmic 76
religious education 151
repentance 145, 146
Republic (Plato) 67–9, 73
ritual 67, 127
Robinson, John 77
Romero, Oscar 105
Rublev's icon 29
Ruether, R. 178n

Sacks, Jonathan 26, 28, 176n, 177nn
sacramentalism 112
sacramentality 113–15
Schillebeeckx, E. 60, 178n, 180n
Schmemann, Alexander 123, 181n
Schmidt, Leigh Eric 181n
Scott, Walter 38, 177n
Scripture *see* biblical interpretation
self-interest 171
service books 101
service of God 119–20
sex, idolatry of 42
sexual continence 45
sexual orientation 44
sexuality 35–46
    and biblical interpretation 38–9
    fear of 42
    and Greek philosophy 36
    and natural law thinking 37
    and personality 42
    positive qualities 46
    and procreation 42, 37, 46
Shalamov, Varlam 88
sin 31–2, 39, 139–40, 159
Smith, Adam 163
Smith, Donald C. 184nn
Sobrino, Jon 125, 126, 181nn
society, utopian views 170
Socrates 1–2, 51, 149, 150, 154, 155
solidarity vs caring 86–7
state neutrality 142
Stoicism 51, 52
stories
    biblical 6, 65, 66, 67
    non-biblical 65–6
Storrar, William 175n

Stout, Jeffrey 12, 14, 176nn
Strain, Charles R. 184n
Strassbourg extermination camp 80
study
    and modesty 68, 69, 73, 74
    and motivation 69
    and reverence 68, 69
Sykes, S. 180n
systems, system building 1, 2, 3–5, 8, 9

Tawney, R. H. 168, 170, 171–2, 185n
Temple, William 167–8
Thatcher, Margaret 50, 169, 178n
theological liberalism 160, 167, 168
theology
    church 144–5
    and detachment 3
    as doxology 97, 102
    fragmentary nature, vii 1, 4, 6, 7, 8, 12, 16–21, 172–3
    as improvisation 1
    and involvement 3
    as irrelevance 49
    liberation 18, 126
    and mass media 147, 157
    natural 160, 163–4, 173
    political 54
    practical 49, 50, 53–5, 148
    public 8, 19, 158, 160–4
    resources of 19
    and story and image 149, 156
    wordiness of 156
    and worship 96–102
theories, theory building 1, 3–5, 6, 18
Titmuss, Richard 166–7, 170
Todorov, Tzvetan 86, 87–8, 179nn
Torrance, Ian 45
Torres, Camilo 131
totalitarianism 73, 142
Trevelyan, Charles 184n
Trinity 28–9, 97–8
Trocmé, André 82
Trocmé, Magda 82
Troeltsch, Ernst 71
truth 2, 11, 50, 55
    and communication 149–53